THE POWER OF CONTINUITY

Ethiopia through the eyes of its children

Eva Poluha

NORDISKA AFRIKAINSTITUTET 2004

Indexing terms

Children, Childhood, Child rearing
Cultural identity
Ethnicity
Family environment
Gender roles
School environment
Social norms

Ethiopia

Cover illustration: Yalle Elehu

Photo: Eva Poluha

Language checking: Elaine Almén

Index: Margaret Binns

© the author and Nordiska Afrikainstitutet, 2004

ISBN 91-7106-535-0

Printed in Sweden by Elanders Gotab, Stockholm 2004

Contents

Acknowledgements

The children, teachers and administrative personnel of the Birabiro school in Addis Abeba as well as those of the Ashena Primary School in Gojjam made my fieldwork in Ethiopia into a fascinating experience. They were all friendly, hospitable and informative, interested in assisting me in my research. While teaching me about life in an Ethiopian school they individually, in so many ways, also showed me what it is to be a caring and concerned member of a social community. My life has been profoundly enriched by knowing them all. I am only sorry that I cannot thank them individually, but I prefer to keep their names anonymous.

During the research and period of writing I have been financially supported by the Swedish Agency for Research Cooperation with Developing Countries, SAREC, a support for which I am extremely grateful. I also sincerely appreciate the financial support from Rädda Barnen, Addis Abeba, which made trips in the city possible and landed me in a grand apartment.

The Department of Sociology and Social Anthropology at Addis Abeba University not only facilitated my fieldwork but affiliation with the Department also allowed me to participate in seminars with very interesting discussions. Almaz Terrefe and Gunder Edström made life in Addis comfortable and stimulating. They not only, for a couple of months, gave me a room with a bed and a view but also included me in their rich social life. In Addis, Agneta Hejll from Rädda Barnen was always ready to discuss new ideas emanating from my observations, discussions usually accompanied by tasty dinners. Johan Stånggren, from the same organization, eagerly followed my work with many challenging questions. Tiruye Admassu, friend and assistant, facilitated work in Gojjam. Transport between Bahar Dar, Dangla and Ashena would have been impossible without the staunch support of Göte Lidvall and the safe driving of Yigzaw Tegenje. The Department of Social Anthropology at Stockholm University facilitated my work both from and in Sweden.

Several friends and colleagues have given me invaluable comments on parts or the whole of the manuscript. Mona Rosendahl has supported me from the first outline to the full manuscript. Mona's comments have always been critical, incisive and constructive, encouraging me to elaborate on vague ideas. Herbert S. Lewis and Tekeste Negash have also read the full manuscript and given me cogent and positive comments highly pertinent to my arguments. Comments by three anonymous reviewers, especially number two, also helped me improve the discussion. Gunilla Bjerén, with a long history of work and research in Ethiopia, has given me many relevant comments and important references.

Some colleagues and friends, like Jónína Einarsdóttír, Karin Norman, Britt-Marie Thurén and Barbara Welles, read individual chapters and all came back to me with thought-provoking comments. While in the field, I had interesting and stimulating discussions with Anneka Knutsson, and at home, with Annika Rabo. An intellectually stimulating term was spent at the Centre for Cross-Cultural Research on Women in Oxford in 2001. I especially benefited from fruitful discussions with Helen Callaway, Anne Coles, Maria Jaschok, Regine Bendl and Shirley Ardener. The Centre provided a wonderful climate for thinking and writing. Participants in the Development seminar at Oxford University, Queen Elizabeth House, and in the c-sap seminar in Birmingham provided many useful comments for which I am grateful. In Birmingham, Susan Wright's comment that 'perhaps there is something positive to hierarchy', stimulated a lot of ideas and further reading. The gender panel at the fifteenth International Conference of Ethiopian Studies 2003, with Emnet Yadeta, Kristina Nässén and Judith Narrowe also benefited my writing.

My sons, Yalle and Daggi Elehu, have read, commented on and discussed key interpretations of the material, supported me with computer advice and, not least, encouraging exhortations to rest. Yalle has also designed the cover picture. Thank you both! Last but not least I want to thank my husband, Elehu Feleke, who has never tired of reading and re-reading my manuscript, always with a critical eye, resulting in many apt and useful comments which have inspired new lines of thinking. With Elehu I share a strong concern about the future of Ethiopia. Neither Elehu nor anyone else mentioned here bears any responsibility for the ideas presented in the book, however. I have taken all comments into careful consideration. Sometimes they have made me alter or sharpen existing arguments and sometimes the comments have forced me to develop new lines of reasoning. The overarching argument, with all its shortcomings is, however, my own responsibility.

Preface

January 1969, Addis Abeba. A multitude of people gathered in Janmeda to celebrate Epiphany or Timkit. Exciting sounds from people singing, playing old instruments, talking and laughing fill the field; beautifully coloured dresses signal a sense of joy, happiness and celebration. Priests from the city's churches have brought their Holy Arks. They chant and dance while children and adults eagerly watch the centuries-old ceremonies. Suddenly, the mass separates and emperor Haile Sellassie can be seen in majestic procession. He moves slowly towards the dais by the pool of water, where baptisms will take place. Their bodies deeply bowed, the crowd expresses great deference and submissiveness. Silence reigns as the thousands of people gathered wait for the emperor to step up and speak. The reverence for the emperor, straight-backed but of short stature is striking, the distance between him and the people bowing is impressive.

February 1974, a small village in Arsi. The 'creeping revolution' has started. In their homes and at meetings, peasants and CADU (Chilalo Agricultural Development Unit) employees discuss the emperor's speech to the nation. He had sounded so tired on the radio, as if he had given up. Later follows the rumour that the emperor has been imprisoned. Everybody suddenly seems to have access to a radio. Few regrets are expressed about his fate or demonstrations held in support of the emperor. People talk about what is happening in Nazret and Addis. Are demonstrators allowing drivers to use the road in Nazret to go to Addis? Are even priests and prostitutes joining in the demonstrations against the old order? Rumours about what is happening keep people talking, the discussions sometimes become very emotional, the speculations appear endless.

August 1974, the city of Harar. A group of lower echelon military officers (the Derg) have virtual control of government affairs in Ethiopia. Their slogan is 'Ethiopia First Without Bloodshed'. People in town queue for newspapers; where earlier there was abundance, the supply is now inadequate. Within an hour the papers are sold out. They contain a wealth of information, not least opinions expressing different, even contradictory, views about the country's possible political future.

October 1974, Bahar Dar. There is a continued shortage of newspapers. Discussions are held everywhere, even in public bars.

October 1975, Bahar Dar. Children go on strike in the secondary school arguing that the current curriculum is not relevant to their needs. They demand to learn about Marxism. Some students are armed. When their demands are accepted they also request automatic promotion to the next class to return to school.

September 1976, Bahar Dar. There are newspapers in abundance. Nobody seems to want to read them; again they have become a mouthpiece of the government.

August 1977, Bahar Dar. Many people are imprisoned; the elected members of the urban dwellers' associations seem to be the main target. Upon reaching the prison a chairperson of one of Bahar Dar's Urban Dwellers' Associations asks: 'What happened, has the revolution been overturned?' Most stay in prison for a couple of months, after which they are released. Some are kept for a much longer period.

Autumn 1977, Bahar Dar. A feeling of insecurity is spreading. There are no longer discussions in bars or at meetings. Fewer people attend demonstrations and those who do seem apprehensive about it. Children in school stop their strikes and start attending classes. Armed adults guard schoolyards and class-rooms. People are getting killed, supposedly by the armed opposition.

Spring 1978, Bahar Dar. The Red Terror of the government has come to town. Previously it was talked about on the radio as something taking place in Addis. I leave Bahar Dar with my husband, one son on my lap, one in my belly and a niece of ours for Addis, where the Red Terror is said to be over.

1979–1980, Ashena, a peasant association outside Dangla. Doing research on the establishment and workings of an agricultural producers' cooperative. Peasant contacts with state officials seem smooth, the officials are open, interested to lis-ten and ready to negotiate with the peasants. But this approach does not last. Slowly the young and not so well educated men in official positions start using new words and change their body language. They become arrogant, order indi-vidual peasants about and threaten them. Some peasants are punished with loss of land or imprisonment when they do not immediately obey the officials. Peas-ants become more and more silent especially in public places. Even Dangla in-habitants are quiet and appear scared. Some friends tell me to be careful about with whom I talk and what I say. I finish my work and leave the field. In Bahar Dar on my way home to Addis I hear that I have been accused of being a spy for the CIA stirring up the women against the government.

Spring, 1995, Ashena, outside Dangla. There has been a new government in Ethiopia since 1991, led by the Ethiopian People's Revolutionary Democratic Front. The 1995 May elections are being prepared. There is no opposition party, no candidate providing alternatives to the official agenda. Old friends in the peas-ant association tell me that they were encouraged to speak out and voice criticism after the government take-over. But today, there is no such prompting. Those who criticise state officials are threatened; a few have been imprisoned; most have withdrawn from official meetings. Everybody will participate fully in the coming election. People have been informed that not to vote will result in the loss of land. It is the same as before, my friends tell me; you do what they tell you to if you want to survive.

These people–state relations, which I have observed for more than 30 years, illustrate aspects of both continuity and change between officials and ordinary people in Ethiopia. Three successive regimes have followed upon each other, one 'feudal', one 'socialist' and one 'democratic', different in name yet the characteristics that their officials exhibit are strangely similar. On its way to power each new government is open, flexible and tolerant and people are optimistic, eager to find out what kind of 'development' the new government is going to bring them. Within a couple of years similar changes occur. The government's need to control the population and curb local and individual initiatives is excercised through the recruitment of loyal young men who report about people and events from ever-lower levels. The citizens who immediately after the change of government were allowed their own opinions and encouraged to express criticism are slowly made to choose sides, either for the government or against it. Only those who express themselves as staunch supporters of the government can be promoted to official positions. The process of making people choose sides is reinforced with intimidations, threats, imprisonments and even killings. The spread of fear and insecurity is almost tangible. Some officials are fired from their positions for reasons nobody seems to know. Others, known to take bribes, or to put people in prison without cause, are promoted. It becomes impossible to predict the consequences of your acts. There appear to be no explicit rules, or whatever rules there are, are applied differently in different contexts. Insecurity affects everybody and spreads all over the country. To protect themselves, peasants withdraw, delegating both initiative and responsibility to government officials. Yet these same peasants continue to be and still are observant. Watching every act, step and intervention by the officials, they are ready to withdraw even further if warranted, or come forward and join in the activities if that seems more advantageous. (See also Poluha 1998, 2002a).

My personal experiences over this long period led to my present research interest, the concrete result of which is this book. In the pages which follow I shall pursue the question of why hierarchical modes of government have such durable forms or why the official treatment of peasants was basically similar even when the individuals occupying the positions in the bureaucracy and the professed ideology changed. The changes of government in Ethiopia were not minor; passing from feudal to so-called socialist, and from socialist to so-called democratic rule are large-scale events in any country's history. Many of the actors in the power structure today were only small children, or not even born, in the late 1960s and early 1970s. In spite of the large-scale changes in the country and the preoccupation with change that has been the hallmark of each successive government the people in power today act in much the same way as the government officials of the Imperial era. In order to understand about the mechanisms promoting such continuity of behaviour I have chosen to focus this study on cultural cognition among children, with special emphasis on hierarchy.

Chapter 1

THEORETICAL CONTEXT

This book is an attempt to identify and understand mechanisms that promote continuity and change in a hierarchical society, with an emphasis on continuity. Social science research in general has tended to pay greater attention to aspects of development and change than to continuity. This can be illustrated by a brief look at the Stockholm University library catalogue, which gives 728 titles for the key words 'social development' and 'social change' and only one title for 'social continuity'. In the larger Libris catalogue, we get 2,340 titles for 'social development' and 'social change' together but only two for 'social continuity' and 385 titles for 'continuity' combined with 'change'. One reason why so much more attention has been paid to change and development may be that they are considered more attractive than continuity; that we tend to associate especially development with positive change in the sense of improvements in life, looking towards the future, while continuity is often thought of in negative terms, referring to conditions in the past. My argument here is, however, that cultural continuity is a more frequent result of human interactions than change and that it also characterizes the way we organise socially, and unless we learn more about the mechanisms which tend to promote continuity, there is little chance of understanding either continuity or change, especially since the two are intimately connected. I shall come back to conceptualisations of continuity and change in relation to schema theory below and return to it in relation to their implications for the individual and the social system in the last chapter.

The method I have chosen, to approach the subject of hierarchical relations and mechanisms that promote cultural continuity and change, has been to study a group of Ethiopian children and look at how they gain cultural competence through their everyday life experiences. What is particularly in focus is the children's learning process, with special attention paid to how they learn and the content of what they learn. The findings about the children will then be related to and compared with the dominant cultural schemas in the society, in particular with the mode of governance of the Ethiopian state since the 1850s. The study revolves around the daily trials and tribulations of children in the context of the seemingly insurmountable economic, political and social problems of Ethiopia and deals both with cultural patterns of hierarchy and patron–client relations and with continuity and change.

Recent research on African politics has given great emphasis to people-state relations. Departing from the necessity for economic development the political situation has often been viewed from the perspective of what possible opportunities there are for democracy. Expressed in different terms the subjects have ranged from the viability of liberal democracy (Beckman 1992), requisites for democratic consolidation (Robinson 1994), the role and effects of authoritarian regimes (Bayart 1993, Yeraswork Admassie1995, Kassahun 2000), civil society as a means for limiting predatory power (Chazan 1988, Bratton 1989, Fatton 1992 and Hydén 1992) to the role of elections (Cowen and Laakso 2002, Pausewang et al. 2002). The methodological focus of this research until the end of the 80s was on political institutions, elites and men. Since the 1990s, however, more interest has been paid to actors, people without power, and process rather than form (Robinson 1994, Haugerud 1995, Monga 1996 and James et al. 2002). Even women and their absence from central political arenas have lately been given more attention (Staudt 1986, Hirschmann 1991, Tripp 1994, Ardener and Burman 1995, Evers Rosander 1997, Mikell 1997, Tsehai Berhane-Sellassie 1997, Poluha 2002b). Still, it is the practices and ideas of adults that have caught the attention of researchers while children have been almost totally neglected.

One major reason for the omission of children from studies of politics may be their age. Children can neither elect nor be elected; they are categorized as politically immature and as children they are not even supposed to speak in public arenas. This condition lasts until suddenly, at a legally and/or culturally specified age, like 18 in Ethiopia, they are assumed to be politically mature. Such an abrupt change does, however, not reflect human life experiences. Women and men mature and change both gradually and individually, not until a predetermined age, but until they die. An arbitrarily defined, so-called 'politically mature' age, agreed upon to regulate affairs of the state and transcend individual differences between citizens has therefore, inadvertently also come to frame research on politics. Obviously, the behaviour adults exhibit in different settings and the way they relate to specific others, is the result of all their interactions and experiences. Thus to exclusively attribute the specifics of an individual's political behaviour to those circumstances and conditions prevailing when she/he is adult, is as incomplete as to say that we can deduce all adult behaviour from knowledge about the conditions prevailing when growing up. Neither statement covers the whole process since individuals from birth to death try to grasp and come to terms with what they encounter and to change or adapt their lives accordingly.

CHILDREN AND AGENCY

In early child research children were considered as rather passive recipients of culture with little agency of their own. This was due to a focus on issues of socialization and lasted until the end of the 1970s. Although the socialization paradigm continues to hold sway in many quarters like all hegemonic discourses that tend to resist change (see e.g. Prout and James 1990:22), it has been forcefully contested mainly through ethnographic research. Descriptions of children who influence each other as well as adults through their everyday interactions have provided the major argument for an understanding of children as active social agents (Prout and James 1990, Thorne 1993, Stephens 1995). Such detailed observations can be found in monographs based on conversations, interactions, quarrels, essays and the children's own comments on what they do. One such study is Heath's (1983) longitudinal research on black and white working class children in the USA. Another is James' (1999) study in a school with four to eight year olds in the British Midlands. Such studies, though rare, allow us to hear the children's own voices, and have inspired me to include interviews with and conversations between children in most chapters of the book. The purpose is to show how children express themselves with regard to questions that concern them, what their ideas are and how they argue for them.

Apart from viewing children as immature and helpless, needing to be socialized, child research has also had a tendency to focus on children as future adults. Thorne (1993), for instance has questioned this approach, arguing that 'children's interactions are not preparation for life; they are life itself' (ibid.:3). Even the paradigm that sees children as future adults has been strong, however, and continues to frame much policy work and research despite being contested.

In recent research children have also been treated as victims of the state, the market or globalisation (see for example the volumes by Stephens 1995 and by Scheper-Hughes and Sargent 1998) and as such as objects rather than as subjects with their own agency. The, 'children as victims' approach has much resemblance with early research on women, who were also often deprived of agency in writings about them. In his essay on power, Barnes (1993) warns us about the dangers of victimizing and depriving different categories of people of agency despite the seemingly 'good' reasons for doing so. Discussing the meaning of power, Barnes argues that 'imputation of power is an essential prelude to the imputation of responsibility' while 'the opposite tendency, which seeks to exculpate individuals by insisting that they lacked the power to act other than as they did' (ibid.:201), may put you in a political dilemma. The reason, as Barnes points out, is that the understanding of people as powerless in certain instances can also be used in other contexts as a 'pretext for withdrawing rights from group members on the grounds that they are not responsible agents' (ibid.:204).

Even if children are now treated as actors on their own, this does not mean that they are considered as 'free agents' independent of or uninfluenced by the contexts and circumstances within which they find themselves. Contemporary research on children has illustrated how factors like gender (Thorne 1993, Rydström 1998), class and caste (Heath 1983, Blanchet 1996) may have a great impact on the individual child. In Addis Abeba I found that gender, age, class and religion strongly influenced how children related to each other. Class aspects are present throughout the study since the children with whom I worked were very poor, a condition that framed their way of living. Gender and age are referred to in most chapters but due to the overall importance of gender for constituting

hierarchical relations and in order to illustrate how such relations can be reproduced, gender is also treated separately in Chapter 6. Religion is discussed in
Chapter 7, where globalisation and especially the workings of the media are also
referred to. Yet, media in Ethiopia have less influence on children than in some
other parts of Africa (Fuglesang 1994, Richards 1996) and much less when compared to the north (Mendoza-Denton 1996, Ambjörnsson 1997, Frisell Ellburg
1997, Frick 1997).

A key issue in the present study is how we can compare manifestations of rank
and status among children and between children and adults with the observation
which initiated the study, namely the reiteration of hierarchical patron–client
relations between state representatives and adults. It concerns the seemingly eter-
nal issue of the relationship between micro and macro or between local events and
large-scale processes, a topic that has been discussed at great length (see e.g.
Poluha and Rosendahl 2002; Knorr-Cetina 1981, 1988, Callon and Latour
1981, Foucault 1980). My approach here has been to study the Addis Abeba children in the environment of the school, as one arena where dominant cultural
schemas have been institutionalised and become part of the children's lives and
compare this with the cultural schema developed historically in the relations between the heads of the Ethiopian state, the state bureaucracy and the people.

School studies have recently been conducted in many countries such as Japan
(Field 1995), Korea (Cho 1995), Indonesia (Shiraishi 1995), Tanzania (Stambach 2000) and Sweden (Narrowe 1998, Bartholdsson 2003). The emphasis in
the present study is, however, not so much on the school itself as on the perceptions of knowledge expressed in the school, on what the children learn, on how
they are taught and how these aspects recur in other spheres of the children's lives.
In this respect the study has more similarities with Morton's (1996) description
of Tongan childhood, where she explicitly relates her findings on child upbringing to dominant themes in Tongan political discourses. Focusing on power relations and value orientations she argues that 'child socialization in Tonga is,
broadly speaking, a political process in which children acquire the values and
skills necessary to function competently in the context of status and power differences' (ibid.:251). There are also some common aspects with Norman's (1991)
study of ideology and upbringing in Germany where she focuses on 'the ideas and
values involved in the formation of children into 'good persons'' (ibid.:1), as these
are conceptualised by parents in the village.

The argument forwarded in the study is thus that children, their patterns of
communicating and ways of relating to each other can, methodologically, be used
as a window onto the society of which they are a part. Their understandings of
how to behave, to show respect and make priorities in different situations tell us
about what happens in the society where they live since both child and adult share
existing modes of existence, communication and ideology. Like other actors children tend to reproduce much of the ideology, norms and discourses that prevail
in their society while they simultaneously contest and even change some of them,

16

including parts of that which seems to be taken for granted and considered as 'normal'. For these reasons, it is argued, children are as important to study as adults if we want to understand about the ideology and politics of a society, about the norms, values and habits that guide people's practices and interactions and about their individual capacity for agency in relation to such structuring phenomena.

The purpose in the following chapters is to provide an ethnography which illustrates how the Addis Abeba school children are active and creative social agents in school and in their homes; to show how they produce and reproduce important cultural schemas or patterns which, in turn, structure and are structured by their practices; to discuss how the children's cultural schemas or patterns can inform about the dominant ideology and politics of Ethiopia and how these processes in which they are involved can help us understand what is behind the power of continuity.

CHILDREN AND CULTURAL COGNITION

Cultural schemas, ideology and discourse are key concepts I use to understand the children and the world that they try to grasp and live in. They are not used by the children themselves, who would rather talk about what they 'should' and 'should not' do or say. The concept of culture was originally developed within anthropology at the end of the 19th century but has for the last decade tended to be avoided by anthropologists mainly for the ways in which the concept has been misused (Abu Lugod 1991, Wikan 1992, Ingold 1993). Interpreted as the way of life of a people, their attitudes, values, modes of perception and habits of thought, culture (and the plural cultures) has, in many contexts, come to misrepresent the relationships between the individuals and groups that it wanted to describe. Through essentializing the concept and making it into a thing, culture has been interpreted as something homogeneous as if every member of a group adhered to the same principles, felt the same degree of belonging and had the same amount of influence in defining what the group stood for, which they definitely did not. Power relations within groups, whether based on gender, class, age or other factors were often concealed when culture was taken to be their common denominator. Similarly, by fixing the stamp of culture on people's behaviour, changes in values and practices taking place in subgroups were not observed and culture came to be represented as static, impervious to change.

Yet, there is no denying the fact that there are groups of people who share a language, norms and a way of life and if we do not call what they share culture, a new concept would have to be invented for it. Thus I agree with Hannerz who argues for 'keeping the concept of culture to sum up the special capacity of human beings to create and uphold their lives together' (1993:109). The point is, however, how to avoid the traps into which some previous users have fallen. One constructive approach to overcome earlier limitations has been developed by

Strauss and Quinn (1997) who define cultural meaning or cultural schemas, as 'the interpretation evoked in a person by an object or an event at a given time' (ibid.:6) adding that 'a person's interpretation of an object or event includes an identification of it and expectations regarding it, and, often, a feeling about it and motivation to respond to it' (ibid.). This 'intrapersonal' cultural knowledge is according to them made up of flexible and adaptable interpretations rather than unchanging rules. It is therefore exposed to change, although, for various reasons, it might not change much.

All these interpretations, Strauss and Quinn (ibid.) argue, take place in each individual separately, although in constant interaction with others, like family, friends, and relatives etc. who represent the 'extrapersonal'. Cultural schemas are thus all the interpretations an individual more or less shares with others with whom she/he communicates on a regular or not so regular basis and/or with whom she/he shares a language, religion, national media like TV and so on. A cultural meaning therefore becomes the similar interpretation evoked in a number of people who share life experiences. In this way, cultural meanings are not separate things but shared experiences and interpretations. They are not bounded since when the sharing diminishes or stops, for example due to migration, interpretations may also differ. Many cultural meanings are also deeply embedded in human beings, who often are not even aware that they have them. Below I shall illustrate how school children in their interactions exchange ideas and experiences and how they reach shared understandings of events in life even if they do not always agree.

Ideology is a different concept used in the text. It stands for the set of ideas that explains the world, may aspire to change the way it is organized, or tries to make things remain the same. In the latter case ideology is often referred to as an 'official' ideology, representing the ideas and acts of those who hold key positions in the state. Through the children I shall investigate the political ideas, culture and acts necessary to implement the ideas. These include norms for correct behaviour and value judgments distinguishing between right and wrong. The fact that people are often not aware that they impute values to certain explanations and sets of ideas but tend to take them for granted and think of them as 'natural', makes the topic even more important and the ideas more difficult to challenge (Rosendahl 1985, 1997, Norman 1991, Encyclopaedia Britannica 1994, Eriksen 1995).

The main approach through which the children have been studied, apart from participant observation, is through an analysis of their discourses as these have been expressed in their speech, essays, diaries and practices. Discourse analysis initially referred to the analysis of language but was extended to cover both ways of thinking and practices. The objective is to understand what makes a certain kind of knowledge intelligible and authoritative. Investigations involve studying what concepts and statements are used together, how they are organized thematically and also how certain social or institutional contexts or specific social identities may promote the acceptance of some knowledge while it will immediately be questioned if coming from other quarters or people (Rouse 1994). The concept 'dominant' discourse may coincide with what is considered to be an official ideology especially when referring to key statements and practices about how a country should be run, which are considered both authoritative and legitimate. A 'demotic' discourse, on the other hand, expresses an alternative, 'of the people', as discussed by Bauman (1996).

The major similarity between cultural schemas, ideology and discourse is that all are based on norms, values and ways of doing things which are often not explicit but part of the subconscious. There are differences between how the concepts are used, however. While ideology mainly refers to politics, discourse may be used either in connection with politics or in relation to any other thematic topic with its own set of ideas, concepts and pronouncements. Cultural schemas, again, refer to all that individuals as social beings have come to understand, feel and be motivated, or not motivated, about in their lives, including political issues. Thus, while ideology is limited to politics, discourse deals with authoritative modes of speech and practice on a variety of topics. Cultural schemas, in turn, cover a broader field, involving all an individual's experiences although emphasising that which is shared, rather than what is individual.

In this study I focus on the children's cultural schemas, especially their conceptualisations of rank and its implications in different contexts. I have investigated their practices, expectations and emotions regarding how they ought to relate to specific others and how they perceived egalitarian and hierarchical relations. I have aimed to identify the norms, values and ideals that guided the children in their interactions and understand how they expected to be treated by others in turn. In relation to these interactions I have looked at what rights and duties individual children felt they had towards specific others and collectives and how they motivated the pattern of rights and duties of which they were a part. As a whole, it has been important to pinpoint what the children seemed to be aware of regarding super- and subordination, their emotions about it, what they questioned, and what they seemed to take for granted because it appeared 'natural'.

The fact that all relations are socially constructed implies that to any meeting between two or more people each will bring their own experiences to interpret the situation. Observations of children's speech, play and interactions will therefore give information about the norms, practices and emotions that are legitimate in their society. Children tend to express their experiences and opinions more spontaneously in speech and bodily behaviour than adults.[1] The latter have often had time to re-phrase, re-think and rationalize their experiences in a way that children do not. And, although even children have often already embodied many experiences and take them for granted, they still vocally remark upon and correct

---

1. Or, as Toren 1993, discusses it, children's meanings can be the inversion of those made by adults.

each other's behaviour in a way that often more crudely illustrates the underlying accepted patterns of norms and values that they usually follow but sometimes also contest. Participant observation has thus allowed me to study the intrapersonal cultural patterns as these have been expressed in children's dialogues, quarrels, insults, essays and diaries. As Holy (1984) contends, 'the social world… is a world constituted by meaning' and 'does not exist independently of the social meaning its members use to account for it and, hence, to constitute it' (ibid.:28). Consequently, meanings, which are constructed in interactions between human beings, are only cognitively available through participation in these activities.

According to cultural schema theory information processing is mediated through both learned and innate mental structures that help human beings organize new information. New information is also sorted or processed according to previous knowledge and experience. This is why people, who have had similar experiences, share many schemas. They are not totally shared, however, but on a large scale since all experiences have individual aspects. Cultural models are in this way, according to Strauss and Quinn (1997) shaped by the learner's specific life experiences, including gender and class, and are sensitive to context, such as with whom and how a particular event took place. In a similar vein, Bourdieu (1977) argues that 'practice' in the form of everyday activities, shapes people's dispositions, ways of thinking and acting, the so-called 'habitus', which in turn governs practice. According to schema theory, the learning process implies that many processes work together in the brain and create patterns for how we behave. When such patterns are well developed we do not need to reflect upon what we want to do, we just do it. Some practices tend to become taken-for-granted and not talked about, as argued by Bourdieu (ibid.), which also implies that they can be difficult to question.

It is obvious when looking at any society and the people that inhabit it, that each person is an individual actor in her/his own right. Simultaneously, this does not deny the fact that the young also uphold many of the values and traditions embraced by the old. When studying children and their interactions I am therefore looking at them as individual actors, who form themselves and influence their environment, which in turn has an impact on them. Focusing on children as individual actors allows us to see how they may differ in their respective values, norms and practices, and also how they may change individually. Furthermore, it makes it possible for us to see the children's active creation of continuity. In their interactions with each other, children recreate many of the traditions and norms that are predominant in their society, somewhat differently (Butler 1990), each in her/his own way, but the end result is that you can often recognize the parents, in the opinions of sons and daughters, even if it is in an up-dated and adapted version.[1]

---

1. Compare also Lewis [1989] (1994) for continuity and change among the Yemenites of Israel.

The whole learning process therefore actively promotes processes of continuity, a re-creation of norms, values and practices. Strauss and Quinn (ibid.) argue that childhood experiences, especially those related to love, survival and security have an extra strong impact on our schemas because they are experienced early in life and connected to strong emotions. All acts and reactions, praise as well as punishments, words, deeds, body language and facial expressions, everything that has an emotional or motivational force, influences our behaviour often resulting in the persistence of prevailing norms and values.

Some ways of acting and behaving also tend to cluster together, and can, consciously, or more often subconsciously, be grouped as themes (ibid.). These themes are repeated in different contexts and can be thought to belong together. They often have a great impact on us without our really being aware of it. Through such repeated ways of acting in different arenas, we not only learn to behave in a certain way in a certain context, but we also learn to think of our own and other people's ways of acting as 'self-evident', that it is 'natural' to behave like this. In this way, traditions, norms and ideals become deeply embedded in us and live on in society as part of our experiences.

Everything according to schema theory is not continuity, although there are powerful forces pushing towards it. Whatever children do is never a complete repetition of what their peers, parents or other adults have done. Neither can any individual's acts ever be the same, since each occasion is new with a change of, for example, context, person or purpose. Previous experiences always appear in new situations and have an impact on them. Thus, small, individual changes always take place.

Major abrupt or institutional change of a familiar environment or of ways of doing things is more rare, though. Such change, as discussed in the last chapter, may be intended, resulting from new agendas and strategies, or unintended, following upon new inventions through repeated use. Major historical change seems to have been the result of a combination of both intended and unintended consequences (Popper 1963, Jarvie 1967). It has for example come about in situations where new groups of people have succeeded in changing the economy thereby impacting on people's daily routines when new jobs and new facilities have become accessible. Yet, even under extraordinary circumstances, it is surprising how persistent norms, values and traditional ways of doing things tend to be. Connerton (1989) here talks of an 'inertia' of social structures. Yet in a global economy a media-dominated society exposing people to never-ending new information may promote quicker change. This, however, is not yet the case in Ethiopia.

THE BOOK

Chapter 2 gives a brief introduction to the setting in Addis Abeba where the children live and to the school, Birabiro, a pseudonym for the school where the study was conducted. A review of the educational situation in Ethiopia illustrates that

On the road to school with all the day's exercise books.

children and teachers all over the country share the problems encountered in the Birabiro school. The fieldwork on which the book is based will also be discussed from the perspective of the strengths of and limitations to the various methods used.

Chapter 3 depicts the children's life in the community. A description of their daily activities, work and value judgments provides the context and content of their lives and illustrates how they through practice and reflections on their experiences, develop their cultural schemas or 'habitus' in interaction with their surroundings.

Chapter 4 presents and discusses the complexities of super- and subordination and patron–client relations, how these are enacted at home and in school and how they are taught and learned. Interactions between children, and between children and adults, are regulated by criteria such as age, gender, adult- and childhood as well as position. The rules are strict and closely adhered to inside the various collectives, like the family, school class or religious group. Yet, these hierarchies hold many attractions for the children.

In Chapter 5 I describe what life is like in the classroom, how different teachers use time, space and school materials in their lessons and how children respond to their teaching. Despite individual variations between teachers and students the overall hierarchical pattern in class is similar. This is due to an interplay of a number of complex overarching factors like norms and values, controlling structures, and above all how knowledge is conceived as limited and immutable, a perception which has an impact on how it is transmitted and received. A counter

Student cum gardener in his garden.

discourse, which suddenly erupts during one lesson, emphasizes the distinctive characteristics of the formal pattern.

Chapter 6 discusses the basis and reproduction of the hierarchical gender order. The children's concern with good and bad behaviour is often expressed in their evaluations of their own and each other's behaviour. Although many do not reflect upon gender as a differentiating factor for children direct questions show their awareness of the implications of being not only a child but also either a girl or a boy. The ethnography illustrates how not only one, but a number of factors contribute to the system's reproduction thereby promoting continuity and making change difficult.

In Chapter 7 three different existential categories of belonging, the group of friends, the religious group and being an Ethiopian are discussed from the children's perceptions of them. Although all categories are part and parcel of the children's conceptualisation of their identity and appear to be stable and fixed, their content and meaning are at the same time in a process of change, being negotiated and altered due to context, participants and national as well as global events.

In Chapter 8 the dominant cultural schema of the Ethiopian state is investigated. Focus is on how the State has developed historically since around 1850 and what its major characteristics are. The salient features of the state are then compared with what in the previous chapters has emerged as distinctive in the cultural pattern created in the children's interactions.

In Chapter 9 I conclude with a theoretical discussion about continuity and preconditions for change, relating this to the experiences of the Birabiro school children and to the reproduction of the dominant cultural schema in the Ethiopian state. The purpose is to summarize our understanding about processes of continuity and to initiate a discussion about preconditions for change, about the kind of circumstances that need to be in place for change to appear possible.

Chapter 2

FIELDWORK SETTING

From my diary, May 2000, 7:45 a.m.

To avoid the Addis Abeba traffic jams I leave home early and park my car in a 'safe' compound not far from the school. What remains is a fifteen minute walk uphill, not so easy at 2400 metres above sea level, but I am slowly getting used to it. The sun is warm but not yet too hot and still shines on only one side of the road. Starting my walk on the gravel road I see a car coming towards me. It stirs up the dust in the street and the wind pushes it in my direction. Hurriedly I cross to the other side. The smell of urine is stronger on this side because the ditch dug along the road to drain the heavy rainwater has become a sewer into which the inhabitants throw all their waste. When the dust has settled I cross back and continue walking.

*Not many people are out in the street yet. A woman comes from one of the lanes to the right and throws some waste into the ditch. She greets another woman, who is arranging a few onions, carrots and tomatoes for sale outside her house, asking her how she has passed the night. She then continues her talk offering news about some other people. Both women are dressed in simple clothes and have no **nettela** (white scarf), which means that they are not going out. They look at me, call out 'Teacher' and ask how my night has been. I thank them and respond in similar terms. In front of me a young toddler is squatting by the street, nude from the waist down, he is doing his morning toilet. From behind a corrugated iron fence I hear a woman shout that he must hurry. Intent on what he is doing he does not react.*

A couple of men come out from a lane as I pass. One is very well dressed in a cloth suit. Two others wear khaki suits, similar to those that were obligatory for government officials during the Derg. Their faces are shining, some water from the morning washing still in their hair. They walk purposefully as if on their way to work but greet each other by name and bow to me. I bow back. On a stone to the left an elderly man dressed in a thick coat sits in the sun, probably warming up after the cold night. Addis is usually cold at night. Further on, a three to four year old boy shouts 'hit it' to his friend and tries to catch the homemade ball that is being sent to him, without success though, since it goes in the other direction. Another little boy carrying a small puppy puts it in the sunshine in the middle of the street and sits down beside it, caressing it slowly. The morning is still young; children are in the process of waking and warming up; there is not much traffic and I have a sense of early morning lethargy, the moment before a working day has really started.

Carrying the anthropologist's foldable chair.

Not so for everyone, though. I have reached the workshop where they paint iron string beds in strong colours. The two boys working there have already put some beds out in the street to be painted. They address me jokingly, imitating my Amharic accent in a friendly way, and say that today the beds will be painted red, not blue the way I like them. Passing a week earlier I had commented that I loved the blue colour they used. I said I was sorry about the colour and wished them a nice day.

Just before reaching Main Street leading to Mercato several children wearing the blue school uniform have congregated. Three young teenage boys are engaged in a serious discussion and move their bodies like adult men; no clinging, pushing or pretend fighting. Elfenesh and Habiba, two girls from my class greet me as I approach. I ask them why they are still standing in the middle of the street. They tell me they are waiting for Meseret, who is unusually late today, maybe she had to help her mother, they add. I leave them behind and turn up to the left on Main Street. In the corner an old man sits begging in the sunshine. He greets some people and begs from others, saying 'For Mary's sake'. Today is Mary's day and many go to church in the morning. I wonder if he is a relative of any of the children in class.

Starting to climb the very steep asphalted road I suddenly feel a small hand in mine. I look down and see Tsigeredda, a six year old, extremely pretty girl in first grade. She greets me with her wonderful broad smile. On the other side is her friend; I ask Tsigeredda how she is and what she thinks of the school and her teacher. She says she loves school and her teacher is very kind, like a mother. Greetings finished, Tsigeredda releases my hand, joins her friend and follows me.

On Main Street there are many children on their way to school. The blue ones from my school and some dressed in red that belong to the government school across the street. Suddenly, three boys run over to the other side and I hear the brakes of a car that almost ran over them. Main Street is dangerous at this time of day. It is broad and allows all cars, especially lorries, to drive very fast. The boys turn around, look at the car and laugh happily. I wonder if they realize how easily they could have been killed. Later in the day vehicles will have trouble passing since the

*market for second-hand clothes, scarves, plastic containers, spices and much else
will occupy most of the street.*

*Just before reaching the school I see the upper part of a man to the left. He is
busy washing clothes from an open water pipe running under the street. He has
already worked for some time and I can see some washed clothes spread out to dry
on the pavement nearby. Approaching the school the stench of urine becomes over-
powering. The school toilets are built along the wall, which surrounds the school
and borders Main Street. Some children have played with the main water tap and
broken it. The school has not had any water for the last two months.*

*To the right as I enter the compound I meet the guard on duty. He checks all
who enter and prevents non-students from coming in. Sometimes, when told to, he
and the other guards also check the students' school uniforms and send all those who
are not properly dressed back home. I greet him with a handshake, and then walk
across the yard towards the office buildings. To the left I pass the toilets and the one-
storey building housing grades 1–3 and to the right the two-storey, L-shaped building, for grades 4–8. Since it is early morning not many children have arrived.
Some young boys try to catch each other and run past me. They shower me with
dust. 'Take it easy', I shout to them. They take no notice. The whole compound is
filled with gravel and dust is a big problem for students and teachers. Reaching the
tiny, fenced-in garden in front of the office I decide to enter and see if the gardener
has had access to water. Kassa and Gebre, two male teachers are already there. We
greet each other and praise the young gardener who has done wonders with the little
garden, maybe he has carried water to school so the plants will not die. The garden
is filled with flowers, bushes and grass. Kassa and Gebre tell me that last Sunday a
wedding group from the neighbourhood had their pictures taken in the school garden. That was praise, indeed. Rich people go to Ghion Hotel or some other hotel
garden to take their wedding photos and pay for it and here some poor people come
to our school to celebrate.*

*Leaving Kassa and Gebre I look to the right behind the office to see if the girls
who make tea and food have arrived in the canteen. There is no movement though
and I enter the office building. Walking along the corridor I pass the rooms housing
the administration and reach the end, which is the teachers' rest and locker room.
No one has come so I sit in the sun at one of the tables and start jotting down some
notes. Another school day will start soon.*

PEOPLE AND AREA

Addis Abeba is a strange city where the homes of rich, middle class and very poor
are mixed in all parts of town. The neighbourhood where the school children
lived is predominantly poor, however, although there are degrees of poverty. The
area borders on and has actually become part of the large major market in Addis,
the so-called Mercato. Many of the children's parents lived from small-scale trade,
buying items in one place and selling them in another, or selling food items prepared at home. A few parents were merchants or owners of small shops, while

some had temporary office employment. Some parents were also beggars. More than 50 per cent of the households in the neighbourhood were female-headed, with the women subsisting on trade. The children came from a variety of ethnic groups and several had ethnically, although usually not religiously, mixed parents. A majority were Orthodox Christians but there were also many Muslims and a few Protestants.

The poverty in which the children lived differed between households but could be found in most. An active indigenous NGO working in the area had, together with the people, renovated the houses, put up lamps in dark alleys and built some communal water toilets and showers. However, the houses were small and simple. Most households tended to live in one to two rooms built of mud, with floors of mud or concrete and corrugated iron for a roof. Some had a separate storage place and even fewer had an additional small room where they could cook. Most families consisted of between five and eight people but there were both larger and smaller households. They all lived, ate and slept in these one or two rooms.

The children's poverty implied that there was a perpetual shortage of money, first of all for food, making it necessary to beg for it or buy what they could afford each day. Bought food also had to be ready-made since they had no money for fuel and cooking ingredients, making the little that was consumed even more expensive. Few children, or their parents, had three proper meals a day. Sometimes when I asked a student what she or he had had for breakfast and lunch, they told me that they had only had tea because there was nothing else at home since their mother had not been able to sell anything the previous day. Many children also had health problems and stayed away from school for shorter and longer periods. Some mentioned that they had had to cut a whole year due to their ill health. When they became sick it was also a problem to find a doctor and even if they were examined, they might not be able to afford the prescribed medicine. Some lacked extra clothes and had to stay at home when their school uniforms were washed. Personal hygiene suffered from the general shortage of water, latrine problems and overcrowding. The precarious economy also affected the school situation and when an exercise book was lost, stolen or finished it could take weeks for a parent to find the money to buy a new one. Meanwhile, the children could not do what their teachers told them to in class and were often considered negligent and careless.

Poverty made both children and parents preoccupied with finding money, food and everything else they needed to survive. They had little energy or time to reflect upon other things in life. The intellectual environment for many children was poor and there was little in their surroundings to stimulate them. Newspapers, books, radio or TV-programmes with news about the world, new scientific findings or discussions that, for example, Swedish children are exposed to daily without thinking about it, had little part in these children's lives. It may be that their lack of awareness of conditions in other parts of the world allowed them the optimism they had about a future with a professional career, something which will be discussed later. They mostly appeared with a smile on their face expressing feelings of comfort, of being loved by their parent or parents and of being protective about them in turn.

THE BIRABIRO SCHOOL

When I started to plan for the research I decided to do it in a school in Addis Abeba having until then mostly experienced work in rural areas in Ethiopia. Even though I planned to do the major part of the fieldwork in Addis I still wanted to visit another school for comparative purposes. I preferred it to be rural since some 80 per cent of Ethiopia's 63.5 million people reside in the countryside and my choice fell on Ashena, a pseudonym for a Peasant Association outside Dangla where I had already been working for some twenty years. Most adults in Ashena knew or knew about me and would not worry about my asking their children questions. I came to spend a total of six weeks divided between three different occasions at the Ashena primary school and have used that information to provide a contrast to the Birabiro children's experiences. This book is, however, mainly about the children in Addis Abeba.

I have given the Addis Abeba school the pseudonym Birabiro, meaning butterfly in Amharic, to try to retain its anonymity even if it would not be difficult for someone who really looks for it to find it. Birabiro is a private school but still very poor. It contains a primary and junior secondary school, covering grades 1–8, and has more than 3,000 students. About 700 of the students have their fees covered by the NGO mentioned above. These students come from extra poor families who cannot afford to send their children to school. A maximum of one child per family is allowed into the programme and apart from the school fee the children are provided with one meal per day, a school uniform and simple sports shoes, exercise books, pens and pencils. The large majority of the students, however, have their fees covered by their parents.

There were about 100 children in each class, sitting 3–5 per bench. The rooms were very crowded, having been planned for half that number and it was difficult for the students even to find table space on which to write their notes. The walls were all empty except for a blackboard in the front, which was repainted every autumn before the school started. The school had no laboratory facilities but a library, which some older students used to do their homework. There was no room for sports and the schoolyard was too dusty to play football. It could only be used for running. The school fees were supposed to cover books in each subject for every child but due to a shortage of schoolbooks in Ethiopia the children were only given half or a third of the books they needed and these were shared with three to four other students. Crowded classrooms and a shortage of books were not problems specific to the Birabiro school but were also encountered in government schools.

The reason for the school's poverty was partly that it lacked government support but also that school fees were low, less than 1 US$ per month per child, which did not allow for any extra expenses. The school administration wanted to increase the fees to improve the overall standard of the school especially to attract more qualified teachers with higher salaries. They were prevented from doing so, however, by the NGO, which felt unable to support all the children if the fees were increased.

Most teachers had a certificate from a Teachers Training Institute, a TTI, and were qualified to teach grades 1–4. Today a grade 12 certificate is required to enter a TTI but previously many students were already allowed from grade 10. The TTI training takes one year. Few of the Birabiro teachers had a college diploma and were thus in principle not qualified to teach grades 5–8 which they still did. Several teachers attended evening school to obtain a diploma, which took them three years or double the time of day students. Many teachers originated from the countryside from illiterate peasant families. Some of these parents had supported their children in their struggle to be educated, and others would have preferred them to stay at home and farm. At a workshop I conducted with all the teachers they told me that to teach the next generation of Ethiopians was one of the most important jobs in Ethiopia, yet, they argued it was one of the least respected today. Many were frustrated, especially when they saw old friends with qualifications similar to theirs but otherwise employed, get much higher salaries. They were also frustrated because they felt that the government did not listen to their experiences when new educational plans were made. The government's treatment of them emphasized, in their view, the low regard in which the community held them.

The administrative personnel at Birabiro consisted of a director, a deputy director, a storekeeper, cashier, secretaries and a messenger. Together they acted as glue to the school's activities, putting the various functions of the school together, making it possible to teach. They took tea with the teachers and the relationship between them was good although each category tended to spend more time talking within itself than with each other. While the teachers' ages varied from 23 to 55, those of the administrative personnel had a more limited span from 30 to 50, a not so remarkable difference. Several of the teachers and most of the administrative staff lived in the vicinity of the school. Thus even if the administrative personnel had less personal contact with the children they knew many of them and their families by name and reputation. The administrative personnel were qualified for the jobs they were doing and had worked for a minimum of 8–10 years in the school.

I worked in Birabiro in the spring and autumn of the year 2000, first with a grade 4, which in the autumn became a grade 5. I also revisited the school for two weeks in the autumn of 2001 and made a brief visit in the spring of 2002. The ages of the children when in grade 4 varied between 9 and 15 years. This was due to the economic problems of some families, which had delayed their children's entry into school. Several children had also been ill, and unable to attend school regularly. The class I came to stay with initially had 105 students, 66 girls and 39 boys. There were both Muslims and Orthodox Christians in the class, but Christians and girls were in a large majority.

EDUCATION IN ETHIOPIA

The reason for studying school children is that a school in any country is a public institution and as such a microcosm of the society where it has been set up while still a milieu with its own structures, rules and regulations. It is a place where children spend a lot of their time and where they have dense contacts with each other, teachers and adults. The institution of the school makes it possible not only to observe children in their various interactions but also to study what are considered to be legitimate norms and values, meaning those which the school wants to inculcate in the children in order to make them into good citizens.

Historically, education in Christian Ethiopia was mainly carried out by the Coptic Orthodox Church. In medieval times, church-based education was restricted to boys; mainly the priests' own sons (Pankhurst 1990) and was based on the reading and recitation of religious texts. Writing was almost entirely limited to religious matters. Today, apart from teaching its own future servants, the church also functions as a pre-school where many Christian children learn to read and write, often a prerequisite to enter first grade in school. For centuries there has simultaneously been education in the mosque about the Koran, mainly for Muslim boys, but increasingly also for girls. This education continues today and has several parallels with church education.

In most countries school is part of the daily lives of almost all children. This is not really the case in Ethiopia. Although the Ethiopian script has a history of about 2000 years, the country's literacy rate is today one of the lowest in the world. The major problems encountered are a low enrolment ratio, lack of teachers in general and of qualified teachers in particular and an insufficient budget to supply the schools with what they need.

In 2000–2001 the net enrolment for the 13 million primary school children in Ethiopia was 48.8 per cent for regular students. Thus, more than half the children in the age group 7–14 did not attend school. There were also very wide variations in enrolment between regions and between urban and rural areas and a large gender disparity with 55.7 per cent boys and only 41.7 per cent girls registered in primary school. In secondary schools the gross enrolment rate was as low as 12.9 per cent of the total age group or 14.8 per cent for boys and 10.9 per cent for girls (Educational Statistics Annual Abstract 2001).

Besides the low enrolment ratio there is also a problem with the quality of education. The emphasis at present is on formal education, something strongly questioned by for example Tekeste Negash (1996), who argues that non-formal education should be promoted instead, since the country's limited resources will never allow all children to be educated with formal education. Furthermore, Tekeste Negash (ibid.) argues that the content of the curriculum has to be adapted to the country's history, local culture and needs, because as it is today it will not be able to promote the kind of development Ethiopia so urgently needs.

Without taking any stand on the issue of the content of the curriculum it is obvious that the formal teaching suffers from a number of very serious qualitative shortcomings. These revolve around issues like teachers having too little education,[1] and the fact that there are too few female teachers, only 30.3 per cent in primary education and 8.2 per cent in secondary education in the year 2000 (ibid.). A weak national economy also results in a deficient production of schoolbooks and very few libraries, laboratories and other facilities. There is also a problem with the language of instruction. In 1963–64 the language was changed from English to Amharic for the whole country. Since the EPRDF took power in 1992, local languages are being introduced as the medium of instruction from grades 1–8. This introduction brings along its own problems, at least for some years to come: some of the languages have never previously been written but now require textbooks; there is a difficulty in developing textbooks with adequate new words where none previously existed; and the costs required for both books and the training of teachers to teach in the various languages are huge while the country's economy remains poor.

The government has introduced some measures to solve these problems. More teachers are being trained; a greater emphasis is given to primary school (grades 1–8) through, among other things, reducing the number of students who continue an academic education, and there is an increase in the intake of students per class. Statistics for the whole country indicate that in 1996–1997 the pupil–teacher ratio was 42, while in 2000–2001 it was 60. In urban areas there are from 100–120, sometimes more, pupils per class. Thus instead of providing a solution, the increased pupil–teacher ratio in towns seems to have compounded the teaching problem.

FIELDWORK

My fieldwork in the Birabiro school was initiated in the middle of January 2000 and the first stay lasted to the middle of May, when I went back to Sweden and wrote a preliminary text on what I had learned until then. In early September the same year I returned to Birabiro before the school actually started and stayed there until the beginning of January 2001. For the first two months I just sat at the back

---

1. 99.6% of the teachers teaching the first cycle (1–4) were qualified, meaning that they had 12th grade plus 1 year at a Teachers Training Institute, while only 23.9% of the teachers of the second cycle (5–8) were qualified, meaning that they had 12th grade plus 2 years of college education and a diploma from a Teachers Training College and 36.5% of the teachers teaching the secondary school (9–12) were qualified, meaning that they had 4 years of university education and a Bachelor's degree (Educational Statistics Annual Abstract 2001).

of the classroom listening to and observing how the children communicated with each other and with the teachers. I was kept busy trying to understand what meanings children and teachers were making in their interactions and I tried to learn what I needed to know to communicate with them properly, keeping in mind the question Goodenough has expressed so well (1967:1203, in J.E. Terrel 2001:808, with Terrel's emphasis): 'What does a person need to have learned if he is to understand events in a strange community *as its members understand them* and if he is to conduct himself in ways that *they accept as conforming to their expectations* of one another?'

I asked the children simple questions when I did not understand what had happened, relating to the daily interactions in the classroom. I watched them chat, insult and fight with each other and I watched them being praised and punished. I learned which children talked a lot with each other; which were the ones who were responsible for order in class; which children never seemed to bring pens and exercise books; which girls and boys dressed well, which came dirty, even smelling; which were clever and which were not. These observations continued during my whole stay.

In the school I participated in some of the English teaching, not only in the class where I did fieldwork, but also in other classes. Some teachers wanted to use my presence in the school to expose their students to another kind of pronunciation of English, and see if the children would understand it and even be able to communicate with me. I was happy to be part of these interventions since it was quite an innovative pedagogical approach in the school, and the children had had very little exposure to spoken English. Sometimes, a teacher later raised what I had said and done in class and we could talk about why I had used certain words or phrases and not others. On some occasions, when no teacher came, and I felt that the students were left too much on their own, I would also teach English in my own class. This put me in the teacher's position and the experience made me realize how difficult it was to keep 100 students silent.

The advantage with doing participant observation in class was that it made it possible for me to observe what the children did, and not only what they said they did, and I could see how their practices, depending on the context, could differ from expressed norms or ideals. I also tried to learn about the categories and criteria they used to be able to communicate with them. I observed their body language and tried to understand what it meant, especially when their bodies seemed to say something different than their mouths. As a whole, I studied their behaviour and speech and came to learn enough to notice variations between different children, how they changed according to context and how some children sometimes questioned the whole pattern.

There were some limitations to the participant observation I could carry out. Thus I could not hang around in the schoolyard, and at the toilets, as I had initially intended to. Being white prevented that. It was impossible to melt into the school crowd with my skin colour. As soon as I came out of the classroom, other school children, not from my class, came forward to greet me, shake hands, wanting to talk. Many simply stared at me, silently, something I found very unpleasant, especially since they were so many.

There were also some language difficulties. Not being completely fluent in Amharic made me lose information when the children had quick exchanges of words. Furthermore, although I met with some parents I visited very few homes. Some of the children were too young to be able to ask me to come to their home. Others were very shy. Some invitations I did not dare take up, because I knew the families were poor and that in the hospitable Ethiopian tradition they would offer me all that they had, maybe even borrow, to be able to treat me properly to food and drink. Thus my feelings were mixed and so were, I think, theirs. My personal characteristics thus affected the research situation. I was a foreigner, but married to an Ethiopian, I was white and as such rich, which strongly contrasted with the children's poor backgrounds and the teachers' low salaries. I was old, which gives respect in Ethiopia, while the children and many of the teachers were quite young. Some of the characteristics thus established me as an outsider creating a distance between the children, teachers, the administrative personnel and myself, while other concerns and interests, not least for the children, brought us together.

My previous experiences in Ethiopia were very useful to the fieldwork not least because they made it easier for me to understand when people hesitated to tell me something they thought could be harmful to them, especially if known by an official. Having a long history in the country also helped me understand why the school director did not want me to participate in the meetings between teachers and administration to which I was not invited. That could have implied that I learned about internal affairs he did not want me to study. As a whole, my personal experiences heightened my sensitivity to anything that 'smelled' of politics, as most things do in Ethiopia. In some instances I noticed that I had censured my questions only to become aware of the fact long after it was done. On other occasions I am sure I exercised self-censorship even if I am still not aware of quite when and how. My sensitivity to political issues could, on the other hand, also force me to pursue certain topics, which I felt were important even though people would hesitate to talk about them. On these occasions I consciously posed my questions in a roundabout way so that the person with whom I was talking would not have to worry afterwards that what she or he had said was going to endanger them. I think, however, that self-censorship and avoidance of sensitive issues continues to be a common phenomenon in anthropological fieldwork but too little discussed in the literature (but see Rosendahl 2002).

In the beginning of the fieldwork everything was new and chaotic to me. Slowly I got used to it and learned to know what to expect. Oftentimes it became boring, especially when the room was warm and the teacher spent the whole period writing a summary on the blackboard with the children copying it. My chair was not very comfortable and just to sit, and sit still, so as not to disturb the teacher and the class, required a large amount of self-discipline. With 100 children in class there were always some who had colds and I seemed to act as a magnet to these colds, having one after another, often losing my voice completely during the school year. Yet, one important event, which took place six weeks after I had started sitting in the class, taught me not to be too presumptuous regarding what I thought I knew about the children. When, one day, the homeroom teacher complained about the students, their laziness, stupidity and ignorance, I argued with him, and said that they were not too bad, some were actually quite smart. To which he said: 'It is because you sit where you do, that you think like that, why don't you move over to the other corner and you will understand what I mean?' I did as he had told me although there was even less space for me and my chair on the other side. But I soon understood what he meant. These were children without basic knowledge, who did not understand his explanations; they always copied from each other, just to get their marks. Although they were in grade 4, some were not even able to read Amharic. The homeroom teacher had re-arranged the seating arrangement many times over the year, he later told me. The last arrangement, which I had not noticed the specifics about, was to seat the children according to school results. I had been sitting with the 20 per cent class elite and had now moved to the bottom. It was a shock to see the difference.

Apart from participant observation, when I wrote down anything out of the ordinary, I also learned about the children and their ideas and experiences from the diaries that about twenty of them wrote for me and on the basis of which I also interviewed them. I conducted both individual and group interviews depending on whether the questions were personal or could benefit from group discussions. The whole class also wrote essays on subjects that I had suggested in order to know them better.

Reflecting on the fieldwork it is obvious that I as a person, with my particular experiences influenced what the children wrote and what they and adults said. My special interest in egalitarian and hierarchical relations also guided the observations, questions, topics for discussion and essays; the whole research process was actually framed by my particular, chosen focus. The advantage with participant observation in this situation was that it also forced me to be guided by the events taking place in and outside the classroom. I had to take notice of words uttered repeatedly, acts committed to which the students reacted in different ways and interactions that had nothing to do with rank. These observations had to be understood in relation to what they meant to the children whose interpretations of them I thus had to seek.

It is more difficult to evaluate what impact my presence and special kind of questions had on the children and adults in the school. I think that some of the questions may have initiated reflections and made some, both adults and children, wonder about things they had previously taken for granted. I also think that my prodding of certain gender topics made some of the girls, and a few boys, rethink certain relationships they had earlier seen as 'natural'. Some boys might, on the other hand, have become even firmer in their beliefs due to my pursuing the issue so persistently.

Although the writing process is not considered part of the fieldwork, it still has a great impact on the outcome of an investigation, whether in the form of a book, report or article and therefore requires some comments. To write means to reflect upon what it is that we know, which events seem to belong together, what kinds of clusters exist and what it all tells us about people's lives. As writers we must impose structure on the material and give it some kind of order. This process gives us insights into the people and societies we study that are of another order, different from that we had while in the field. When structuring the material, we see new patterns and become aware of some of the practices which we might have taken for granted, or looked upon as natural. The whole drafting, writing and re-writing process is therefore simultaneously a process of interpretation, of trying to make sense of and to impose structure on the experiences and data while analysing them in the light of and in relation to what others have written about similar contexts. The unequal relations in the field are thus most conspicuously brought to light in the writing process, as Hastrup notes (1992), since it is the anthropologist who chooses what should be included and how that which is included is to be formulated, while other actors have no say in the matter. This book is thus a result of my personal experiences at the Birabiro school. It is based on what children and adults in school did and said, interpreted by me in the light of my 30 years' experiences of the country and readings on related subjects.

Chapter 3

THE WORLD OF SCHOOL CHILDREN – PRACTISING CULTURE

To enter the world of the Birabiro school children let us start by taking a closer look at their social life outside the school. Three themes, which repeatedly came up during fieldwork and which I realized structured much of their lives, will be used to describe their way of living. The first theme relates to the children's daily activities and gives an idea of the location and the people with whom they spent most of their days. Excerpts from diaries and interviews are used to illustrate where individual girls and boys were, with whom they associated and what they did, discussed or just talked about.

The second theme focuses on how children related to work. Most children spent a lot of time out of school doing various jobs without, it seemed, thinking of it as work. This part depicts the kind of tasks girls and boys did, their opinions about the tasks and how they were distributed by gender. The discussion is based on diaries, individual and group interviews.

The third theme deals with aspects of right and wrong, normative judgements that were an essential part of the children's lives. Group discussions on stealing, a subject children in class often complained about, and on sex and abortion, a topic not publicly talked about but important to their future, will illustrate the children's opinions on these topics. The discussions not only tell us what they thought, however, but also how they reasoned about the issues and what aspects in life they took into consideration when stating a point of view. Elements of great concern that were often referred to in their talks were their own family or household and the social associations to which the household belonged, indicating that ethical opinions were closely bound up with these collectives.

The social world of children, the specific people with whom they interacted and the content of the interaction had, as we shall see, a structuring effect on how they could live their lives; and as such, the place, time, people and content of an interaction usually did not vary much between the children. Despite many similarities between them, however, the local context also allowed for their individuality to be recognized and all children emerged as separate persons, each with her or his experiences. What became apparent through these actions, interactions, musings and reflections was how *'habitus'* (Bourdieu 1977) or 'cultural schemas', as argued by Strauss and Quinn (1997), through practice and reflection were built up in the children's minds and bodies and how they as agents adapted to, re-created and also innovated the cognitive and practical knowledge expressed in their environment.

LIFE AT HOME AND IN THE NEIGHBOURHOOD

A timetable constructed from diaries and interviews with some twenty girls and boys will provide an overview of and basis for a discussion on how the children used time and space on school days.

Approximate time table for grade 4 Birabiro school children

7:00–8:00   Children woke up and washed their faces. Some prayed at home, some went to church. Some ate breakfast if it was not a fasting day and if they had any food at home.

8:00–8:30   Friends and neighbouring children congregated to go to school together.

8:30–8:40   In school the flag was hoisted and the national anthem sung. Sometimes children from the mini-media, a school club, presented jokes, poems and recent sports results.

8:45–10:45 Three periods without break. Grade 4 had seven subjects, four theoretical, which they learned every day, namely Amharic, English, Mathematics and Environmental Science (*yeakababi science*, physics, chemistry etc.) and three skill-oriented subjects, which they had three days a week, namely sports, art and music.

10:45–11:10 Break. Tea and buns were for sale in the teachers' rest room for teachers, and in the cafeteria for children. Very few children could afford them. Most played in the yard while the older ones sat and talked; some did homework or copied from each other's exercise books in the classroom.

11:10–12:30 Two more periods.

12:30–2p.m. Lunch. Children went home and sponsorship children, who got free lunch, first went home with their books in order not to lose them and then to the auditorium where food was served. After lunch they again went home to pick up the afternoon books.

2:00–3:20   Two more periods and end of school day.

3:20–6:00   Most children went home after school, took off their uniforms, changed into civilian clothes and left their school books at home. Some went to the church or the mosque, others played in their yards and some farther away. Many helped with tasks at home or did their regular jobs. Most were home by 6 p.m. when it gets dark in Ethiopia.

6:00– 8-9:00 The children did homework, had something to eat and helped with tasks at home. Some listened to the radio, those who had access to it, watched television. The younger ones usually went to bed around 8 or 9 p.m. while the older ones may have stayed up as late as 10–11 p.m.

From this time schedule we can see that going to and from school, attending lessons and doing homework took some 8–10 hours of the children's school day, a substantial amount of time making up more than half their time awake. However, to learn more about the children's activities, where they went and with whom they met, out of school where I rarely saw them, I prepared diaries for some children to fill in. Twenty children, girls and boys, Christians and Muslims of different ages were asked to write a diary for from one to three weeks. Some children were selected for this task because I had found them to be unusually active in class during my first two months, and some were selected to provide a good variation in age, gender and religion. The children were told to fill in the day's date, the time when they met with somebody, with whom they met, where the meeting took place and what they had talked about or done together with the person in question. Most children managed to fill in at least some of these details and were, after the first week, asked to continue for another two weeks. A few, very young children, however, were not able to understand the form itself, maybe because they had no clear concept of time and space, and were therefore not asked to continue.

The diaries became very interesting, both for the factual knowledge they provided, and for the way children of different ages and intellectual maturity responded in them. From all categories, some gave very brief answers, but had at least filled in some of the blank spaces for a consecutive period of time. What they wrote depended on their individual experiences. Since I interviewed all of them when they handed over the diary to me, it was possible to ask them to elaborate on the answers. The younger students gave brief answers in the written diaries, but could provide a lot of information about many of the people they had met in a day and what they had talked about or done. The very young ones were often a bit confused about time, whether it had been morning or afternoon, and also about the dates. Older students were good at filling in the form properly, but they did not tell about many of the people they had met during the day. To me it appeared as if they mentioned those with whom they had played for any length of time or with whom they had had a serious conversation; something that had been important or made an impact on them. They might also have chosen to tell me of events that they felt could make an impression on me.

Ahmed was a young boy of 10, and one of the students who wrote a diary for three weeks. As we can see from the excerpts below, when Ahmed was reading and explaining his diary notes to me, he was very careful when he wrote his diary. He included many of the people he had met and he also mentioned what they had discussed. No one was as careful as Ahmed in describing their meetings, nor in noting the topics that had been discussed. What stands out in his diary is, first of all Ahmed's whereabouts. He spent most of his time at home, in school, in the mosque or on the road between these places either going there or running some errands. Over and above that, however, what we repeatedly hear about is what seemed to be Ahmed's major preoccupation in life, namely trying to understand how different things in the world function. The following are excerpts from Ahmed's diary and his own explanations when showing it to me.

At 7 a.m. With my father, to eat breakfast and to read the Koran. First we pray, then we read and then we have breakfast.

At 8 a.m. With my friends we go to school. They study here too (at Birabiro) *and we talked about different subjects. We talked about seals* (stamp **mehatem**). *I did not know what a seal was and I asked him* (one of the friends) *to tell me about it.*

*At 1 p.m. With my friends from the neighbourhood. One showed a **Kerar*** (an Ethiopian string instrument) *he had made and I was allowed to try it. It was made of plastic and it gave a nice sound.*

At 1:15 p.m. With a friend, we discussed about the flag and how you get it up and how you can make it so that it gets different colours. I would be very happy if I were allowed to hoist it (the flag in the school compound).

At 1:30 p.m. With Benjam, when we went to have lunch. We talked about the holiday. Some get clothes.

Eva: Do you also get clothes?

Sometimes I get them, but sometimes I do not since they (the parents) *are poor.*

At 2:30 p.m. In class with a friend, we discussed if the lion is bigger than the elephant. Which is bigger?

Eva: The elephant is bigger than the lion.

At 3:30 p.m. With a friend, we were talking about rulers. Some (shops) *give very thin rulers. Some also have erasers, which break the pages or make them black. In school, when we walked back from school, we talked about rulers and erasers because I wanted to buy some.*

At 8 p.m. With my father. We met at home. We talked about order, order in the house. Like in our house, my younger (brother) *he disturbs. So my father is saying, do not disturb. He gives us advice.*

With my father at home. How is your school? He is asking if I am learning or if I am just going there. He gave me a study programme and a playing programme. He told me from when to when that I should play and from when to when that I should study, and when I should read the Koran. With play, play about one hour and then it is time for the mosque, and then study. And if we say no (in a lowered voice) *we will be whipped.* (In a normal voice) *That is nothing. This was at home, and my father was asking about the exams.*

At 8:10 p.m. When I was sent on an errand I met with a relative outside the neighbourhood.

Next morning

At 8:15. With a school friend to school. I asked him, letters, how do you send them? Letters in our house, we sent them to our relative. That is, since I have never seen a letter being sent. If you have seen it, please explain it to me, I told him.

At 10:30. With my friend in class. We discussed about how to become clever in class, how to come out first and second and to make our families happy.

At 11:00. With my friend in class. We discussed which exercise books last long and which do not. I bought exercise books that I thought would last long but they were very thin and break easily. So when that one was finished, I wanted to buy a new exercise book and ... (brief silence) so in the shop they say this is better this lasts long. Then I will look and see if it breaks easily.

*At 4 p.m. With Abebe, my friend, on our way to the mosque ... When we were walking what we were discussing, about our education, about our teacher. A good teacher. Who is a good teacher and who is not a good teacher. What we study at the mosque, we study ancient education (***tint temhert***) all is ancient education.*

At 9 p.m. With my brother, in the house, about our bed, how it is made and how it has been made strong, that means.

Eva: Is there a problem with your bed?

No, it is good. Just how it has been made, to find out about its strength.

Next day (a holiday)

With my mother in the house. We met to talk about our home village. One house in our home village had been destroyed by fire. Since it had burnt down, she had gone there. It was her mother's house. So, she called me to tell me about it. Whether she will go or not, that she will go to the home area.

At 10 a.m. With friends, I discussed how stones are made and that there are different kinds of stones.

At 4 p.m. About a film on TV in the neighbourhood house.

The persons with whom Ahmed met during the days were mainly the members of his family: his father, mother, uncle and younger brother and his friends from the school and the neighbourhood. Ahmed was a bit confused about tenses. I think he meant to say that his mother was planning to go to her home area because her mother's house had burnt down and she wanted Ahmed to know about it. We also learn from the diary that religion was an integral part of Ahmed's life and daily routines, something he did not reflect upon as being special or unusual. Here, and in other contexts, Ahmed also showed a great awareness of his parents' poverty. They might not have had money for new clothes or special food at the big holidays, as many of his neighbours did, and which was part and parcel of celebrating a big holiday. Yet, he seems to have received money when he needed it for school essentials. Ahmed, like many of the children in class, had access to a television even though there was not one in his own home. What I have found is that in Addis Abeba those who have a TV often allow neighbours to watch, and in middle class families, servants and their children also come in to watch television when it is on. Thus the number of watchers is much larger than those owning the television and their immediate family.

Ahmed's major daily preoccupation was a perpetual search for and sharing of knowledge. All his investigations became like minor research projects: he looked into which pens or erasers were better for what exercise books, and he studied the quality or function of things he intended to buy and for which he often also compared the price. Whatever Ahmed himself had learned, from personal experience, from friends or from adults, he shared with his young friends. Ahmed's diary illustrates how all the time he was engaged with his friends in on-going evaluations and discussions about things, people and events. In the process, they came to share their understandings about how various things functioned, like what good teaching was all about and how they should behave to get good results in school and make their families proud.

A girl with somewhat different preoccupations was nine year old Yetnayet, who lived with her mother, father, one sister and four older brothers.

8th month, Miazia 4

At 10:50 a.m. Recreation time. With my friend Selam in school. That we play together. During recreation my brother and his friend came and asked me to play with them.

At 10 a.m. With my friend Betlehem in the classroom, that we do homework together.

At 8 a.m. With my brother Solomon (aged 12) at home, that we go to school.

At 1:30 p.m. With my sister at home. I had been to the mill.

At 8 p.m. With my mother Emebet, at home after having had dinner, she told me to take medicine.

Eva: Were you feeling sick?

Yes I was having a headache

At 4 p.m. with my brother Solomon, that he bring me a doll.

Miazia 5

At 10.30 a.m. In class with Selam, when we had done our homework, that we study together.

At 11:50 a.m. With my friends, Selam and Betlehem at school, that we play together.

At 8 p.m. With my father Girma at home, since I was sick. When I was sick I ate with my father, meaning after I had eaten with him that I take medicine. My mother had not come.

At 4 p.m. With my sister at home. Since she was ill she asked me to make her coffee.

At 6 p.m. With my relative, in the neighbourhood, that I run an errand for her.

At 6 p.m. With my brother Solomon in the neighbourhood, with his friends, that we play. He had brought his friend.

Miazia 6

At 8 a.m. With my mother Emebet at home. Since I was sick that I eat my breakfast, meaning that I was fasting, since I am a Christian. I was fasting, but since I was sick, I should eat my breakfast.

At 7 a.m. With my brother Solomon at home. He told me to watch a film, the film on Saturday.

At 11:50 a.m. With my friend Selam at school, that we play together.

At 5 p.m. With my friend Tezeta in the neighbourhood, that we play together.

At 6:30 p.m. With my relative Fanos, at home, that I feed a child. She has a child she wanted me to feed it. She has a sewing machine.

As we can see from this diary, Yetnayet was confused about times, maybe because she forgot about what she was doing and only registered certain meetings later, when she remembered them or because of her age or for some other reason. Although only nine, Yetnayet fasted, meaning that like other Orthodox Christians she did not eat anything until after Kedassie, that is the church ceremony, which finished around 1 p.m. during Lent. After Kedassie she could eat whatever was available apart from milk and meat products. What she indicated in her diary was that the fast could be broken when somebody was sick and/or needed to take medicine.

Similarly to Ahmed, the major arenas where Yetnayet met with people were her home and the school. At home, the most important people were her mother, father, sister and her 12 year old brother, Solomon. She was very close to Solomon and her whole face came alight when she talked about him especially when she mentioned that he asked her to play with him and his friends. In school, Yetnayet had a few close girl friends and they always seemed to make a formal decision about with whom and when to play or to study. Yetnayet did not attend any religious school. The girls and boys who went to church to learn about the faith of the Christian Orthodox Church were usually older. What seems to be a major difference between Yetnayet and Ahmed is that while her main concern was the people she met and played with, he focused on how things functioned. Although Ahmed and Yetnayet cannot be used as a basis from which we can generalize about girls and boys as a whole, it seemed from the other children's diaries as if there was a tendency for girls to focus more on relationships and to describe and analyse these while boys put a greater emphasis on how things functioned, on football teams and on how to study with friends.[1] But there were also exceptions to these tendencies, boys who talked a lot about their family, neighbours and friends, and girls who discussed water quality, education in school etc. Thus all tendencies that seemed to indicate that female and male preoccupations were different always had their own exceptions.

What both Ahmed and Yetnayet were doing can be seen as part of a cultural learning process. Through his persistent questions, Ahmed shared the knowledge his friends already had and from other interviews I understood that they also learned a lot from him. Yetnayet and her friends, on the other hand, shared another kind of knowledge. They were interested in qualities of friendship and

---

1. Compare with Gilligan 1993 for similar observations of girls and boys in the USA.

learned from each other's experiences how to organize their social lives and treat friends.

A girl who elaborated even more on her relations with other people was 11 year old Batnori, who lived with her mother, grandmother and younger brother. Now and then, she met with her older sister, who lived with the father. To give a more extensive description of what could be talked about between people who meet, I shall give two excerpts from the interview with Batnori in connection with her diary.

> *At 3. p.m. I went with my mother and sister to a relative's party. Afterwards we talked about how good the party was and that all our relatives had come. Their hospitality was also good and the mother, the father and the children were all present, and that all the children who had come, were sitting in a separate room and* (had) *soft drinks, bread and* **injera** (Ethiopian bread), *and that the adults* (were) *by themselves, when they were eating. They had* **tella** (local beer) *and arrake to drink and were talking with a lot of feeling about the problems and ideas they had. It was nice to talk about this. We* (Batnori, her mother and her sister) *met to talk about this regular meeting of relatives to which we have grown accustomed and that it is both a duty and something we love to do* (**gedetana wedeta**).

> *At 9 a.m. With my mother at the new market, when she was buying soap. We talked about that my mother washes all the clothes in the house and that I help her and then that I warm up water and wash myself and my hair. We see each other daily and help each other with work and with ideas.*

In the way she told me about the family reunion later it seems as if the exchange of ideas between Batnori, her mother and sister had also taught her about which elements were important for such a reception. Telling me about it she emphasized the fact that everyone from the inviting family was present, that children and adults were put in different rooms, that it was a lavish party with a variety of drinks and that the talk between adults was good. This way of discussing and evaluating the party, appears to me to reflect the mother's categorizations, which had already become part of Batnori's own conceptual framework and way of interpreting what a 'good' party is, something which also corresponded with what I knew as the local understanding or definition of a 'good' party.

In the second comment on her notes, Batnori illustrated her relationship with her mother. From this and many other exchanges I understood that they had a close and warm relationship. This was also the case with her grandmother who lived with them. From her explanations it seems as if Batnori and her mother carried out some kind of self-reflection about what they did and that it was pleasant to work together.

All the diaries showed where the schoolchildren spent most of their time and few went outside the triangle, which the home, school and mosque or church came to constitute. Some boys went to the stadium and some boys and girls went further into Mercato, the big open business market not far away from their homes. A visit to a distant place usually implied that they went with their parents or some relative. The geographical area, within which the children moved, was therefore quite limited. Older boys but fewer girls tended to know more places outside this triangle, than the young ones, and some of the youngest girls had no experience of places outside. Girls were, in general, more confined to their homes than boys. The persons with whom the children met were relatives, those with whom they lived and those that came visiting or they visited with or without their parents. The children also spent a lot of time with their friends, who usually lived in the neighbourhood, or classmates from a bit further away. In school the children encountered teachers and school personnel and in the mosque or the church, religious people and their neighbourhood friends with whom they often went there.

Many of the encounters at home were made up of admonishments between siblings and orders from adults to work or study. There was also praise when the children had done something good. Mothers and fathers often attempted to follow up on how their children were doing in school and worried that they misbehave. Girl friends talked of playing or studying together, while boy friends discussed playing football. Some children had particular friends with whom they studied. I heard of no girl with a boyfriend or any boy with a girlfriend.

The most important unit to which the children referred was the household, especially the mother but also the father, siblings and other relatives, either living with them or with whom they often met. Children worried about their parents, especially when they were unemployed. They felt supportive of the family, both parents and younger siblings and strived to make the whole family proud of them.

WORK AS LIFE

In their diaries the children made very little mention of the work they carried out outside the school during the day. The many daily responsibilities they had been given and also taken upon themselves were only revealed to me, when I started cross-questioning them, in relation to the diaries. During the interviews I learnt that they had tasks and responsibilities not only at home but also that some worked to earn money for their subsistence. The fact that none of this was initially mentioned in our talks or the diaries may be a sign of their taking these tasks and responsibilities for granted. Since so many were surrounded by poverty and work and money were a perpetual topic in their homes, it seems possible that the children took it for granted that they contribute with whatever they were capable of. While tasks related to the school were the same for boys and girls in the same class, what had to be done to keep the home running was strictly gender defined. The tasks that some of them performed to earn cash were less divided by gender but more dependent on the individual and her/his situation at home.

Work at home

Amarech was one of the schoolgirls who took a great responsibility for her home. Once she said to me, 'Since my sister died, I am the only one for my mother, and she cares a lot for me'. The mother worked now and then in Mercato buying and selling items that could bring a small income to support her family. Amarech's father was mostly unemployed, but had previously worked as a builder. Both Amarech and her younger brother, Girma, who was in the same class, told me that their father was often depressed since he had no job but that they tried to give him moral support and cheer him up. One of their older brothers sat for his 12th grade examination in the spring of 2000 and was afterwards employed for a couple of months outside Addis. His results were not good and he was not admitted to further education, as he and they had hoped. When the work was finished he had nothing to do, and came back to the family in Addis. The second brother was in grade 11, and studied very hard, according to Amarech. 'All four of us', she told me, 'are clever and get good results in school.' She also had a young, four year old brother.

Since the mother was away most of the day Amarech, although only thirteen, took responsibility for all the cooking and cleaning at home. Her brothers sometimes assisted her, but the home was her responsibility. Neither the father nor the brothers got involved in the daily activities apart from the boys running some errands or drawing water. Girma did not always help with these tasks either and told me that his older brother sometimes beat him for not having helped Amarech. According to Girma everybody in the family liked Amarech. She worked hard at home and was very obedient, doing what they asked her to. 'Amarech never makes mistakes', Girma said. On many occasions I found that she had not done her homework properly. Once when I asked her why, she said that it was due to all her other work at home. Amarech once expressed resentment at having so little time for her schoolwork and commented in an essay that 'girls should not be disturbed during study time'. She also resented that Girma had a higher rank than she in grade 4. He came out 12 while she ranked 19. However, Amarech herself, her mother, father and her brothers all took it for granted that she was the one who should take responsibility and do most of the work at home. She had grown into it, learned it and was also proud of the knowledge she had which no boy or man could match. Through practice she had become an experienced and responsible person who could run the household as a very able Ethiopian housewife.

Amarech worried a lot about her family's poverty though. Not the fact that she had little to eat, or that she could not afford a doctor when she had a rash with sores all around her lips, but because the family would not be able to celebrate Easter properly, not being able to afford the required food. I paid her and the other students five Birr a week, in total fifteen each for her and her brother, when they wrote a diary for me. While Girma, the brother, bought trousers and a watch for his money, Amarech gave it all to her mother. I later understood that it was common for girls to give most of their earnings to their parents, while boys spent more on themselves.

Being such a hard-working and obliging girl at home, one could have expected Amarech to be shy and silent in class, but she was not. Amarech was the most outspoken of all the girls in class. She was never afraid to work at the blackboard, or to answer the teachers' questions. Her whole behaviour in class was bodily outgoing and quite conspicuous. The students in class also respected Amarech. They elected her monitor and, together with female representatives from other classes, she got extra lessons about how girls and women could improve their situation. In her behaviour in class, Amarech questioned many of the traditions stating what was acceptable female behaviour such as, for example, that girls should be shy, silent and not conspicuous in any way; actually supporting the way that Messelesh, the so-called 'bad' girl we shall discuss in Chapter 6, behaved in class. On the other hand, Amarech was a firm believer in the gender division of labour at home. I tried hard to provoke her and two other girls in an interview about work and gender since I had found the division of work gave many girls too little time to study. Both Amarech and the other two girls stuck to their opinions about what girls and boys could and could not do, as for example when I asked them what happened when relatives came for a visit. Maryamawit then said:

> Maryamawit: ... And when relatives come, the girls will come and work and the boys go out and play.
> Eva: Aha, do you think this is how it ought to be?
> Amarech, Birke, Maryamawit, all together: Yes.
> Eva: Is it good that the boys go out and play and that the girls work?
> Amarech: Yes! What do boys know, what can they do?
> Amarech 14, Maryamawit 15, and Birke 15

From other things Amarech told me, I understood that she was quite a gate-keeper regarding girls' work. Thus she said she would laugh at boys who asked if they could help in the kitchen and make them feel so ashamed that they would leave.

Amarech's home situation was typical for most of the girls although some of them came off with less work, because they had a mother, sister or some other female doing the work at home. Girls were expected to spend their time after school at home and help run the house. Girls cooked, cleaned the house, washed dishes, made coffee, ran errands and did some of the shopping. The work could take them several hours. Boys, on the other hand, were expected to haul water and run errands. A few boys would also sweep the floors, make coffee and clean the house. Usually it took them between ten minutes and half an hour. But as within all such patterns there were wide variations. Several of the girls, who had a mother or older sister at home, or whose parents could afford a maid, did not have to help with the daily tasks, but were encouraged to study. Thus, for the girls, their opportunity for study and play was closely related to whether there was any other girl or woman, in the house, who could run it.

A few boys helped quite a lot at home, like Alemu:

> *Alemu: My older sister, if she has to do the **injera** and all the other work, she studies at the government school* (where they learn in shifts), *then in the afternoon I help to wash dishes, I wash the clothes I can wash, shoes* (sport), *socks and if the house has not been cleaned, I clean and wash the floors.*

Another boy, Mohammed, also helped a lot at home because he was the only child and had to assist his mother in the daily tasks. When she washed clothes on a Saturday or Sunday, he was there with her, hauled the water and washed some of the lighter things like socks. He often made her coffee when she came home late at night, to allow her to rest. There were other boys as well who helped their mothers, but only with men's work. At the same time, there were some boys, who seemed to do almost nothing at home, apart maybe from running an errand now and then. Some of them were very young, and not expected to help, mostly, however, they did almost nothing at home because they had sisters who did the work. Not only gender, but also age, were thus basic criteria for deciding who should do what at home.

The social and educational background of parents also had an impact on what was required from the children and parents with a high school education tended to give their daughters time to study without being interrupted. The income of the parents was furthermore significant since a steady income could allow a family to hire a maid. These factors did not affect the situation of sons as much, though. Unless a boy was an only child he could study and play as much as he wanted to and it was only when the family was very poor that the boy had to go out and earn some money.

As mentioned, girls and boys had very strong opinions on the gender division of work, and to my surprise, most supported it. I had expected more girls to question such a division, since it took so much of their time. But like Amarech above, I heard both girls and boys say that this was how it ought to be. Discussing how she would bring up her own children in the future, 12 year old Judith told me, somewhat defensively:

> *Judith: I am not going to tell him to make **injera**! So long as he is a man, I don't know, if he comes into the house, men's work, he can wash clothes.*
>
> *Eva: Is that men's work?*
>
> *Judith: Yes.*

Later on Judith added:

> *Judith: I don't want them* (the sons) *to go into the dough and I don't want them to make stew. I don't know how it is in your country* (addressing me) *but in Ethi-*

opia to tell them to work with the dough or to make stew (**besmaam**) *in God's name, that is very bad.*

Manassebesh and Rebqa, the other two girls who participated in the interview, agreed with this statement although they disagreed with much else that Judith said.

Later in the conversation Judith added:

> *Judith: In the Ethiopian tradition, boys should play football, they do this and that, and they are not told to work like we are. For example if I am making stew, the boy, the Ethiopian men, especially if they are big and strong, if they are told to do something else, I don't think they will agree.*

As we shall see in Chapter 6, adherence to a gendered division of labour was also common among older girls and boys in class. Most children seemed never to have thought that things could be done differently until I provoked them with my questions. A few of the older Muslim children were more open to change, however, and thought that it could be a good idea not to follow old traditions.

Discussing how his future son and daughter were to be brought up Ibrahim for example said in a group interview:

> *Ibrahim:* (Girls and boys) *it is the same. What a girl does, a boy should also do. For example if the girl is sick, she cannot work, then the boy must be able to do the work. He should not go out to eat. He can go out and play a little and so can she. And so they can work and play, turn by turn. One should not differentiate between boys and girls. For example if I get married and am out, my wife may be pregnant or about to deliver, then I will do what I can* (at home) *and if necessary I will hire a worker to help at home. So a girl should not be the only one to work. The boy should also help, according to his capacity.*

Ibrahim himself helped a lot at home. His sister had taught him how to do various household tasks, and they worked together. Seeing this, his mother encouraged him, saying, 'yes, she (the sister) should not work alone, you should work too'.

One girl who strongly favoured change was 16 year old Fatima, from the Somali part of Hararge. She lived with her aunt, the aunt's daughter and son and another male cousin whom she liked a lot. Fatima and her cousin had been brought to Addis to study and also to get away from the long-drawn-out war in which many of their relatives had already died. When I asked Fatima and Mona, another Muslim girl, how they were going to bring their own children up, and what they were going to do about girls' work and boys' work, it was mainly Fatima who responded.

> *Fatima: Me, the girls' work I will teach to the boys as well. Now girls' work and boys' work is beginning to disappear, isn't it? The boy is learning from the girl to cook stew and he has to do that.*

Later in the interview Fatima mentioned one of the problems for men who cook at home.

> *Fatima: If for example a man cooks in his own home, people will tell him, are you a woman? When there is a woman, how come you cook? So, he can stop doing it because he wants respect, otherwise he can do anything he wants to. There is no reason for this division, but he will be afraid of being insulted, of being called a woman. It is when I came here* (to Addis Abeba where she first learnt Amharic), *that I heard the saying,* (**set ketemarech behwala tedafferalech**) *if a woman studies then she will be more daring.* (Which can be interpreted as, it is dangerous to allow women to study because that can make them question the gender order and the subordination of women.)

Fatima spoke from her own experiences when talking about boys never learning to cook and do other kinds of work.

> *Fatima: And since they* (the boys) *are not told to make coffee or food they have time to study and they rank better. But for us it is not possible. I myself, for example, if I take out my exercise books to study, then my aunt's daughter will call me to do something and tell me, you can study later. Then she will tell me do this, do that, clean my shoes, wash my clothes and a lot of things. Then I get very angry, I don't even know what to say. When for example he* (her much liked cousin) *is studying I may ask him, can you do this for me? Then he will do it very quickly for me. Then the daughter will tell me, do this and that and say, you will study afterwards. When everybody is silent you can study. She is the one who calls me all the time. She herself finished 12th grade, but she didn't get good results. When she was studying she didn't like people disturbing her studies. So I usually do my homework in class. And when my brother* (same as the one called cousin above) *helps me at home and we do things together, then she comes and tells me, what, you! Isn't he a man? So long as you are a woman, what does he do with this kind of job? Then I feel frustrated. Shouldn't a man do any kind of job?*

As we can see both from what Fatima tells us and what we learnt about Amarech's working conditions, it is obvious that girls spent more time on work at home than boys, that this is considered 'natural' but that it also gives them less time to study. This may be one reason why girls' ranks in class in general, are lower than those of the boys, as Fatima mentioned above.[1] The workload is not only a question of work being gendered and most of it attributed to girls, however, but is also due to the fact that girls are supposed to be in the home. Being inside the house, as good girls should, makes the girls available to others at home. Just by being present they will be asked to help with different tasks, especially since girls with school or exercise books in their hands tend to appear unoccupied to those around them.

---

1. For a similar argument see Gennet Zewdie 1991.

Homework

Homework is part of the work that children are expected to do daily for the school. Some students seemed to do their homework, but most appeared not to. The reason why, may have been that they really had not done it. But it may also have been that the children did not know how to study. The fact that so many children talked of study programmes, and yet, when in class, appeared as if they had not done their homework could be due to the fact that rather than neglecting their homework they were not efficient when they studied.

Some of those who seemed to study hard, had parents who encouraged them. There were also children who, although coming from poor economic backgrounds, took their studies seriously. Mekonnen, for example, came from a poor home. His mother was illiterate and his older brothers and sisters only had temporary jobs. Mekonnen was big enough to earn money through folding papers into cones to wrap up spices. He had, however, decided not to use this opportunity despite his mother nagging him about it. Mekonnen concentrated on school, studied very hard and gave priority to homework even over football, despite the fact that he liked football a lot. Another young boy, Ermias, 15 like Mekonnen, also came from a very poor home with a single mother, younger siblings at home and two older sisters who had gone abroad. Ermias' school attendance was irregular, however. He would come for certain lessons and then disappear and he never attended any of the extracurricular activities that were offered by the school. When I asked Ermias why he disappeared and why he did not take part in the extra lectures, he said that he did not have time. He had a job in a small kiosk that he had to attend to. Although he seemed as convinced as the others of the importance of schooling, he chose not to spend much of his time on schoolwork.

Another such pair was Maryamawit and Birke, both 15, who were also best friends. Birke lived with her mother, sisters and a nephew. Her father was dead. Birke started school early and reached third grade with excellent results, she told me. Then she became ill and could not go back to school for a year. When she returned she was told to start from grade 1 again, which she did, and which was the reason why at her age she was only in grade 4. The fact that she had been returned to grade 1 had discouraged her and made her lose some of her interest in her studies. Birke now helped her mother in the house preparing spices (**berbere**) that the mother sold in the market. Birke had two sisters at home who did most of the cooking, thus her work at home mainly consisted of helping her mother. Birke sometimes came late to school, because she had helped her mother carry the spices to the market. Sometimes she did not come, because she had a headache. Yet, Birke had quite good grades. For Easter Birke and her sisters started to fold papers, which one of the sisters sold in the market. They wanted cash to buy paint and brushes to repaint the house for the Easter holiday. Birke said that she would stop working afterwards, but she continued folding papers in grade 5 too when she was absent from school even more than in grade 4. I asked her why she continued with the papers and if it did not encroach upon her study time, but she answered that she wanted the money to be able to buy small things that she needed and things they needed at home. She agreed that it took time away from her studies but did not think that it would have any impact on her school results.

Maryamawit lived with her mother, sisters and brothers. I do not know how they survived because no one in the family seemed to have a job, although one brother had some daily work in Mercato. The family was very poor, like Birke's. Maryamawit did not help much at home; her mother did most of the household work and allowed her to spend her time on studies. Maryamawit was very concerned about her school and told me that she really loved it. She was hardly ever sick, late, or absent. Maryamawit improved her school results during the second semester in grade 4 and ranked ninth. She also became less shy in class over the months that I was there. I might have influenced her because I tried to encourage all the girls around me to speak up and not be afraid. Maryamawit told me that she thought Birke was fantastic who helped her family by earning some money. To this I responded that I was worried about her education now that she was working so much. Maryamawit said that maybe it was possible to do both, so I asked her if she herself had ever considered folding papers to earn money. Maryamawit responded that her mother had actually asked her to do it but Maryamawit had told her mother that she just did not know how to. Both had left it at that. The mother had not insisted and Maryamawit did not seem to feel obliged to earn money or have any remorse for not doing so. It thus appears as if both Birke and Maryamawit had a choice and chose differently, one focusing on her schoolwork exclusively, the other continuing with her studies but also spending time to earn money.

Among the children who did not seem to study some were not even able to follow what happened in class and could neither read the Ethiopian, nor the English script properly. One reason why they did not study could be that they had economic problems and had to work outside to get cash, or at home to help their mother. It is also possible that the environment from which some of the children came, with uneducated parents, some begging, or being so poor that they did not know whether they would have anything to eat, made studying impossible for them. Their environment was not only unfavourable to schooling but may have made them too tired and worried even to think of school.

Despite their home situation and their results in school, all the children I talked to seemed utterly convinced that education was necessary to get a job. It was not enough to go through a few classes, they said, they had to finish 12th grade and have something more. Many of their sisters, brothers and friends who spent most of their time in the street had finished 12th grade but been unable to get a job afterwards. The Birabiro children were therefore aware that good results in school were important. I also felt, that the fact that they had lived with so much insecurity due to their parents' being unemployed, made them even more convinced that without a job, they had no future. The students expressed such concerns when I asked how many children they wanted to have in the future. A great many girls and boys answered that they wanted two. When several of them repeatedly had said two, I asked who had talked to them about this limitation to two children? They responded that they had learned in grade 2 that it was good to have only two children if you really wanted to bring them up properly. This message had made a strong impression on them due not least to the status of the teachers. But what they had said, was strengthened by the children's own experiences at home. Thus Ibrahim, the 14 year old, articulate boy, with nine people in the house, said:

> *Ibrahim: There are many problems with having several children. For example one parent might not have work. So the child cannot study properly. When she asks for an exercise book and there is no money for it, where will she go? Then she will go out into the neighbourhood and what she sees there, she will put into practice* (he referred to theft and prostitution). *So I don't like it when there are too many children. One boy and one girl is enough.*

Despite being convinced that school was important, the children appeared not to be studying hard, or as mentioned above, they might never have learned proper study techniques. Whatever the reason, their school performance was not good, neither were their results. What surprised me, however, was that despite the low results, their hopes for a future career were without limit. They imagined that they would get jobs, even jobs requiring advanced training and yet they knew that it was very difficult to be accepted at a college or university. Their ideas about what the future had in store for them initially appeared totally unrealistic to me since their expectations were in no way related to their results. It was only later that I began to understand how they were thinking.

Work for cash

Most children who worked for cash did so within their homes. They engaged in folding paper into cones that were sold to shopkeepers who used them to package spices for their customers. Those who worked at home were usually not responsible for selling the cones, but an older sibling would do it for them and distribute the money according to their shares. The young ones helped in folding as much as they could. A few children, who either had no older sibling, or whose older siblings were engaged in other activities, sold the cones themselves in the market. These children were from around fourteen and above. The ones who did paper work belonged to the poorest section of the class, but as discussed above most of the children were poor. It was not only a question of poverty, however, as illustrated by Mekonnen and Ermias, Maryamawit and Birke, there was also a choice. They evaluated their respective situations and their need for money, gauged the time they felt they needed for school and made different decisions.

Ermias, who said he worked in a kiosk, also said that he had another job. Some of the others said that he just lied and I do not know whether what he said was true or not. Yenur, another 12 year old boy had contacts with different dressmakers in Mercato. They made clothes on sewing machines and he helped them sewing by hand. Yenur went to work every day at around 4 p.m. and stayed working until 7 p.m. He was paid by the week and earned about 10 Birr. Yenur gave 8 Birr to his mother, paid one to the football team and used one when he relaxed on Sundays. Yenur was satisfied with his work, it suited him, he said, because it was not heavy, and he found the responsibility light. There was no mention of any other jobs that children were involved in.

The reason why all these children were engaged in cash work while going to school was, they said, because they needed to help their families. They felt a lot of responsibility for the family and wanted to bring some money home. However, I think their ideas about cash work were mixed. They did want to help the family and to many this was necessary and when they succeeded they felt good about it. But, there was also the advantage of the extra money that they could use for themselves. Thus, Yenur certainly felt a strong responsibility for the upkeep of his family but he also wanted his own pleasure and used his money for the football team and for his relaxation on Sundays.

Some, even poor children, were critical about young school children working to get cash, however. Thus Ahmed, 10 years old told me:

Ahmed … [M]y family says, do not work, then your school will suffer and it will make you stupid. And if you get used to money you will become stupid. Yes, if I get used to go to Mercato there are **doriyes** (vagabonds) there. Some will tell me to stop school. So if I start folding papers it means that school will be left behind.

Ahmed 10, boy, spring 2000

This opinion about cash work was unusual although it coincided with my own, or rather my worries that the children would not be able to study properly and would not be able to get a salaried job in the future. There was one exception though, Mulat did cash work and was also one of the highest ranking in class. He folded papers with his brothers at home, studied hard, often worked as a monitor and was good at sports. Some said that his good results in sports improved his rank, which is possible but he was also good in other subjects. Thus as the case of Mulat shows, it was not impossible to combine work and school education.

ETHICS AND SOCIAL LIFE

Early in the fieldwork I noticed that children had very strong opinions about their own behaviour and that of others. Normative judgements were often passed, especially on others, in a sad tone of voice. To learn more about these opinions and how the children reasoned around and about them I asked them in group interviews to discuss some cases that I had devised. The cases concerned stealing, over which the children frequently lamented, and sex and abortion, a subject not openly discussed in Ethiopian homes and especially not by young children, but which due to the frequency of unwanted pregnancies and AIDS I found to be an important subject.

The children had talked about the frequent stealing in the classroom and that they could not even turn their heads without finding that pens, exercise books and even school books had disappeared. At the same time I knew that stealing from people in your community was a very serious offence for which not only the person who had done it but her/his whole family could be punished. Theft could result in exclusion from the local social organisations and in becoming ostracized from community life. Life in Ethiopia, as I had been repeatedly told, is dependent on your neighbours and friends; you must live a social life (**mahaberawi nuro**) and do so through membership in various social associations. When you yourself, or a member of your family, become sick or die your association will help you manage socially, financially and morally. To steal from somebody in the community is therefore a grave social offence. Not only an offence, however, theft is also considered to be a sin. This idea, however, was more common among the children in Addis Abeba who attended religious education than among those who lived in Gojjam.

Stealing and its consequences

To discuss ethical values and particularly theft I presented the children with the following case:

Your sister has stolen something from a neighbour. You know about it, what do you do?

Then I asked the same question about a brother and sometimes I took the brother first. The following excerpts are parts of the discussions between the children in the various groups.

Rebqa: Is she my older sister?

Eva: Okay, what is the difference?

Rebqa: If she is my older I will first advise her, find out why she did it etc etc. If she is my younger I will be very angry.

Judith: I will give her advice … (silence). I will go around the issue and talk about many things until her 'moral is touched' and she will admit that she stole it. Until then I will talk to her and argue with her.

Eva: And your younger sister?

Judith: I will advise her like this and I will be angry with her.

Manassebesh: According to the best of my capacity I will advise her if she is my older sister.

Eva: And if she is your younger sister?

Manassebesh: I will be angry with her but for me I am not going to beat her. I will advise her but not beat her because she is not going to be any better because we beat her.

Manassebesh 10, Judith 12 and Rebqa 12

Amarech: I tell my family, my father. I make my father punish her. Then I tell her that not even from her own home and even less from outside should she steal. Even more than stealing, people will say about her that the daughter of so and so is a thief. That is very bad not only for her but for her entire family. Thus whether it is from home or from the neighbour nobody should even take a cent or a thing.

Eva: So you will first tell your father?

Amarech: I will first give her advice as a sister. If she doesn't return it I will tell it to my brother. He himself will punish her. Then to my father. Then it goes outside the house. Then the name will be an insult.

Birke: I will advise her. It is bad to take things from people. And to steal and take things is very bad in this country. And tell her not to take anything and to return what she has taken. Now she has done it and that from now on she should not do anything like this in the future. And I tell my mother (Birke's father is dead) *and ask her to give her advice so that she doesn't do things like this. And if she says yes, it means that she listens to our advice. And if she says no, then she will stay like that. What can we do? But we will give her advice. But it is very bad when it is said that so and so's child has stolen. It is better if it is said that she is begging. If she refuses then she will have to be punished by law.*

Amarech 14 and Birke 15. Maryamawit 15 was also present.

About a brother:

Berhanu: Is he younger or older?

Eva: Is there a difference?

Berhanu: No.

Eva: But why do you ask if there isn't any?

Berhanu: Well there is, because an older one he will hit me.

Mekonnen: Yes, he will say what have you got to do with it, what do you do with my affairs?

Eva: So he has to be younger?

Mekonnen and Berhanu unanimously: Yes.

Berhanu: Yes, if he is younger, then I will ask him from where he got it. If it is a neighbour's I will tell him this is not correct, one shouldn't steal from people, it is very bad. Go there and ask for forgiveness and return it, I will tell him.

Mekonnen: Just like I gave advice to the girl I will give him advice. I will explain to him that if he starts like this, what will happen to him in the future. He will get used to having money and he will be harmed in different ways.

Berhanu 13 and Mekonnen 15. Teku 14 was also present.

Another case of stealing that I asked the children to discuss was an adaptation of 'Heinz dilemma' as devised by Lawrence Kohlberg and used and discussed by Gilligan to measure moral development in adolescence (Gilligan 1993:25ff). While in North America the answers given by girls and boys differed a lot, this was not the case in Ethiopia. I shall not make any comparisons between children from Ethiopia and the USA, however, but will give a few excerpts of the Birabiro children's discussions to illustrate their way of reasoning about how to avoid stealing in Ethiopia.

The case that I presented to the children was as follows:

A woman is very sick, dying, but there is a medicine that would cure her. Her husband has a job but does not earn so much. The pharmacists want to earn money from this disease because it infects many people. So they have increased the price of the medicine to get more profit. The husband cannot pay the price that is asked in the pharmacy. What should the husband do? Steal the medicine?

Mulat: No he should not steal. He will see to it that he gets a paper that identifies him as somebody who is poor and that she should be given the medicine. This paper he gets from the Kebbele (the urban or rural dwellers' association). *Then she will be sent to the hospital and treated.*

Eva: Okay, but this medicine can only be found in private pharmacies (not unusual in Ethiopia).

Ibrahim: If that is so, the people in the neighbourhood will pay. For example in our neighbourhood if somebody gets sick and he is poor, people will help. In all Ethiopia it is like that. Each one will pay a little and they will help each other. So I will talk to her, she must be willing to do it and then I will advise him to inform the neighbourhood about the problem and that he should take what he gets. And when he has enough, he will have his wife treated.

*Mohammed: In some places there is **Idir** (burial association) and there is **Ekub*** (savings association) *and he can ask his Ekub to give the money to him first. And if he informs his Idir they will also help him.*

Eva: So you don't believe in him stealing?

Mohammed: If he steals he gets into worse problems.

Ibrahim: She will not be treated, he will be taken (by the police) *and she may die. So where will that take them?*

Mohammed: Both of them will be in problems it means. She will not regain health and he will be in prison.

Mohammed 13, Ibrahim 14 and Mulat 14

Maryamawit: Borrow from his friends.

Eva: But if it is not possible, they do not have this much money. Does he have to steal?

All three: Oh no, that is not necessary.

Eva: Then she dies.

Maryamawit: But he can go out and beg for help.

Amarech: He can go to all the churches and ask for help.

Eva: But if he doesn't get enough?

Amarech: If he doesn't get enough he can add what he gets from his friends.

Maryamawit: If he goes to all the churches his relatives might be able to help, but he can get 1 Birr and 50 cents even from very poor people. If he goes to all the churches and he writes about his situation he will not lack for money.

Eva: If even that is too little, then what?

Maryamawit: That will not be too little.

Amarech: If one pharmacy has added to the price there will be another that has a lower price.

Eva: No, they have all raised their prices.

Amarech: Well, let God take her then.

Eva: Either the woman has to die or he has to steal?

All: No he cannot steal.

Amarech: As God made her he may take her.

Maryamawit: May God who made her take her.

Eva: Then she dies.

Birke: Then it will be like God took her.

Maryamawit: He has done whatever he could to get the money, what remains is only to steal but to steal is not possible. So if God takes her, may it be so.

Amarech: But if he steals for her he will suffer even more by going to Hell, into the fire. So isn't he as important as she? If she is leaving (dying) *let her leave.*

Amarech 14, Maryamawit 15 and Birke 15

In the above and other discussions the children's negative associations to stealing are obvious. It is a sin; a person may burn in hell for stealing. We can see that most reactions to these questions were similar. First the children asked whether it was a younger or older sister or brother. I had not thought of making this distinction, but quickly realized that age was important to the children in this situation as well. The students were mostly asked to deal with the younger sister or brother first. Then they told me that a younger sister or brother would first be asked if they had really stolen something from the neighbour. When this had been verified, they would be advised about how wrong it was to steal and told that if the community learnt about it, the sister's or brother's name would be associated with stealing for the rest of their life. And not only her or his name, but also the rest of the family would be associated with it. It would become like a stigma attached to the family. Then they would beat the younger sister or brother up, and make them return whatever they had stolen. They also might inform their parents about the theft.

An older brother or sister would be similarly advised at great length and told to return whatever they had stolen, but since they were older, and especially the brother most probably stronger, the children would be more careful, show more respect, not try to beat them, but tell their parents, who would do it instead. The beating was necessary, according to most, because without it their sibling would never understand the seriousness of the matter. They also told me that there would be no difference in their treatment of or advice to a sister or a brother because both were the same with regard to stealing. What was most important about stealing was the bad name it gave the person who had done it, and not only her or him, but the whole family from which she or he came. Theft could affect neighbourly relations, choice of marriage partner; indeed, it could have an impact on almost any social interaction. It was even better to allow a close relative to die than to be caught stealing for her or his sake. To be called a thief was among the worst epithets the children could imagine and something that should be avoided at all costs.

From their discussions we can see how both Muslim and Christian children immediately referred to friends, relatives, neighbours, members of the social associations etc. for help. They took it for granted that all these people were ready to help when one of them was in serious need of assistance. The **mahaberawi nuro**, social life through associations, was already an important part of the children's lives, actually their social security, even though the **Kebbele**, or urban dwellers' association, today also provides some assistance to those who live within its area.

Sex and abortion

The other topic I discussed with the children concerned their opinions on sexual relations. Like many others I am worried about the spread of HIV/AIDS in Ethiopia but I was also afraid of the effects that unwanted pregnancy could have on young teenage girls and their schooling and wanted to know how girls and boys reasoned and motivated their opinions on these subjects. Having read Gilligan's book 'In a Different Voice' (1993) where she discusses the issue of pregnancy with young North American girls I made some of these experiences into a case, adapted it to the Birabiro situation and presented it as follows:

> *Your sister who is 16 years old is an extremely bright student. She has found a boy-friend and now she has become pregnant with his child. She has the alternative to have an abortion at a hospital* (this is not allowed in Ethiopia, but was the only means to provide a realistic option, since local – **habesha** – medicine against abortion was known by the children to be very dangerous to the woman and therefore would not have been considered as a real choice) *or give birth. She asks for your advice, what do you say to her?*

Then I slightly changed the question and asked them as follows:

> *Your brother who is 16, and is extremely bright in school, has made his girl friend of the same age pregnant. She is also an extremely bright student. He is wondering whether he should advise his girlfriend to have an abortion in hospital, so that they both can continue their studies, or whether he should tell her to give birth to the child. He asks you, his sister/brother for your opinion, what do you say to him?*

All the students found the questions very difficult to respond to. 'How can I give advice on such issues', many said. Yet, I could see that they were challenged by the questions, took them seriously and reflected upon them to give their best advice to the imagined sister or brother. The answers were not as unanimous as those concerned with stealing. First the children discussed what to say to an imagined sister.

> *Maryamawit: After it has happened it has happened.*
>
> *Birke: We would not like her to have an abortion, that is how we should advise her.*
>
> *Maryamawit: If she has an abortion she will suffer a lot. She may die.*
>
> *Eva: No, it is not like that. If it is done in a hospital or a clinic nothing will happen to her.*
>
> *Birke: Yes there …* (silence).
>
> *Amarech: Well not with **habesha** medicine.*
>
> *Eva: No if it is done properly nothing will happen to her.*
>
> *Birke: But even then, if she doesn't have an abortion it is good.*
>
> *Maryamawit: Yes it is good.*
>
> *Birke: The child may become someone very big.*
>
> *Amarech: How great he may become she does not even know.*
>
> *Birke: When he grows up he may become a ruler, he can become anything.*
>
> *Maryamawit: That is not known. He will grow up with her effort.*
>
> *Birke: He can help her and he can help other people. If it has happened, it is good if she doesn't have an abortion.*
>
> *Maryamawit: After it has happened it should not be repeated. With God's help this child may become anything, but it should not be repeated.*
>
> Amarech 14, Maryamawit 15 and Birke 15, autumn 2000

> *Mekonnen: I will not tell her to have an abortion because it means that she will have killed someone. She has made a mistake and I will advise her about what she should do in the future. If the boyfriend has a job and if he has a good character and if he can take care of her and the baby I will tell her that it is good if they get married.*
>
> Mekonnen 15, Berhanu 13, and Teku 14, autumn 2000

Yenur: It is better to give birth. If she has an abortion it is a sin. It means that she killed the child. That is why it is better to have the child. Otherwise she has committed a sin.

Eva: So she has to give birth even if it means no more school?

Yenur: Yes, she has to give birth.

Yenur 13, autumn 2000

The above responses came from some of the Christian children. Some Muslim children's responses follow, first, however, the mixed group of Mulat 14, who is a Christian and Ibrahim 14 and Ahmed 13, who are Muslims.

Ibrahim: If she has no husband and if she is a student I think it is better if she has an abortion in the hospital. This is what I will advise her. First she has no husband and then she will lose her name. Even while she is a student and before she is married, to get pregnant is another thing. When she is married there is no problem. But to do it in the hospital ... (silence). If she gives birth, it is known. There may be many other people who will want her. But if they hear about this, they will leave her. So I think it is better if she has the abortion in the hospital.

Ahmed: For me it is the same as Ibrahim said. If there is no problem when she has the abortion, then I think it is good. First of all there may be problems to bring up the child, to get all the things he needs. And her family may also be poor. And also she will not have to stop her schooling.

Mulat: I think the same as they do. If she doesn't have any problems from having the abortion then I will advise her to do it in the hospital and continue the school.

Eva: But doesn't it say in all religions, I think, that what God has created we have to accept?

Ahmed: Yes it is said like that.

Eva: But you mean that sometimes it is not necessary to follow this?

Ibrahim: Yes sometimes it is not necessary.

Ahmed: Most important is to think about this beforehand.

Eva: Yes, that is a good idea.

Mulat: Once it is done, what He has brought we have to accept and she has to give birth to the child.

Ibrahim: While she is a student?

Eva: Are you changing your mind?

Mulat: Not that, but when I see it from the point of view of religion.

Eva: So I brought in religion and you changed your opinion?

Naema: (I will ask her) why did you do like this first of all? Without having asked your mother for permission? Your mother she will see to it that you have a wedding if you are mature. But like this, without any kind of ceremony, not even **Nika** (the Muslim marriage ritual). *The boy will be very much insulted afterwards.*

Eva: Do you mean that she will be insulted?

Naema: No, not she, yes she will be insulted to start with, that goes without saying. But the child after it has grown.

*Tekia: The child is called **Dikala**.*

Naema: Now for example if she is pregnant with him and she says to him let us take care of the child together and if he says no, the child will be in problems. If they don't bring him up together the child will be insulted and she will be insulted, but not he. Why, because he is a man.

. . . .

Eva: So what advice do you give her then?

Naema: … If she gives birth the child will be strongly condemned. Yes, I think she has to have an abortion. So that the child will not be condemned everywhere and also he will be hated, such a child will be hated, one who is made without a marriage is really hated.

Eva: So what is better, if they get married or if she has an abortion?

Tekia: If they get married.

Eva: But she is very young?

Naema and Rekik: It is better to have an abortion.

Rekik 10, Tekia 10 and Naema 11, autumn 2000

Fatima: For me, if she is a very good student, first of all she should have been careful, but she wasn't and she got pregnant. So she has to have an abortion. That is how I think about it. If she has a baby today people will talk about her, that girl has a problem, so it is better to have an abortion and for her to reach a high position. But in the beginning she should be careful and if not, have an abortion. She can also make use of other things.

Mona: I think like Fatima. Instead of stopping going to school it would be better for her to have an abortion.

Fatima 16 and Mona 16, autumn 2000

The above discussions dealt with a pregnant sister, below follow some excerpts from discussions dealing with a brother who has made his girlfriend pregnant.

Yenur: Until he finishes they have to help each other. Some boys they just drop them and leave.

Eva: They say it is not mine, do they? But he knows that it is his?

Yenur: Yes he does.

Eva: So you mean that they have to help each other?

Yenur: Yes they have to, meaning that he has to pay money and buy other things for the child, that he has to do.

Eva: And after the child has been born, what should he do, the father?

Yenur: They can get married when they have the proper age.

Eva: How old should he be then?

Yenur: He should be more than 20.

Eva: And she?

Yenur: She should also be more than 20.

Yenur 13, Christian, autumn 2000

Mulat: If he accepts my advice I will tell him to agree with and live with the girl or talk with her about having an abortion in the hospital. If she agrees to carry through the abortion and if she doesn't discuss it with the family, and to have the child and not to run away from it.

Mohammed: Some who are afraid to tell their families will run away from it.

Ibrahim: The boy may run away. First he may be after her and when finally she says yes, and then when she tells him that she is pregnant he may run away. So before this happens it is best to be careful.

Mulat 14, Christian, Mohammed 13 and Ibrahim 14, Muslims, autumn 2000

Fatima: Whose child are you going with and making pregnant? Be careful! Even if she doesn't get pregnant she may have another disease that she can pass on to you. So I will tell him to advise her to have an abortion so that her family doesn't worry. And then make use of something else.

Mona: First I will tell him not to do such things. People will talk about him, so and so's child did this. And don't let people talk about your parents! So I will advise him to tell her to have an abortion without people knowing about it.

Eva: You will not tell him to marry her?

Mona: If she is a good girl he can marry her, but if she isn't he shouldn't.

Fatima: Now this girl is pregnant and her family and our family might not agree with one another. They may think that he is poor and that he shouldn't marry their daughter. They might not agree. And then the girl herself may be worried. And if he very much wants to marry her we, his family, will not let her in, we don't want her. Without getting advice from the family to make somebody pregnant and then to ask her to marry, I really don't know.

Fatima 16 and Mona 16, Muslims, autumn 2000

Regarding abortion, the Christian girls and boys in Addis Abeba were adamant that it was out of the question. 'Abortion is the same as killing and that is a sin according to God', they said. 'Furthermore', many of them argued, 'you never know what he (i.e. the baby) will become, maybe a doctor who will help many sick people or a leader of the country. He may become something really big.' The potential baby was always a he, unless I suggested a she.

Muslim girls in Addis Abeba were in favour of abortion. Partly because they thought that if the sister or girl and the brother were such good students, it was better for them to continue their education. Partly also, as they told me, because a child who is born out of wedlock will never be fully accepted by the families. Most Muslim boys also supported an abortion, commenting that the girl would lose her name if she had a child without being married, but also because it would be a waste of the girl's capacity when she was so good in school. She might never return to school afterwards, but she could always have a child later. A few younger Muslim boys thought that abortion was a sin and the sister or girl should give birth instead.

In the countryside in Gojjam all the children were Coptic Christians, Yet their experiences varied distinctly from those of the Coptic Christian children in Addis Abeba who had been much more exposed to religious preaching. All the six young girls in Gojjam supported an abortion for a bright female student, whether a sister or a brother's girlfriend. To these Gojjame girls schooling was such a new, unusual and extraordinary opportunity for girls, that they could not imagine leaving school to have a child. Once the girl had finished her education and had a job, she could have children, but if she stopped her education in the middle, she would remain a farmer and that would be a real waste when she had been given the opportunity to study. The boys in one of the group interviews in Gojjam had similar opinions, saying that an abortion was the best alternative for the girl. The other group of boys thought that it was better if she gave birth. Not because an abortion would mean to sin but because the child might become 'something big'. And the girl could just give birth and go back to school after ten days. Either the mother's or the father's parents or siblings could take care of the baby. When I suggested that she could not just come back after ten days, one of them said, 'Ok, even if it takes a year it is a very short time, but if she is clever she has to continue her education, otherwise she will remain a farmer and that is not good'.

Another thing that came up in the discussions was that a boy could always disclaim parentage. Neither the girls nor the boys I interviewed supported such behaviour from their imagined brother, but it was obvious that it happened quite frequently and that many young men did not take responsibility for their child. Yet the children interviewed said they wanted their brothers to act as a father to the child, if it was his, and not shy away from it.

Abortion and stealing were thus discussed by the children in somewhat different terms depending both on their gender, area of origin and religion. Abortion to the Christian children in Addis meant to sin against what God had given, something which was unthinkable to them. Although some Muslim boys had similar ideas about abortion most Muslim boys and all Muslim girls thought it would be better for the girl to study and get married in a proper way. To them giving birth without being married would be shameful for the girls and would negatively reflect on the whole family and most of all on the child. In Gojjam all the girls and half the boys favoured abortion although like the Christians in Addis they felt that a child out of wedlock would not be shameful either to the girl or her family.

Both with regard to stealing and abortion the children's reflections remind us of the importance of the collective for them. If one family member stole the whole family could be ostracized from the community. And, according to Mona, a boy who made a girl pregnant could give a bad name to his family. Thus, whether you liked it or not, you were part of the collective, primarily the family, as a unit and you would share in both the positive and negative reputation that developed around and adhered to it. This did not mean that all children experienced the duties to the family and in some cases, the association, in the same way. Some could attach greater importance to personal interests and neglect those of the collective. Yet, whatever choice they made, the children were aware of what the norms were and if they then had given priority to personal rather than family or group interests they might have difficulties living with such a decision.

CONCLUDING REMARKS

In the preceding pages we have had some glimpses of the Birabiro children's social life. Their daily interactions took place with members of their extended family, with neighbours, friends, and classmates and for some with their religious teachers. These people and the places where they met together constituted the everyday social world of which the children had their first hand experience; the arenas where they heard, observed and saw how things were done and where they acted and tested opinions and saw how they functioned. Within these arenas the children developed their *habitus* (Bourdieu 1992) or cultural models (Strauss and Quinn 1997). There were obviously other influences on the children's lives directly and indirectly via television or radio, friends or relatives some of whom might have travelled, but it should be emphasized that the children's own first-hand experiences, as illustrated here, were gained in their homes, the neighbourhood, school, religious institution or in the roads between these. Their ideas and opinions were, in this way, developed in the local context.

The importance of the local for the individual has been emphasized by Hannerz (1996), who argues that the local often stands for continuity as it is made up of everyday, repetitive and practical acts. The face-to-face relations, which these acts are filled with, become emotionally important to the individuals. Thus people often characterize local experiences as real, in comparison with those they have read about, heard on the radio or seen on television. The local as the basis for the individual's experiences has also been underlined by Eriksen (1995), who believes that the global is always locally interpreted because the global itself lacks place.

Many of the children's views and opinions resembled what I had heard and observed from adults in and outside the school. In the dialogues and diaries it was therefore possible to recognize a presence of continuity with norms, values and traditions that prevailed locally; with the hierarchy in the family and in relation to God; with the importance of gender for what to do and how; with the feeling of protecting the household, especially the mother, but also the knowledge that everything you do reflects back on the family; and with the necessity to belong to various associations, implying that you ought to abide by their rules to obtain social security.

While emphasizing continuity, the diaries and dialogues also illustrate that to these children everything was in a process. They were not yet ready with their opinions but formed them on the basis of previous experiences, the reactions of their environment and also on small interventions like how I framed my questions. In some exchanges my influence on what they said is quite obvious. Above all, however, we see an on-going dialogue between the individual children and their surroundings. The children tested what they did, said or bought to see whether it functioned. They evaluated the responses and tested their ideas or things or behaviour again, maybe in a slightly modified way, and then they tried to gauge what the new reactions might imply. Their practice was a never-ending process. And yet, despite the fact that each individual was a different person with her/his own distinctive experiences, likes and dislikes and position in the opportunity structure (Wallman 1984) the framework or social field within which all the interactions took place was similar for all. They shared a geographical area, a school, and as either friends or enemies they were guided by similar norms and values. Their actions as human beings were thus constrained by the social and cultural order or the existing structures (Ortner 1984, 1996), which they themselves constituted in their interactions.

Chapter 4

GROWING UP INTO HIERARCHY – LEARNING OBEDIENCE, RESPECT AND CONTROL

Modes of child upbringing can be seen as expressions of cultural and individual conceptions of how children's psychological, physical, intellectual and emotional growth can best be promoted. Such conceptions vary between societies but in most they are manifested by the use of rewards and punishments. Common forms of rewards are sweets, money, favours, verbal encouragement, love and appreciation while punishments vary from beatings, scolding, reprimands to threats of the loss of love. There are also often clear rules about who can punish which child, allowing some and preventing others from inflicting punishment. In Ethiopia as elsewhere it was common to have quite a permissive attitude towards infants. Up to the age of about two to three, children were showered with love and affection but after that they were sometimes gradually and sometimes abruptly required to conform to accepted behaviour.

The argument in this chapter is that child upbringing, or the pattern of relations between adults and children, as well as between siblings and among children in Ethiopia was often explicitly hierarchical. Age, adult status, physical size, strength, gender and social status were the more noteworthy aspects determining super- and subordination. Depending on the issue interactions were carried out within various kinds of collectives such as the extended family, the school, school class or the religious group within which members had rights and duties towards each other expressed in the form of patron–client relations. Key words used by Birabiro children for what their own behaviour towards adults ought to be were **obedience** and **respect**, while they expected adults to exercise **control** or **supervision** over them. The duties adults and children performed for each other were related to these concepts and evaluated according to a combination of general ideals for behaviour and individual idiosyncrasies.

What initially appeared to be a rather simple, clear-cut stratified system turned, however, into something more complex when taking a closer look at what the children meant with their concepts. The hierarchical relations were not carried out in some un-determined reality but conducted within various collectives where the idea of different forms of redistribution predominated. Within the hierarchy expressions of super- and subordination were strictly upheld yet the system was flexible and children appeared to be more aware of its options than its restrictions.

OBEDIENCE AND RESPECT

Children and adults

It is the disagreement in our house, there is no agreement. By that I mean that my younger brother does not obey my older brother and my older brother does not obey my younger brother either. In short, we do not respect each other. We groan when we are told to run errands and we do not have any agreement in our house, and what I say is, that it is not good when it is like this.

Essay by Mulat on good and bad decisions at home, spring 2000.

Tekia:… But not to obey your mother is not good, then your work will also not be good. If you don't obey it is bad.

Eva: Do boys obey?

Tekia: Even if boys do not obey, it doesn't matter, but when girls refuse it is disgusting.

Interview with Tekia, Rekik and Naema, autumn 2000

To be obedient to your parents implied, according to the children, that they should do what their parents told them to, come home on time, run errands, help in the house, get water, and fulfil whatever duties had been assigned to them. Obedience was never talked of in negative terms, rather as something, which was natural or self-evident to the children, 'you should obey your parents'. This relationship between parents and children was reflected in the loving and respectful terms in which the children talked about their parents. Even in one case, where a father spent most of the family's money on alcohol and in another where he beat his children inordinately, even hitting their mother, the children talked of him in a forgiving tone of voice, implying that somehow he could not help doing what he did.

The mother was the most important person in the children's lives, though. When I asked children 'which adult has been closest to you in your life?' almost all answered that it was their mother, even when they had a father living with them. The reasons put forward were that she spent more time at home, together with them than the father, who even when unemployed was mostly outside; she also worried about them, asked them how their day had been and served them food when it was available. Their mother was also mostly the one who saw to it that they had money to buy pens, exercise books and whatever they needed for the school. Many of the children's mothers worked, selling small items in the market to get money for food and other necessary items. Daughters and sons observed this and talked about it in interviews and essays, some saying that she was working outside all day and when she came home, tired in the evening, she started to cook for them, 'she is really doing everything for us', they repeated. In turn, they were, at least in theory but often also in practice, prepared to do whatever she asked them to. Since many of the fathers were unemployed, they had little to offer the children to assist them in their needs. Yet, according to what many children said, their fathers were concerned about their education and kept themselves informed about it. The children felt that they should obey their father, irrespective of his contribution to the household

To obey a parent was to show respect. Someone who did not obey a parent, or an older sibling, did not show that parent or sibling due respect. The children took it upon themselves to obey, although there were obvious variations in how they interpreted their parents' wishes or orders. Some of the boys often admitted to 'having forgotten' to go home directly after school because they got lost in their play, usually football. It was not that they had intended to disrespect their mother; they just found the play so engaging. From the interviews, for example with Tekia above, it is also obvious that girls often took the obedience more seriously than boys, and that adult women and men, as well as boys, expected girls to be more obedient than boys.

Obedience, as a sign of respect, is also what ideally should characterize the relationship between a student and a teacher:

Eva: Can you describe a good student to me?

Ermias: It is one who studies well and who respects the teacher and who gets very good results.

Eva: And a bad student?

Ermias: One who derogates the teacher, who insults him, who gets bad results.

Eva: What surprises me a little, not only about you, but also about the other students, is that nobody mentions that a good student, as in my opinion, should help the others, those who have not understood, a person who, more than respecting his teacher, helps his fellow students?

Ermias: It is good to help the other students, but it is more important to respect the teacher than the students.

Interview with Ermias, 15, autumn 2000

Obedience to a teacher implied that a student should bring pens, exercise books and textbooks to class; that she or he did their class and home work, was silent and listened to the teacher when the latter talked. When I asked why so many students did not bring their exercise books and pens, and in this sense showed disobedience, the students mostly answered that it was really not the students' fault, the reason was that so many of them could not afford to buy these things. When I insisted that the really poor students were supplied with exercise books and pens when term started, I was told that there was much stealing in class. Pens and exercise books were repeatedly stolen, sometimes it would be enough to look to the side and when you looked back your things would be gone. When this happened, some students might have to wait for several days, a week or more, until their mothers would be able to sell something extra in the market to get the money for a new pen. Textbooks were like cash and easily sold in the street. The fear of theft made many children organise groups who took turns to bring the necessary books to class allowing the others to leave theirs at home. In this way, poverty could force you into disobeying the teacher, the children argued.

Obedience from the students and mutual respect between students and teachers was thus the norm for their relationship in school. This was also in line with the expectation that a teacher should act as a parent or older sibling towards a student. There were, however, teachers who not only did not fulfil their role expectations but also insulted and abused the children, especially by beating them on the head or in other places that could harm them forever. The children did not respect such teachers, even if they did not show their lack of respect openly.

> *Amarech: One day this teacher he insulted me,* (this was several years earlier) *he said you sack, you* **Attela** (what you throw away after having made the local beer), *you* **Lambula** (what you throw away after having made local honey wine). *I didn't say anything. The next day he hit me in the face. Still I was silent. I cried but I was silent, but* **kim yazkubet.**

> *Eva: What do you mean by that, kim yazkubet?*

> *Amarech: I was very sorry, I felt a grudge against him, I was filled up with it and felt I could not forgive him. Then he starts greeting me. He had forgotten what he had said. But I, until today, I have it written inside here* (pointing to her head), *I have not forgotten it. I answer him when he tells me to, but if I am standing talking to somebody,* (and he comes by) *I tell them, what he has done. I shall never forget it.*

> Interview with Amarech, Birke and Maryamawit, autumn 2000

After having heard other critical assessments of teachers by students who expressed ideas similar to what Amarech had said, I started to see a pattern for how relations between teachers and students were conceptualised. Students looked up to their teachers, respected them and expected the teachers to treat them with the same concern that they would their own children. According to the students, teachers could be critical of them but they should never make derogatory remarks about them. This pattern was well characterised in an interview with the students' homeroom teacher, Girma, and it also illustrates the power teachers have over their students.

> *Girma: No teacher should advise his students in such a way that the students feel frustrated, that they lose confidence in themselves. Students' minds are just like a white paper. They catch everything, which comes from a teacher, even the personality of the teacher is important. The students will always identify the teacher with the insult the teacher has given the student. I am afraid of insulting the students because they are very childish. In Amharic there is even a saying that what a child has learned from you in his childhood, he will always associate with you.*

> Interview with Girma, spring 2000

Children should respect not only parents and teachers but also adult neighbours and kin. Not all of them, but those who were close to you, who cared for you and those who could not manage on their own. These people might need assistance because they were old, childless or sick. To such people many of the children were also helpful and expressed their obedience and respect through running errands for them.

> *Birke: All the people in the neighbourhood they like me. When I was small and now as well. Even when they die, they die blessing me. I run errands for them. One Gurage woman she blessed me when she died. I agree with everyone and since I run errands for them they all bless me.*
>
> *Eva: You mean the adults in the neighbourhood?*
>
> *Birke: Yes.*
>
> Interview with Amarech, Birke and Maryamawit, autumn 2000

> *Yenur: In the evening with my mother, she said, Wzo Azeb, she is sick isn't she? Yes, she is sick, I told her. Then what happened to her, she asked. Well, she is in bed, I told her. That was* (what happened) *when I met my mother.*
>
> *Eva: So you were asking about your aunt?*
>
> *Yenur: No, she was asking me.*
>
> *Eva: Was she asking you?*
>
> *Yenur: Yes.*
>
> *Eva: Do you know more about your aunt than your mother?*
>
> *Yenur: Yes, since I always visit my aunt, I know.*
>
> *Eva: What do you do at your aunt's, why do you go there?*
>
> *Yenur: Since my aunt has no child and has nothing. Her children are abroad. And since she has nobody at home who runs errands for her.*
>
> *Eva: So you are the one who runs errands for her.*
>
> *Yenur: Yes.*
>
> Interview with Yenur in connection with his diary, spring 2000

The children might get some food or something else for doing errands for these people. Mostly, however, the adults were all so poor that they could not pay the children either in cash or kind. What they could do to thank them, was to give them their blessing.

Modes of showing respect

It was not only by running errands and doing what was expected of them that children showed adults respect and obedience, however. Words of address were also an important means to communicate that you respected somebody. Thus children could address their elders with the respectful you, **antu** or even **irswo**.

They could also give an older sister whom they liked a new name, like **Abebaye**, meaning my flower, and an older brother **Gasheye**, meaning my shield, even though the person already had a given name. Body language was also used to show respect. Children stood up when an adult entered a room. They did not look adults in the eyes, but bowed their heads in front of them. They let an adult enter a room first, and allowed an adult they knew, to walk ahead of them in the street. They also seemed to unconsciously shrink their bodies in the presence of adults, this was especially visible with boys, who when alone in the street with their friends seemed to let their bodies expand but when adults they knew approached, they somehow became much smaller. Girls were almost always more circumspect and withdrawn than boys in the street; and in the classroom they covered their bodies with several layers of clothes.

Another way of showing adults respect, especially when other adults visited the home, was to avoid them:

> *Eva: When adults meet in your home what do girls do and what do boys do?*
>
> *Judith: It is not proper for children to sit with the adults, so long as they are kids. And kids should look for their equals and play with them and not sit with adults. In my opinion that is not good. When guests come, then I myself, if I sit with my father and my mother, then I will show them respect, greet them and then go outside.*
>
> *Manassebesh: When guests come, if there is food, they will eat, and do what they want, and then when they have finished my mother wants to sit with the guests. And she wants us to go out when guests come. One day, I didn't know about this, guests had come and I was sitting with them, then she said, Manassebesh, go into the back room. I didn't know about it. So I did what she said. And afterwards, she said, don't ever again stay when guests come. Go into the back room. And after that, when guests come, it is not a question of me sitting and listening, but I go into the back room.*
>
> Interview with Manassebesh, Judith and Rebqa, autumn 2000

Children and adults repeatedly stressed the importance of children leaving the room when guests come. Upon enquiring about why this was necessary the reason was given some clarification by Ibrahim, and was later also repeated by many other children:

> *Ibrahim: Adults do not want the small ones to be close-by.* They (the adults) *may tell about some secrets, and then the little ones may suddenly jump into the conversation, without knowing anything.* Then (again) *the young child may tell about the secret at some other place. A small child cannot keep a secret.*
>
> Interview with Mohammed, Ibrahim and Mulat, autumn 2000

I became curious about these secrets, but although I repeatedly asked children what the secrets could be about, nobody seemed to know. Maybe it was that children could not distinguish between what could be told outside the home and what could not. Most children took it for granted that children should go out when adults arrived. That was as it should be and when I asked the children about the future when they had their own children, would they then tell them to go out when they had guests? They answered 'of course, otherwise our neighbours will say that our children are not well brought up'. The consensus was that good children leave the room when adults come for a visit and ill-bred children do not.

To do what you are told, or even what you know that adults expect of you, shows that you are a good child in the sense of caring, loving and respectful. But it also shows that you are a child with good manners, one who knows how to behave. Children used the concept respect, **makber**, when they talked about adults with whom they had a close relationship. The respect implied that they would try in every way to fulfil the wishes of these adults. From discussions I understood that it was not only the wishes, which had been verbally expressed, that the children should fulfil, but many also took it upon themselves even to sense and implement the unexpressed needs of adults.

The specific adults towards whom the children showed obedience were the mother and the father, if he was present. With other adults the behaviour was more dependent on the individual relationship between a specific adult and the child. Thus a particular child could have more respect and feel greater propinquity to teacher C, as compared to teacher A, B and D, and towards a mother's sister, rather than towards the mother's brother or father's sibling, even though, in general terms, all adults should be shown respect.

Children thus respected adults through being obedient and through doing what they were told to, especially by running errands and helping in and around the house. Children also expressed their respect through their body language and in their way of addressing adults. And, not least, children who inconspicuously left the room when adult guests came showed them great respect. These were the norms that all students verbally adhered to. When it came to implementing them, however, life often proved more complicated; some boys forgot themselves and did not run errands or come home on time; some fathers who were unemployed did not engage themselves in their children as much as the latter had hoped for; some teachers beat children badly and without cause. There were also girls who did not follow the norms, even though they told me that they subscribed to them. Poverty was another reason that could make you disobedient, especially when there was no money with which to buy the necessary school essentials.

CONTROLLING ADULTS

Parents were expected to supervise and control what their children were doing. This was how, according to the children, parents expressed love and care. It was not only the duty of parents, however, also other adults including teachers were expected to daily supervise and see what happened to the child.

Getting instructions for sports.

Eva: Why is it that some children come without having done their homework, without bringing pen or pencil?

Mekonnen: Really, it is because they have no interest.

Eva: Is it because they are not interested?

Mekonnen: Yes, some are not interested. Some also forget.

Eva: Whose fault is it? Is it the children's or whose? That they behave like this?

*Mekonnen: Parents have to supervise (check, **mekottater**) these things. What have you done? What have you been given as homework? They have to ask (questions like) these and follow up daily. These ones, (the students) they forget about school when they are playing, and some are also not interested and when the parents don't supervise them, then, really ... (silence!)*

Interview with Mekonnen, 15 year old boy, spring 2000

At home, parents should control their children. They should tell the students in their face to study whatever they learnt during the day. They have to prevent the children from playing on the asphalt road. Furthermore, children should do what their parents tell them to. Students should study from 6 p.m. to 8 p.m. After that they must go to sleep, after having washed their feet and had their dinner.

Essay on good and bad decisions by Teka, a 13 year old boy, spring 2000

Batnori: Yes, she (her mother) looks at my exercise book and at all the corrections and everything and by this she supervises me. And also that I don't fight with the neighbourhood children, she checks that too.

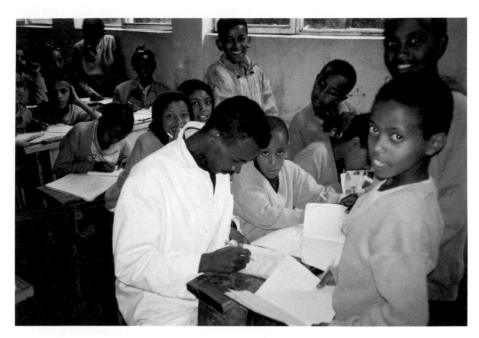

Teacher correcting exercise books in class.

Eva: If you fight with another child?

Batnori: I have been fighting. Once, when I was very little, well, when you are a child there is fighting.

Interview with Batnori, a 13 year old girl, spring 2000

If parents don't control their children it will be devastating for their life. For example, if you go back home late at night, there is a possibility of being stabbed or assaulted. It is bad not to check such things. When parents send their children on errands, and if the child refuses to go, then if this person (who wants to send the child) *is an elderly or older woman, she will curse the child. Cursing invites failure. This is very bad.*

Essay on good and bad decisions by Ahmed, a 10 year old boy, spring 2000

One of the major tasks that parents had vis-à-vis their children was to check or supervise everything that they did. According to adults, and to the children themselves, children were thought to be easily led astray and always take the easiest way out, like playing ball rather than doing homework. Therefore it was the parents' duty to see that they did what was expected of them. In the morning, good parents should check that the children were clean, dressed in their uniforms and had pens and exercise books when they left for school. And when the children came home, parents, or older siblings, should look at their exercise books, see that they had been checked by the teachers, and corrected by the children. A majority of the children with whom I talked told me that in the future, when they had their own children, they would make study programmes for them. The outline of this programme was similar for girls and boys. Children would be allowed to rest for an hour after school and then they should study according to the programme, at least for a couple of hours each day beginning from grade 1. Educated parents already made such programmes for their children while for others, older siblings made them and more ambitious children made their own programmes.

Although the children's school performance was the most important task for parents to check, parents also had many other duties towards their children. They should see to it that their sons did not play on the asphalt roads where they could be hit and hurt by cars. The roads were tempting for ball play and boys often played there especially when there were no fields in the vicinity. 'Good' boys, the children said, were expected to play close to, or inside the compound, while good girls, if they really had to play, should only do so for a few minutes, and then inside the compound, in order to be able to help in the house when required. When the children played at home, it was also possible for mothers, more seldom fathers, to check what kind of friends their daughters and sons had. There was a strong belief that a friend with bad habits, who preferred to spend time in the street rather than go to school, could easily lead the most disciplined and well-intentioned child astray. Parents should therefore check the friends of their children.

Control or supervision was in this sense a key concept like obedience and respect in the children's terminology. A parent who really cared for her or his child would control it. This was an ideal, however, of which the children were very much aware. The fact that many adults, usually mothers, were single and had all the responsibility for the children made it difficult for them to supervise their children properly. Children also seemed aware that the shortage of cash in the family made it hard, sometimes impossible, for many parents to behave in expected ways. However, the norms and ideas about how it ought to be were vivid in their minds.

Even teachers were expected to exercise control over the children, beyond what adhered to the teaching process.

Eva: What should a good teacher do, how should he behave?

Amarech: He is someone who follows up on cleanliness.

Eva: Is it the cleanliness of the classroom or of the students?

Amarech: First for the classroom, but also for the students, that they wash themselves and their clothes and come clean.

Interview with Amarech, Birke and Maryamawit, three girls of 14, 15 and 15 respectively, autumn 2001

The other thing is the uniform. At one time it was said that we could not get into class without a uniform. This was good. Yet, I don't understand why it was lifted. They are not checking it right now. This has helped those students who do not want education; they can stay outside (the school compound) *and need not follow their education properly.*

Essay by Fatima, a 16 year old girl, spring 2000

Many students also expected their teachers to check that they bring exercise books, pens etc. and that they do their home and class work. Some children believed that this was the duty of their teacher who ought to act like a father or a mother to the students. As we shall see below, teacher Girma now and then checked up on the students to see if they had brought their school materials and done their homework. Older students, between 13 and 15, gave more emphasis to teaching, than to checking up when characterizing a good teacher. Although the expectations or ideals for good teachers were clear, the fact that several children in their essays complained about teachers who did not follow up on the disciplinary rules shows that practice could differ from ideals. It was even possible to detect an implicit student critique of teachers, who first stated what the school rules were, maybe punished one or two students who did not follow them, and then seemed to forget all about them.

Control was in different contexts a key component of how children conceptualised their relations with specific adults. Parents and teachers who controlled or supervised what the children were doing were understood to love their children and those, who did not, did not really care for them. Control could be ambiguous, however, because older children who thought that they required less control than their younger siblings or classmates resented too much of it. It was therefore up to parents and teachers to choose and exercise the right degree of control and through their acts decide how they wanted to express their individual love and care for specific children.

INSTRUMENTS OF SOCIALISATION – PRAISE AND PUNISHMENT

Students, teachers and parents looked upon praise and punishment as the major means which adults and elders could legitimately use to make children learn and conform to accepted behaviour. Yet there were different kinds of both praise and punishment and strict rules regulating the exercise of them. There were also norms defining who had the right to do what to whom.

Praise and rewards

Excerpts from interviews with Batnori, a girl of 13, Ahmed, a boy of 10 and Mulat, a boy of 14, illustrate different forms of praise.

Eva: Your mother and your grandmother, if they bless you, what is the reason?

Batnori: Well, if at school I get a good result they will say, good my girl, may you grow well (**gosh yene ledj, e'degi**). *And she will kiss me and buy me clothes and shoes, gifts of happiness. They get happy. Even my little brother becomes happy.*

Eva: Aha, when you get a good result, what does he say?

Batnori: My brother?

Eva: Yes, he who is your little brother, can he praise you?

*Batnori: He cannot! He can say clever (**gobez**), and kiss me, but clever and …
(silence), well he can praise a little.*

Eva: How old is he?

Batnori: He is 5.

………

Eva: Do you praise him sometimes, your brother, your little brother?

Batnori: Yes.

Eva: What do you say to him?

*Batnori: Well, when I study and things like that and tell him don't touch my
things, and he says yes, I say, you are clever my brother, and so on, so I praise him.*

Eva: ….. Can you praise your older sister?

Batnori: No, I cannot, that I cannot! I would be afraid. An older sister!

Eva: Thus, a child cannot praise an older sister or brother or parents?

Batnori: No they cannot, that is according to the custom of this country.

Interview with Batnori, a 13 year old girl, spring 2000

Eva: Do your parents bless you?

Ahmed: Yes, they bless.

Eva: What do they say?

Ahmed: May you grow big, go and play.

Eva: Does your older brother praise you?

Ahmed: No.

Eva: And your sisters?

*Ahmed: If I run errands for them and what I was sent for is something to eat and
they will give it to me, I will eat it.*

Eva: Can you praise an older brother or sister?

Ahmed: No, that is not possible.

Eva: Your little brother?

Ahmed: Yes, when I teach him and he is good, I say, clever.

Eva: Can a young child praise his parents?

Ahmed: No that is not possible.

Eva: Why?

Ahmed: Because he does not know how to do it.

Interview with Ahmed, a 10 year old boy, spring 2000

Eva: When do your parents bless you?

*Mulat: They bless me when I come home with good results from school and when
I pass with good results, with a good rank, they will say, may you continue to be
strong and they may give me a prize, she will make me feel strong.*

Eva: So it is your mother who blesses you?

Mulat: Yes, but also my brother, there is my big brother.

Eva: And he is also concerned about your education?

Mulat: Yes he thinks about my education.

Eva: But your father doesn't care?

Mulat: Yes he doesn't care.

Interview with Mulat, a 14 year old boy, spring 2000

Mulat had told me earlier that when he had finished grade 1, his father stopped caring about his schooling. The father did not even want to know what happened to him in school. Mulat did not know why, only that his father wanted him to earn money.

Eva: Do your parents praise you?

Girma: Yes, they praise me when I run errands for them. They say, may you grow big.

Eva: Can brothers and sisters praise you (they are all older than him)?

*Girma: No they cannot! But they can give you strength, encourage you (**maberet-tatat**).*

Interview with Girma a 12 year old boy, spring 2000

Children who were given a blessing attached great value to it, yet from what I saw and heard children often showed no sign of even having heard it. Nothing in the child's posture changed when the blessing was given and her or his face usually stayed very serious. It was only when children told me afterwards, in interviews and informal talks, that I understood how important these blessings were to them.

Mona: If I come from school with good results, then they will bless me. Sometimes they will also bless me for what I have done at home. They will say like, grow big, or grow up well.

Eva: When they say things like that, what do you do?

Mona: When they say that I do not answer anything, but I thank them in my stomach.

Interview with Mona, spring 2000

In many situations children's relations with adults and older siblings had similarities with what are called patron–client relations in which respect for the patron is a key element. Thus a young person must never lack respect for an older one and a child could not bless her or his parents or older sibling since that would be both disrespectful and inappropriate. Younger siblings could, however, congratulate a sister or brother for having done a job well or for getting good results in school. They should not be too much younger, however, or it might be taken as

Copying notes from black board.

an insult by the one being congratulated. Older age was, in this context, an important marker, delineating who could say what and how and also in relation to whom. Age was furthermore important in the distribution of rewards, because a higher age often entailed access to some kind of money, however little, or goods like food, which could be used as remuneration.

Schoolteachers usually did not bless the students. They might praise a child for being diligent or for having outstanding results, but did not single them out otherwise. Teachers had no other access to rewards, since the school had not provided them with any, but the school gave a prize to the student who had the best results in each grade at the end of the year. Thus, in grade 4, the best out of about 600 students was awarded a prize. Teachers could, however, give students extra marks for hard work.

Punishments at home

Very small children were usually not punished by parents or other adults. It was no use, they said, if the children did not know their own minds (**nefs sayaweku**), meaning that if they did not understand that they had made a mistake they should not be punished. Children were usually thought to become aware of what was right and wrong between three and five. Then, if they made a big mistake, especially if they had previously been reprimanded for it and told not to repeat it, they would be swiftly beaten or else, it was feared, the bad habits might set and

Waiting for the teacher.

be difficult to get rid of. Most children mentioned that they were physically punished at home until the age of 11 or 12, but usually not later.

Eva: At home, if you commit an offence what will your father or mother do?

Ahmed: If I commit an offence, if for example I play when I should run errands I will be beaten, so it is better to run the errand.

Eva: So they never get angry with you?

Ahmed: Now and then they get angry with me, if when while playing I make a mistake ... (silence).

Eva: What kind of mistake can you commit?

Ahmed: For example when I help my father I may break his tool, but last time he didn't say anything to me. He may also give me advice. But there are days when I will be beaten. But mainly it is my brother, he beats me a lot, but my father ... (silence).

Eva: Why does your brother beat you?

Ahmed: Sometimes when I make a mistake he beats me and when my younger brother imitates me and I beat him, he will cry and when he cries then the other one hears and he beats me.

Eva: So the older beats the younger?

Ahmed: Yes and sometimes my father will beat me.

Eva: Why, what is the reason?

Copying notes from the black board.

Ahmed: I broke two yardsticks. When I broke the first, he did not say anything, but when I broke the second, he beat me.

Eva: Where did he beat you, on your hands?

Ahmed: No, by the bed, on my legs.

Eva: With what?

Ahmed: With his belt.

Eva: And your brother, how does he beat you?

Ahmed: He, since he does sports, he just hits me like boxing and so on.

Eva: And does your mother beat you?

Ahmed: No, she does not beat me. But sometimes she beats me. If I make a mistake, she beats me.

Eva: What about your sisters (also older than Ahmed)?

Ahmed: They also beat me, that is by kicking me, and also as a joke. And if I beat my younger brother and my older brother is not at home, they may kick me.

Eva: There are a lot of beatings.

Ahmed: Well it was mostly when I was in third grade. This year, but for my brother, my father never beat me this year.

Interview with Ahmed, a 10 year old boy in grade 4, spring 2000

Maryamawit: One day I was hit. I think I was playing outside with the children. Then she (her mother) *got angry with me, asked why I was out playing with the children and pinched me. I was 12. Before that she had never pinched me. Then I cried. I will not forget it.*

Eva: Because you were unhappy that your mother had pinched you?

Maryamawit: No because it hurt so much where she had pinched me. Since then she has not pinched me.

Interview with Maryamawit, Amarech and Birke, girls of 15, 13 and 15 respectively, autumn 2000

Manassebesh: For me, my mother will slap me only sometimes. But that is not when I have made some mistake but it is because without her permission I go to the church or to the library or if I go somewhere else without telling her. Then she will say, why do you go places without telling me and she will slap me.

Rebqa: And me, if I fight with my brother for a pen or a pencil. When he takes mine and hides his own and then he says give me, then I will hit him. Since he is my younger brother I hit him.

Eva: Aha, and then your father hits you?

Rebqa: No, that is not so, my father will hit both of us.

Interview with Manassebesh, Rebqa and Judith, girls of 10, 12 and 12 respectively

Fatima: If there is anyone who punishes me it is my aunt's children, the bigger ones. One will for example send me on an errand or tell me to do something and in the meantime, before I finish, the other one will tell me, come and do this. When I say, okay, let me first finish and I will come, then there is one big boy (the male cousin) *who will beat me. And I get so angry, he hits me so much.*

Eva: Now as well?

Fatima: Yes, now as well. Sometimes he will say, prepare the house I will bring a guest. Then his mother may ask me to go and get water. Then he will say, why don't you listen to what I tell you and he will hit me with his fist. He will hit me on the head, then he will push me to the corner and beat me against it. And my head aches. I often had headaches, but they put butter on my head so now I am better. Then she will be angry with him and shout at him, but up to now he has not improved at all.

Eva: How old is he?

Fatima: I don't know, I think about 18 years old. He is very big.

Eva: And doesn't he listen to his mother?

Fatima: He doesn't listen to her and she always says to me, be silent my child, big boys are big boys. There is nothing we can do about it.

Interview with Fatima and Mona, 16 year old girls, autumn 2000

Those who meted out physical punishments in the home environment were mostly fathers. Mothers could slap or pinch the younger children but tended to advise them, telling them not to do something, not to repeat whatever bad deed they had done. Neighbours could also give advice, but did not have the right to physically punish somebody else's child. When parents were worried about their children not coming home, or irritated with them for breaking things or fighting with their siblings, they might, sometimes without warning and sometimes after repeatedly having advised a child to be more careful, slap him or her in the face, pinch or beat him or her. No children in the interviews criticized their parents for having punished them, instead they appeared to understand it as both the right and the duty of the parents to do so. According to the children's way of reasoning, their parents did it because they cared for them, not because they wanted to harm them. The fact that older brothers or cousins beat the younger ones could some-times be an issue, though. In many families, older siblings, girls and boys, beat those who were younger and this was usually not understood as abuse. Even when the punishment was considered a bit too harsh and not suitable for the deed, it was part of the sibling relationship. In some instances, though, young siblings or cousins felt that they were being abused, that physical violence was being perpe-trated against them, beyond the rights of the one who did it, and without them having done anything to deserve it. This, they found, was not correct.

In this way children distinguished between punishments meted out by par-ents, who did it because they loved and cared for their children, punishments be-tween siblings which were somehow considered legitimate because you knew you received them when you had done something wrong, and not really legitimate punishments by parents, siblings and other relatives which were harsher than the mistake committed. What Norman says for Germany is also applicable to how many Ethiopian children reasoned, 'Punishments must not be meaningless, a child must learn something from it' (1991:32) and 'beatings were talked of as having been deserved' (ibid.). The children also talked of abuse, however. Those siblings or relatives who took advantage of their age, size or position in the family and demanded extraordinary services or punished severely were usually considered to be abusive. They were judged in this way when they meted out punishments that were harsher than what was considered normal and acceptable. Children questioned such acts, but felt powerless towards those who executed them.

Punishments in school

The pattern of punishments in school had both similarities with and differences from what was happening at home.

> *Eva: There is beating in the classroom, are there other punishments in class?*
>
> *Ahmed: There is beating and then they twist your ear like this* (showing me) *and that really hurts a lot.*
>
> *Eva: Does teacher Girma do that?*
>
> *Ahmed: No, he does not do that.*
>
> *Eva: Is it good, to beat and so on, do you think it is necessary?*

Ahmed: Yes it is necessary. To start with there must be advice, do not disturb and so on, he must say, and in the second instance again, to give advice, and thirdly, if they do not listen, to beat.

Eva: Is there no other solution?

Ahmed: No.

Interview with Ahmed, 10 year old boy, spring 2000

Batnori: He (the teacher) *beats them.*

Eva: Is that good?

Batnori: It is correct. You see he doesn't beat us to harm us. He beats us so that we become better and so that we work. Today we are beaten and tomorrow we do our homework to make him happy. So he gets happy, but it is not to harm us.

Eva: So because of that, it is correct, you must beat?

Batnori: Yes it is correct.

Eva: Is advice not enough?

Batnori: Advice is necessary, but it is better to beat.

Eva: It is better?

Batnori: If they are advised; they don't understand if they are not beaten. Some who are beaten hard, what, here (pointing to her hand).

Eva: On the hand?

Batnori: Yes, once I was very badly beaten by him and it came out like this (illustrating a swollen hand) *and I showed it to my grandmother. What happened to you, she said. I committed an offence, I said. But teacher, our teacher hit me, I would never say that. She massaged me and so on, she did, now it has healed. It is there no more.*

Eva: And if you had told her, your grandmother, what would she have done?

Batnori: She wouldn't have done anything, you see.

Eva: She wouldn't have come to school?

Batnori: She wouldn't have come. You see the rule of this country, to say the teacher has hit my child, is really forbidden, it is bad manners in this country.

Interview with Batnori, a 13 year old girl, spring 2000

I understand Batnori's comments both in the sense that a student must have done something bad if the teacher hits her and in the sense that you should not complain about such treatment from a teacher, who has the right to exercise it.

Birke: When I was in grade 1, one teacher beat me. Then I cried and asked him why he did it, now you have done too much and I haven't done anything. Then another one, who heard me, beat me. After he had done that I was sitting in class crying. Then I started to think about what I had said, and I realized that I had not spoken properly myself. I should have been 'shy' of the teacher. I did not respect him properly. And when the second teacher called me and after he had hit me (the same incident as she mentioned previously) *he advised me that a teacher is like your father. Today you are big and there are young ones who are watching you and will follow your lead and insult the teacher tomorrow. When I thought about that, I found that the advice that the teacher had given me was correct. If I don't respect a person, others who are younger than me will not respect that person either. So advice is always good.*

Interview with Birke, a 15 year old girl, spring 2000

All three, Ahmed, Batnori and Birke found it both correct and necessary for teachers to beat the children, especially if they had shown disrespect, which was what Birke thought of her own behaviour. Mohammed, however, questioned the teachers' right to physically punish the students.

Eva: The teacher punishes the students, doesn't he?

Mohammed: Yes, he beats them. Those who talk, he beats them, and those who don't do homework, he beats them so that they will not leave it again. If they do this today, today they are punished. Tomorrow they will be advised so that they will not do it again. Our teacher, when he gives us homework, he really, really warns us, don't come without having done your lessons. All of you must do it, he says.

Eva: And is it necessary, to beat and so on? Is it necessary do you think?

Mohammed: With us, not to beat is not necessary. But what, the problem comes from the students. When they are given advice some don't listen. And the punishment is not to harm them but so that they stop doing what they were doing. That is why he beats them.

Eva: Does it help, or are there other sanctions?

Mohammed: To send them out from school, ask them to sign. First teacher calls them, gives them advice, and then they are beaten. The next step is to sign. From now on he (the student will sign a paper stating this) *says, I will not commit this offence and if I do, they will send him to the administration here. Then they will talk with the Director and after the Director, they sign a second time and then they are sent out from school. They are not allowed to study.*

Eva: Is this better than to be beaten?

Mohammed: This is better than to be beaten. Why, if they are sent out, the problem is his own, if he doesn't study he will not reach anywhere.

Eva: Yes that is true, but is it necessary to beat now and then do you think?

Mohammed: According to me it isn't. Why because I can be injured by the beating. Since they are people's children, and when we beat them, when Teacher Girma for example beats, it is on the hands and on the back, but he doesn't hit other places, why, because they may be harmed, he thinks.

Interview with Mohammed, a 13 year old boy, spring 2000

Yenur, who had experienced his brother stop going to school because he was hit and injured by a teacher, questioned teachers who abused their right to physical punishment in even stronger words:

> *Yenur: There is one teacher I don't like, … when he beats, he takes hold of the hand and then he hits the person on the head and because of things like that, that he takes hold of the hand and beats, that is why I don't like him. And the reason for it can be that he* (the student) *forgot his exercise book.*
>
> *Eva: Does he do like this?* (I touched lightly with my hand on his head).
>
> *Yenur: No, not with his hand, with a stick. And then there is this other teacher who also hits us, even worse than this one. He even hits us when our homeroom teacher sends us on an errand. He hit me on the head so I was bleeding. That was yesterday, when I went into the classroom with the exercise books Teacher had sent me with.*

Interview with Yenur, a 12 year old boy, spring 2000

Sometimes the beating took place in the yard and some teachers were known as real hard and dangerous beaters. Not all the teachers used physical violence, though. Many of them refused to walk around with the stick made of a rubber water pipe. These teachers told me that they did not believe in beating the children. In 1988 (Swedish Save the Children 1988:8) the Ministry of Education forbade the use of physical violence in school, but it was still common in many schools and a majority of the teachers in Birabiro had such sticks. From what was obvious in the interviews students did not question the use of violent punishment as such. Teachers did not do it to harm them, they said, but like their parents, teachers did it because they loved them and wanted them to become good students. Some students were a bit more questioning about physical punishment, though, believing that a greater emphasis should be given on advice to the students. Most, however, found that the physical violence did not really injure them, and beatings on hands and arms rather than on the head were necessary for those who never listened and changed their behaviour. Not any kind of violence or beating was acceptable, though. Good teachers should not beat hard or in places where the students could be injured forever. Something that hurt for the moment was all right, but abuse was wrong. However, the children said that they could not do anything to change it and the thought that students as a collective, together could question the abuse of teachers was never mentioned. What they could do as individuals was 'to be careful'.

In May 2000, there was a discussion in the classroom between teacher Girma and the students about punishments, the only such discussion on this topic that I heard. At the time, the students were told to rank different punishments from the lightest to the most severe on a scale of five. The lightest punishment was stated as being beaten, but which part of the body that could be beaten was not discussed. The second lightest punishment was work, like cleaning the toilets, the classroom, the blackboard etc. More severe was the loss of marks, five per cent. Many students shook their bodies and groaned when this punishment was mentioned. It appeared that they found it very hard when marks that they had earned through studying hard were taken away from them. Fourthly came information to a parent about the student's bad behaviour. The last, and most severe punishment was to inform the administration of a student's bad conduct for which she or he must first sign not to repeat it, and if it was repeated the student might be expelled from school.

Teacher Girma also asked the students to elect a committee to follow up on the possible misconduct of the students and see to it that punishments were meted out in accordance with the priorities made. A committee was elected and students made the same mistakes, as previously, that is some did not do their homework, others did not bring pens, exercise books etc. Yet, I never saw the student committee give their fellow students any punishments.

Parents and teachers used praise, rewards and punishments to keep order, control the children and instil in them how they should behave. The relationship was not only made up of rewards and punishments, however, both children and adults understood it as a mutual relationship based on love, care and respect. Those who were older and in a parental or teacher position had certain duties towards the children attached to which were rewards and punishments which they could use when it was required. Adults' right to use praise and punishment was considered natural and was deeply embedded in the minds of children and adults alike. Abuse of punishments was, however, questioned. Abuse usually took place in school, and the student community knew those teachers who had made it a habit to badly punish children.

Praise and punishments were not only used between adults and children, but also between children of different ages. In the attribution of praise and punishments age seemed to be the most important marker for who could praise or punish whom. Older children could praise and were also often given the right to punish the younger ones, whether they were siblings or classmates. Strength was another criterion in the sense that you would hardly beat somebody who was stronger than you. Strength also affected gender relations since girls of the same age as boys were often both smaller and weaker and beaten more often than their male peers.

REPRODUCING A PATTERN – MONITORS AND BULLIES

From my diary

The bell has rung in for the first period in the morning. I enter 4a with Girma, the homeroom teacher. Everybody quickly moves to his or her seat as we come in. One student gets my chair and puts it up at the back. Girma starts with roll call from number 1 to 105, ten students are absent. The first period he teaches mathe-

matics and starts by asking the students 'Who has not done the homework?' Eight students stand up. 'Come forward', he says, and they walk up to the blackboard and kneel on the floor. 'Up with your hands', he says and standing on their knees they lift their hands to the ceiling. Meanwhile, I hear Ermias from behind me saying 'It is better to walk up peacefully' and he too goes forward and kneels. Next, Girma goes from row to row, checking the students' exercise books to see if they really have done their homework. When his back is turned towards the blackboard all the students kneeling at front let their hands come down. They are only up when Girma looks at them. Ermias pulls up the sleeve on his right arm, showing all of us that he has hidden the maths book under the sleeve. Twelve more students, who have not done their homework, are told to go up to the blackboard, kneel and put their hands up in the air. Now the lesson starts and all the students become involved in it.

Now and then Girma looks at the kneeling students and their hands come up. Mostly he does not and the hands are down. It does not seem to be important to him whether they follow the admonition to hold their hands up or not. In the middle of the lesson there is a knock on the door. Girma is called outside to talk with a parent coming with his son. He stays outside quite a long time and the sound in the classroom increases, making Mulat and Teku, the two monitors come forward. On the way, two boys give them sticks, and Mulat and Teku then go around the benches beating the small, middle-sized and slightly older children, both girls and boys, when they talk. When they don't stop talking at once, they beat them again, harder. Mohammed joins them and Mulat takes a piece of paper and a pen from his pocket and writes down the numbers of those who don't stop talking. Rekik, a 10 year old girl, shouts to him 'Please don't write my name, I haven't done anything'. Mulat takes no notice of her or others shouting to him but continues writing. When Girma finally enters Mulat gives him the list and the lesson continues.

When the bell rings and the lesson is finished, the students who have been kneeling stand up and lift an arm towards Bellete. He beats each one three times with his rod, then they return to their seats. Some of the children show signs of suffering when he beats them, but as soon as they run back to their seats they are all smiling. It is difficult to know if he beats them hard.

The above notes from my diary give an example of how the hierarchical and violent treatment of children was reproduced in class by the monitors who punished younger and smaller children. Monitors fulfilled a key position in every school class. Primarily they were guardians of order whenever the teachers were absent or busy with some other activity like correcting exercise books. They also assisted the teachers with small tasks like collecting the students' exercise books, cleaning the blackboard and informing the teacher when children were absent. Sometimes the monitors were selected by the teachers and sometimes elected by the students. Similar criteria seemed to be used by teachers and students alike; for monitors to be appointed or elected, they should be physically big, among the oldest, and preferably better than average academically, i.e. they should be serious about their studies.

Although girls were elected as monitors, they took no part in keeping order in the classroom. I asked Maryamawit, one of them, why she and other female monitors did not try to uphold order like the boys. 'Well', she said, 'it is difficult for us, the students are not afraid of us and don't do what we tell them to. Also I don't like to beat them. I don't want to beat anyone. That is why I don't want to be a monitor.' From my observations the female monitors did not seem to have any particular duties, but were elected or appointed more as a token of equality.

Male monitors, and those who took it upon themselves to be monitors, were vested with power over the others. They often beat them with their hands or with sticks; they sometimes made them kneel in front with their hands in the air, just like Teacher Girma had done, beating them when their hands came down. What the students feared most, however, was to be registered. Only the elected monitor could register the name of a student that he found disturbing, or disobedient. The list was then given to the homeroom teacher, who transferred the names to his register. Several such registrations could lead to a reduction in school marks.

Usually, the ones who were punished by the monitors were the younger, smaller and medium-sized boys and girls. I never saw a monitor hit either a girl or boy of their own age. One of the small to medium-sized students, 12 year old Yenur, who was often exposed to them, commented:

> Some of them, they just beat you, especially Ermias, even if you have not done any-thing. And he is not a real monitor! Mulat is better, he only beats when you have done something. Still, even he does not punish the big ones, like Ermias, when he disturbs. I think they are afraid of their own age-mates, so they never register or punish them.

The reason why I say that the monitors were vested with power is that teachers never stopped them or made any comment when monitors beat their fellow students in the teachers' presence, neither did the students who were beaten ever complain to the teachers about the monitors being violent. All shared the knowledge of how the system functioned (Barnes 1993) and seemingly took the procedure for granted.

What thus became conspicuous in class was the hierarchical use of violence; teachers used it against students but very seldom against elected and self-appointed monitors; big boys used it against their younger classmates. Men and boys thus institutionalised the hierarchical use of violence through repeated use. It also acquired legitimacy because teachers did it and did not react when they saw monitors and other big boys follow their own pattern.

INSECURITY AND COUNTER-DISCOURSE

Children put a lot of pressure on themselves to abide by the rules, but they also expected adults to reciprocate. The rules and regulations guiding the hierarchical, patron-client-like behaviour between children and adults were strict. Adults set the agenda in the relationship and informed the children what they expected of them. It was also the duty of adults to control the children and see to it that they did what they were supposed to. Children should never question these close adults but defer to them and show them respect. The super-/subordination, not only between adults and children but also between children of different ages, was expressed both verbally and in body language, and if the children did not understand it from advice, they were taught how to behave through physical punishment as in the case of Birke, who was beaten by a teacher so that other students would not learn disrespect from her. The mutuality of the relationship also implied love and care and was expressed through praise, practical tasks and gifts.

Within this normative pattern there were variations. Some adults were criticized, especially those who did not comply with the rules, gave too harsh penalties and beat the children where it could injure them or without cause; others because they gave the children too little praise when they had run an errand. Also teachers were criticized when they 'touched the children's morale' by, for example, ridiculing them in front of the others in class. All these adults stood to lose the children's respect and children were emotionally upset when adults did not fulfil what children saw as their mutual responsibility. This was not the case with mothers and fathers, however. The indulgence towards especially fathers, whether unemployed, addicted to alcohol or not caring for the children, was great. Furthermore, I never heard a child say that her/his own mother did not do her best towards her children. Talking about their mothers, children indicated that mothers spent most of their time working for and serving their families. The children always had a reason for why a mother was not around.

The relationship was unstable though, such as patron–client relations are, and I could sense a feeling of fear among some students, a fear of losing the love of the respected person, a fear of punishments, of dislike and of being ridiculed. Children worried that even if they fulfilled their part of the deal they would not be rewarded in the way they had hoped for. They often experienced relationships to be more complex and less straightforward than norms would have them. Some children developed their own coping strategies to solve their insecurity thereby coming to rely more on themselves for survival, while others spread the risks through turning to more adults. A few children thus had adult friends, who were not part of the nuclear family. These were people with whom they could discuss problems and who could explain issues relating to the school. Such adult persons, in whom they could confide, were often a relative, a grandmother, aunt or a neighbour, mostly a woman, for both girls and boys. Some boys also had an older male friend.

Waiting for the teacher to come.

In this hierarchical relationship children were often expected to be invisible. They were neither to be seen nor heard in the presence of adult guests. They ought not to initiate conversations with adults and there seemed to be few informal or spontaneous exchanges of ideas between children and adults. Out of respect children should avoid them. The social distance between children and adults, sometimes including parents, made it difficult for students to look at adults critically. When asked whether they had seen an adult commit any wrong or any kind of mistake, many children, even 15 year old girls, answered that they knew that human beings could commit mistakes but they could not give any examples of adults doing anything wrong. Exceptionally, some older boys were more aware that adults commit mistakes, and even gave me some examples, mostly relating to intoxicated priests.

There were a few counter-discourses, which contradicted the norms and ideals about children always having to show respect, be quiet and avoid adults. These came out in essays in which some girls expressed the need for change. One 13 year old girl for example, wrote that she wished to learn more therefore she wanted to talk to adults, not avoid them.

> *I don't support this saying at home that says a kid should not talk with a gentleman or with adult people. What I like to do at home is talk to adults. It is because I want to know, what I do not know, that I want to talk to them.*

Essay by Miriam, spring 2000

Another girl believed that not only did shyness with adults inhibit the child's intellectual growth, but also that children through school could obtain new knowledge, not known to adults, whereby children could become the teachers of adults.

> *Children should speak with the elders on an equal level. In our Ethiopian culture, there are some things that are counted as impolite. But this culture should be improved. I will explain how, by giving examples. (.....) If a child in a family cannot grow up asking and talking to his parents, he will have a behaviour, which will not leave him easily. This shy behaviour will prevent him from asking questions in school. He does not answer. He will have difficulties even if he is asked forcefully to answer. (...) If our parents have wrong ideas about AIDS, or if there exists a person infected by the disease, and if parents speak of not touching that man's doors, any person can imagine the advantage it can have, if the child who knows the ways of transmission, teaches his parents and cares for that man. Generally, since children are the future bearers of the country, they should grow up talking to fathers and mothers properly, with equality, and then they can protect our culture and history in a proper way.*

Essay by Banchialem, a 14 year old girl, spring 2000. Her father is a teacher.

Such ideas were exceptional among the children, however, and would have been considered heresy by many of them and not least by adults in their surroundings.

HIERARCHY AND PATRON–CLIENT RELATIONS

The relationship between Birabiro adults and children and also between children of varying age, gender and strength has, as we have seen, many similarities with that between patrons and clients. Both types of relations are established between persons who have something to offer the other, although the value of what is provided by the super-ordinate is usually considered to be higher than that of the subordinate (see also Poluha 1989:109–110). Furthermore, in both child–adult and client–patron relations the hierarchical bond is expressed in acts, body language and words of address.

The fact that most children and adults subscribed to the same norms and rules, that they allowed these to guide their interactions with each other, and that they considered the hierarchy legitimate makes it possible to talk of them as a collective sharing a cultural schema. Within the collective there could be abuse by those of higher rank and children could complain of individual excesses; seldom, however, did they criticize those close to them, like their own parents or home-room teachers. The children's respect for the authority of these specific adults and for their right to distribute punishments and rewards seemed to be greater than their expectations of so-called fair treatment. There were sometimes complaints by children mainly against those of a similar age who abused their position in the house but against whom they had few means of redress. Apart from such criticism and a few, exceptional counter discourses, the children did not question the hier-archy; the rules were followed and the order seemed to be accepted.

Hierarchy, and its opposite, equality are not unequivocal concepts, however. In a discussion on inequality and equality Béteille (1994) outlines two major forms of equality. On the one hand, he argues that there is equality as a moral philosophical value, something that people may believe in even if they do not practise it and, on the other, equality of condition with regard to the distribution of money and wealth. Béteille refers to Dumont's discussion in Homo hierarchi-cus (1966) and Homo aequalis (1977) where Dumont argues that Western soci-eties have an egalitarian ideology, meaning that they are egalitarian in intention, but not that they have attained or are even likely to attain equality in the distri-bution of resources. The two forms of equality, with respect to ideology and to resource distribution, may even develop in opposition to each other, like in West-ern Europe where the belief in democracy grew at the same time as the inequality in the distribution of resources increased.

While equality is associated by Béteille with individualism, which stresses the autonomy and dignity of the individual person as against any kind of collective, hierarchy is associated with the collective in which the individual is an integral part (1994). Typical collectives that Béteille refers to are the European feudal estates and the castes in the Hindi religion. Such collectives and hierarchies usu-ally imply that the individual's status is ascribed. Individualism and equality, on the other hand, are mostly associated with achieved status and emphasize compe-tition.

The double meaning of equality brings about a number of seeming contradic-tions: the historical spread of democracy combined with an increased inequality in the distribution of resources; the stress on equal conditions for all in democra-cies when applying for schools or jobs, which through a process of competition and individual achievement again leads to hierarchical relations, especially since human beings are different and unequally endowed. Equality and hierarchy, as argued by Dumont (1966:239–258 [1960]) do not exclude but presuppose each other even though our egalitarian ideals tend to obscure this fact. Thus, hierar-chical systems, which are highly stratified with regard to position, influence and power, might exhibit a more egalitarian redistribution of resources within the col-lective than egalitarian systems like democracies in which assets may be redistrib-uted in a more hierarchical way.

Competing for his team (sports hour).

The kind of hierarchy that we hear about from the Birabiro school children relates to the various relationships within the collectives to which the children belonged, like the extended family, the school class and the religious congregation. All these were distinctly stratified by criteria such as age, size, gender, strength and status, which defined the form and content of the relationship such as who could give orders to whom or inflict punishment on whom. The same criteria also determined the pecking order in school and among schoolmates. Not even praise was excluded from the hierarchical system but prevented a younger or subordinate person from conferring it on somebody above her or him. Children's ascribed and lowly status in the various collectives therefore strictly limited their scope for action. On the other hand, the hierarchy within the various Ethiopian collectives also had other characteristics, which rendered them attractive both to children and adults.

The collectives to which the children belonged usually provided them with social, emotional and economic security, a sense of safety, which was similar to what clients expected to find in their relationship with their patrons. In the extended family parents should accordingly protect and control their children the way patrons looked out for their clients. It was also the duty of those heading a collective to see to it that opportunities made available to them were redistributed to the members and put to good use. Children expressed such patron–client like ideas in interviews and essays saying that when they got jobs after school it would be their turn to pay for the education of siblings and other members of their collective. It was assumed that anyone getting a job would work hard and use the income for the benefit of the extended family. The economic redistribution of assets within the collective was thus something children understood that they themselves would carry out in the future, as soon as they were able to, but they also expected those who were already in such positions, to do it today.

The importance of the collective and its redistributive functions is not an idea unique to Ethiopia but can be found in many other social groups. In a Swedish study on refugees from Syria and Iraq, both Muslims and Christians, von Hirsch (1996) made similar observations. Parents in the study found their children's school situation in Sweden to be very different from their own experiences in the home country and difficult to cope with. They thought that much of what their children learnt and did in the Swedish school was wasteful, even wrong. What the children encountered in school, according to von Hirsch, was a promotion of Swedish individualism with emphasis on independence, freedom, equality and self-reliance where the self was considered an autonomous independent unit, who could learn and form opinions very early in life, all in line with Swedish pedagogical theories. To this effect school children were for example encouraged to move around in the classroom, look for information in encyclopaedias, reports and books and communicate with schoolmates to form their opinions about different statements and problems. The Arabic-speaking parents had their own pedagogical theories. According to them, knowledge should be transmitted from teacher to student and a good teaching method was to use repetition since it facilitated memorisation. While learning, however, students should not be distracted by a lot of noise and movement since that would prevent them from concentrating. There should be order in the classroom and students ought to sit still.

Over and above this, the Arabic-speaking parents felt the integrity of their family threatened by the way money was given to children in Swedish families. Swedish school children were provided with pocket money, sometimes the full amount of the parents' children's allowance from the state. This was done to gradually teach the child how to handle and take the responsibility for her/his own money while still under the supervision of her/his parents. Economic individualism was thus enhanced to make it easier for children to manage on their own later and not be dependent on the family or on other people. Muslim and Christian parents clearly disagreed with this idea. von Hirsch quotes what one Muslim mother said about her daughter:

> Why should I give her her own money? She gets everything she needs from us. …… We are a family and we share what we have. It is the parents' duty to make sure that children

have what they need. Not only that, they must decide *what* the child can have, otherwise it (the child) will become too selfish and forget that we are a family with many needs which must all be taken care of (1996:86).

Another mother showed a similar concern about the family, rather than the individual, as the important unit:

> ... The day they start deciding over their own lives we are no longer a family. Children must not make decisions which parents are to make (ibid.).

The Arabic-speaking families were furthermore concerned about the lack of respect between Swedish parents and children and between teachers and students. For them respect was a requirement for order in the classroom and also necessary if the children were to learn from their teachers. Respect was promoted by a combination of fear and love. According to a Swedish understanding, respect is based on the idea of all people's equal worth and to show respect is to show the other person's equal worth. In contrast to the Swedish socialisation goals mentioned above and encountered in school, the immigrant families had their own socialisation objectives of which the most important was 'to imbue in their children the *respect for authority,* a sense of *family-responsibility, family honour,* avoidance of family *conflicts, obedience* and *acceptance* of their religious laws' (ibid.:84, italics in original).

Similarly to the Arabic-speaking families in Sweden Birabiro children referred to their various collectives, especially the extended family, as the most important unit with which they identified and which gave them social and emotional security. The collectives were hierarchical but within the hierarchies assets were expected to be redistributed. Thus, as argued by Dumont (1966), we can understand the Ethiopian collectives as associated with a high degree of economic equality among the members even if none of them stated that they subscribed to the idea of equality as a moral philosophical value. On the contrary, the hierarchy in the Birabiro children's context was strictly upheld and one of its basic tenets was that members should show utmost respect towards those above them.

These representations of collectivism and individualism, of forms of equality and hierarchy illustrate the great complexity that can hide under seemingly unambiguous concepts. Thus, the Western moral philosophical meaning of equality as each adult citizen's equal value and right to speak out and influence decision-making in the collective, irrespective of background, has its own empirical limitations. First, children and youngsters are by definition excluded from this category. Second, it is restricted both with regard to gender and class since a majority of the women (Phillips 1992) and men with little education or from poor families often lack experience and trust in themselves to speak in public arenas. Third, the stress on the individual's right and duty to compete with others on equal terms to achieve her/his own status, is contradicted by experience, which shows that family connections or networks of different kinds often provide a non-competitive person with schools, jobs and positions above her/his results and that actually competition seldom does take place on equal terms. Experience has also shown that competition on equal terms is a paradox because competition by definition results in inequality since, as Dumont (1966) argued, the concepts presuppose each other.

In a hierarchical system the status of individuals is ascribed but even when the ascription is strict, the collective may be attractive because of the redistribution of assets taking place within it. In Ethiopia there is furthermore the idea that hierarchies are flexible. Despite being hierarchical children perceived the collectives as arenas of opportunities where they and anyone else through hard work and good luck (**edel**) could reach the top (compare Messay Kebede 1999). According to history, Ethiopian kings have always obtained their positions through fighting for them. No one could expect to get a position through inheritance and no one could be sure of keeping whatever post he had reached but everyone had the chance to reach the top. In this way, although all perceived the social system as hierarchical it was also understood to be flexible and allowed for a lot of social mobility, contrary to Béteille's (1994) 'typical collectives'. This understanding of the collective was also part of the children's cultural schema and may have been one of the very reasons why they were so optimistic about their future, insisting that they could become 'anything' if they only worked hard enough and their luck was with them; just like any un-born baby who should not be aborted because of his possible bright future. All these aspects made the hierarchical system attractive to both children and adults.

Chapter 5

THE TEACHING–LEARNING PROCESS

Pedagogy, or modes of interaction in classrooms, illustrate the structure and content of the relationship between teachers and students. The pedagogy in use can also explain the characteristics and quality of the relations and what their implications may be for children, teachers and the learning process as a whole. The argument in this chapter is that the perception of knowledge expressed in the Birabiro school, and in today's educational system in Ethiopia, defined it as something bounded and unchangeable, and that the way in which it was communicated was hierarchical. These two aspects of the learning–teaching process in turn promoted continuity with two important Ethiopian traditions, on the one hand, an acceptance of hierarchy as a legitimate social order, and on the other, an understanding that taught knowledge should not be questioned nor a search for new information encouraged.

The teaching-learning process in use in the Birabiro school and in Ethiopia as a whole can partly be traced to the philosophy and educational approach used by the Ethiopian Orthodox Church. The Church has been a powerful institution for more than a thousand years and was historically closely allied to the state. The long history of the Church and the fact that it has been spread over large parts of the country has made it possible for the institution of the Orthodox Church to influence millions of citizens. Seeing Church education as one of the local knowledge systems and as such important to the present educational approach Bridges and Ridley (2000) discuss its major characteristics in an article, basing themselves on texts by Girma Amare (1967), Alemayyehu Moges (1973) and Hailu Fulass (1974). From these texts Bridges and Ridley conclude that some of the distinguishing features of traditional church education are the memorisation of texts in a foreign language, Ge'ez, which neither students nor teachers properly understand; a relationship between students and teachers which is characterized by the students' obedience, humility and respect for their elders, who may give the students a blessing as appreciation; and that 'initiative and inquiry are considered as defects, which have to be discouraged at every manifestation by severe chastisement' (Girma Amare 1967:7). In church education there is also a heavy dependence on rote learning and a low requirement for understanding, expressed by Hailu Fulass as 'The traditional system of education is based on the theory that the present state of knowledge is all that could ever be attained' (1974:19). From this Bridges and Ridley argue, that a distinguishing feature of the teaching–learning approach in the church is 'the mastery of what is essentially a stable body of

Girls skipping rope.

knowledge passed through the generations – there is little sense of knowledge as dynamic and changing, of the need for creativity and invention….., or for the personal construction of knowledge' (2000:149).

A more positive description of church education is based on the text of Alemayyehu Moges (1973), who argues that in the third stage of church education, students learn about evaluation, about critical thought and about how to criticize others and defend themselves. Alemayyehu Moges also upholds the idea that there is a good relationship between teacher and student; that there is an intimate connection between learning and doing; and that older students are used to teach the younger ones (Bridges and Ridley 2000:155). Although I saw many teachers treat students with utmost respect, I did not see anyone teach about critical thoughts and arguments or show older children how to teach younger ones, or use a hands-on approach in class. What was more conspicuous was the habit of rote learning, subservience and discouragement of initiatives in class.

This is not only the case with Church education though; there are also resemblances with how the Koran is taught. The Koran is read in Arabic that children and teachers often have a limited understanding of. The script is foreign and not used in other contexts, while the Ge'ez script is at least used to write most other Ethiopian languages. Rote learning of the Koran verses is the means through which children get acquainted with the holy text. The Koran teacher is usually a strong authority figure who expects subservience and respect from the children and does not prepare them to have independent thoughts or question the holy text. The similarities between the religious education carried out in the church

Girls skipping rope.

and that carried out in the mosque with regard to both perceptions of knowledge and its transmission are thus striking.

In her study on Arabic speaking Christian and Muslim children, mentioned earlier, von Hirsch (1996) describes their school experiences as quite similar to what has been written about the Ethiopian Orthodox Church. Both the Arabic-speakers referred to and the Ethiopian teachers conceptualised learning as the transmission of knowledge which ideally took place through memorisation, imitation and repetition, methods which were understood to be the best means to obtain the main educational goal, namely to fill the students with the required information. To the Arab-speaking parents it was of utmost importance that teachers functioned as role models to the students and that they took an active role in their moral education.

In this chapter I shall use observations and interviews to depict life in a Birabiro classroom in the year 2000 and to describe some of the structures that regulated interactions between students and teachers and teachers and their supervisors. The concept of 'participation' is used to discuss some characteristics of the teaching process. 'Participation' was introduced by the government to modernise the educational system, but acts and opinions of students and teachers illustrate that the original meaning of this Western concept was differently interpreted in the Ethiopian setting and that it was even transformed during its implementation into something that fitted better with the country's own historical experiences, practices and cultural schemas. There was some room for questioning, for alternative behaviour, however. Although the children's ideas, acts, norms and values were deeply embedded, the rigid structures were suddenly over-turned when there was a chance of obtaining a coveted asset – school marks – and for a moment we can see how children questioned their taken-for-granted, embodied behaviour, illustrating that change was not impossible.

STRUCTURING SCHOOL LIFE

From my diary, autumn 2000

The bell has rung in after tea break. I take my little chair and enter 5a. Some of the children rise to greet me. I lift my hand and sign that they do not have to, they can sit down. I tell them so in Amharic too, when I realize that the teacher has not come. I go to the back row where there is room for my chair and me. The students who are outside also join the class. Looking around I see that again a few children close to me have been re-located, but there are still some children I know well close-by, like Mekonnen, this year's monitor, to my right and Heywot to my left. In front of Mekonnen is Amarech and in the next row are both Birke and Maryamawit, evidently still allowed by the homeroom teacher to sit together although they are old friends and often talk to each other. No teacher has come and I turn to Heywot, asking her how things are and if she is going to attend the extra-curricular teaching that the school will provide for grade 5 girls. Heywot lives with rather demanding relatives; her mother is dead and her father lives far away in the countryside. 'No', she says, 'they don't want me to attend. There is too much work to do at home'. 'But you know it could be useful for you', I say, 'especially since you are so few in class during the extra teaching. Don't you think it is possible to explain this to your relatives', I ask her. 'It's no use', she says. 'They won't let me join anyway'. 'I'm sorry about that', I tell her. The students sitting close by try to listen to what we say and I do not want to continue our talk. It is impossible to conduct a private conversation of any length in class since all those around are so curious to find out what I might say and what individual students might say to me.

The noise in class rises and at times, like when Elfenesh shouts to her friend at the other side of the classroom to bring her books, it even becomes painful and I have to hold my hands over my ears to keep it out. Mekonnen, who has been busy finishing his maths from before the break also notices the noise and goes forward. On the way some students give him a stick. He takes it and heads up front, facing his fellow students. He doesn't say anything – even if he had tried he wouldn't have been heard – but looks around and slowly starts moving to where he sees students talking and shouting, then, quickly he hits them with the stick. He is soon joined by Mulat, last year's monitor, coming from the back with his own stick, and now also Mohammed, somehow self-appointed but also accepted by teachers and students as something of a monitor. All three swiftly hit those who talk and after a couple of minutes there is silence in the classroom.

But where is the teacher, I wonder. Whispering I ask Heywot 'What subject are you supposed to have?' 'Music', she says. 'Is he around', I ask. 'Well he was outside before' she answers. The monitors look at us and I become silent so as not to get Heywot into trouble. The rest of the class are silent, just a few whispers. The children gaze at their desk or in front of them, their thoughts seemingly elsewhere.

When around fifteen minutes of the period have passed, the music teacher enters. 'Take up your music exercise books', he says and there is a lot of noise, talk and commotion. He goes to the blackboard and starts writing selected parts in Amharic from the music textbook. The students borrow, lend or get their own pens and start copying what the teacher has written. Silence soon reigns. Not everybody is writing, however. I can see a couple of students just sitting, but when the teacher turns around, they pretend to write. Probably they have no book or pen. I hope he won't see them. The writing, copying and silence continue for about fifteen minutes, when the music teacher has filled the blackboard. Without saying anything he opens the door to the classroom and walks outside. You cannot see him. He might have gone far away or be standing just to the side of the door. Some students start talking to each other but most continue writing. After about five minutes the music teacher re-enters. 'Have you finished', he asks? 'No', say some. 'Yes', say others. Most seem to have finished or are at least not writing. For three to four minutes he then gives some explanations of the text. Then he goes outside again. Mekonnen quickly finishes his copying and goes forward, foreseeing maybe the noise that will come when some 90 students are left unoccupied. Mulat and Mohammed soon join Mekonnen. They hit those who talk with their sticks, sometimes lightly and sometimes hard. After another couple of minutes the period is finished without the teacher re-entering the class.

Lesson plans

The music teacher was not unusual in the way he spent most of the period writing on the blackboard. All teachers wrote notes although the time they spent on it varied between teachers and subjects. As a whole, between one third and half the teaching time was spent on writing notes. Most teachers came and left on time, however, and the music teacher's late arrival was unusual. Teachers made their own summaries of the major points in the textbooks and wrote these on the blackboard. These summaries were what the students had to study and know for their examinations. The reason for writing the notes and not requiring that the students make their own summaries was that very few students were given textbooks to take home and study with. The shortage of textbooks was similar all over Ethiopia, at least in government and poor community schools. Better off private and community schools distributed textbooks to all their students. There were also textbooks available in the government-controlled shops, so the shortage was not absolute.

Judging from the time spent on writing notes, it was obvious that all the teachers attached great importance to the written word. For some of the children all this writing was a problem since they lacked the capacity to copy the notes. While a few wrote as fast as their teacher, some with beautiful handwriting, others might not even have finished when the period was over. The slow students usually borrowed their friends' exercise books to finish copying during the break. Some children, sitting at the back, were always copying from their neighbours. They might not have been able to read at this distance and maybe they needed glasses. But no child wore glasses. In the whole school with more than 3,000 children I only saw one girl wearing glasses. Spectacles were a luxury out of reach for the majority. Even the thought of having their child's eyes tested for glasses would not occur to parents, unless the child was almost blind.

While writing notes could take up to half the teaching time, the teachers' explanations covered about one third or less. The rest was filled up by questions and answers or other kinds of interactions between teachers and students. All these activities were regulated by the curriculum and structured by the teachers through their lesson plans.

All the teachers prepared lesson plans for their respective subjects each semester. The semester plan was divided into monthly, weekly and daily plans where each lesson should have its own objectives, texts and pedagogical means described in writing by the teachers. This required a lot of both time and energy. At the beginning of the semester teachers had to submit their lesson plans to the head of the respective departments, the plans were checked, and if found acceptable, signed. The deputy director also checked the plans. A copy of each semester plan was then put in the archives. Again, each week, every teacher did not only have to write a plan but also a report of what she or he had done and if something stated in the plan had not been accomplished give an explanation for it. The teachers' reports were checked and signed by the department heads as well as by the deputy director and put into the school archives. Showing me his report book and explaining all the details he had to fill in, Girma, the homeroom teacher, told me that this elaborate reporting system took so much of his time that he could not prepare himself properly for his classes.

Apart from teaching, teachers also had to check and correct the children's exercise books at least once a month. With about 100 students per class and five to six different classes, or as many subjects with the same class, these corrections took several hours weekly and sometimes had to be done during the lessons.

Control through the written word

For each of the two semesters teachers prepared, corrected and marked three monthly tests and one final semester exam. The three monthly tests could give 10 marks each, while the final semester examination could give 60 marks. For class activity and keeping their exercise book in order students could get 5 marks each, which made a maximum of 100 marks per semester and subject. As is obvious from these figures, the written word and doing or learning what you have been told to, was given utmost emphasis when students were evaluated, especially when only 5 marks out of 100 were attributed to class activity. This emphasis was also, although indirectly, an admonition to teachers to focus on the written word. Even in skill-oriented subjects like music, arts and sports, priority was given to the written word. Teachers provided notes for each subject and tests and semester exams were developed on the basis of the notes.

Each semester all the students were ranked in relation to their classmates, in grade 4 from 1 to 105, and all the marks, including those in skill-oriented subjects, had equal value. With 100 students in class, one student was bound to get the last rank and all competed with each other to be the best. They also competed to pass. A minimum of 100 marks was required as a pass for the whole school year. Up to grade 4, promotion was automatic, but from grade 4 on a student might have to repeat the class.

Teachers of skill-oriented subjects not only gave notes, however. Sports teachers also took the students out into the yard to do exercises. In grade 4, the music teacher asked students both to bring musical instruments and showed them how to make simple instruments themselves. They often sang, individually and together, with a lot of smiles and gusto.

The music teacher of grade 5, described above, did not engage the students in a similar way. This could be due to the curriculum and that they were expected to have a more theoretical approach to music in grade 5. It could also be due to lack of knowledge of the subject. Almost none of the teachers in skill-oriented subjects had any kind of training, or even special interest in the subject assigned to them. At the beginning of the school year they would be told to teach e.g. grade 4 sports or grade 5 arts, without any previous experience of the subject. The easiest way, and the one in which the students were later to be tested, was to read the book prepared for the subject and give the students relevant notes.

Teaching was done in a similar way in the entire school, irrespective of class. Students sat at their benches and the teacher stood by the blackboard. When teachers turned their back to the students to write something on the board, students were silent and copied what was written, if the teacher was writing notes. If he or she was only going to use what had been written as an illustration or explanation, the students soon lost interest in the writing and started talking to each other.

As illustrated by the time spent in writing notes and the importance attached to the written tests it was clear that the written word was central to all aspects of the teaching process. It was not any written words, however, but usually those employed by the teachers and found in the books. Students were not encouraged to give their own interpretation of what they had read or heard, or express themselves in their own words, but were expected to be able to repeat the key words used. This focus on the written word was a means for the teachers to control the students; to know whether they had done their homework and whether they had listened to the explanations; as a whole, to check whether the students had been mentally as well as physically present in class.

The written word was, however, not only a means for teachers to control students, but can also be seen as a way in which the teachers' own superiors within the school and the Ministry of Education forced the teachers into a specific mode of work, into a way of structuring their lessons so that they could be accounted for at every step. The elaborate reporting system can therefore, through its system of structuring rules, which regulated the control process, be interpreted as a means of effectuating subordination.

TEACHING AS A PROFESSION

In the old days, teachers were very much respected (in Ethiopia). *Parents held teachers in high regard. But today, in this new generation, the students themselves do not respect teachers much and they always say that whatever mistakes they make, are the fault of the teachers. If for example one student is lazy, he complains about his teacher. And when the parents hear this from their children they also lose their respect for the teachers.*
Interview with female middle aged teacher, 21.11.2000

Today I think that the attitude of society towards teachers is going down. Before, the profession of the teacher was respected but not so much now. I don't know why it was respected before. Now, since there are many types of jobs with varying salaries not many want to be teachers. Today the Ministry of Education gives lower salaries than other ministries and offices and I think that the salary is one of the reasons why the respect is going down. Due to this most of the teachers are leaving this profession and joining others.
Interview with young male teacher, 4.10.2000

From what I hear when I talk to important people the status of the teacher used to be very good. But now people don't want to be teachers. If you compare with other offices, teachers' salaries are very low. Secondly, the students themselves have no manners. Thirdly, the number of students per class is much too high. Even if you love your job it makes it impossible to carry it out. For example compared with one who has 100 children in the class, the one who teaches 50 will be happy to do it, thus the number of students is very important. Together these things create a situation where nobody wants to be a teacher. If they say that a person is a teacher, nobody wants to know him. But before a teacher was very much respected. My father is a teacher and he tells me of how he used to be respected.
Interview with a young female teacher, 10.10.2000

In the school year 1999–2000 there were 43 teachers employed by the Birabiro school, 35 were men and 8 were women. In Ethiopia it is still men who fill up the teaching profession, especially in the higher grades. Female teachers usually teach in nurseries and the lower grades in school. Six of the women in the Birabiro school taught the lowest grades, while one taught biology from grade 5 up and one was the deputy director of the school.

Despite the low esteem in which teachers felt that society held them, many of them still took their work very seriously. They saw themselves as models or surrogate parents, whose behaviour had a great impact on their students. In this, they shared the model with their students, who expected them to behave in a strict, proper and loving manner. Some of the teachers with whom I conducted personal interviews described this in the following words:

I want, all in all, to be a good model for my students: morally, psychologically, physically and intellectually. I want to be very skilful in my profession. Then the students accept you. You can understand their emotions, their feelings towards the teaching. Then the teaching becomes interesting both for you yourself and for the students.

Young male teacher, 4.10.2000

A good teacher must carry out his responsibilities and be guided by his plans. Good teachers should be models to their students. They should know their subject matter. Their character and morals must be good, starting from their way of dressing to their way of speaking in order to be good models. They must also be careful when they speak to the students and not harm them. They should also have good contacts with the administration and the parents. So a bad teacher is the opposite of this.

Young female teacher, 11.10.2000

A good teacher is someone who can teach the students what they need to know according to their grades and the books that have been prepared for them. He will know what they are required to know for their level. Secondly, he must be able to control the class, especially since there are so many. (…) Then, apart from teaching, a teacher has to watch his personality, meaning we are all created differently and we cannot change that. But we have to take care of our hair; our clothes must be clean and so on. Then it is good if a teacher doesn't drink or smoke or take chat. (…….) It is also important for a teacher to have a long-range plan, to know what should be done during the whole year. If you only have a short-range plan you will not be able to finish your teaching within the available time.

Young female teacher, 10.10.2000

First of all a good teacher must keep his personality, he must be well disciplined and know his subject matter well. He should relate to the students as a father or a mother, a brother or a sister, not more than that. He shouldn't be aggressive. He should always read something and be in touch with the outside world.

Young male teacher, 9.10.2000

These statements illustrate the teachers' wish to understand the students, their points of view and feelings. Many worried that they might mentally harm the students. This preoccupation surprised me somewhat and when I asked them why they worried, they referred to their own bad experiences from when they went to school. To be a model, implied, according to the teachers, that they intellectually wanted to be good as teachers, which was exemplified by giving students the expected knowledge according to the overall plan and by providing them with good, illustrative examples. Personally the role model implied that the teachers maintained good hygiene, were well dressed and polite. Although all the interviewed teachers expressed such ideas as an ideal, not everyone implemented it, as we shall see from the children's comments below.

Conceptualising children's learning

Sometimes I wondered how much the children actually understood of what they were taught and to what degree the teachers could fill them up with knowledge. One such incident that made me wonder took place when I had given the students the title of the first essay, 'Me and My Home' on which Girma had elaborated, telling them to write about how they lived, with whom, what they were doing etc.

> Heywot, 13 years old is sitting beside me. When everyone's attention is focused on the teacher she hands me a piece of paper and asks in a subdued voice, 'Is this what you want?' Her information about her home is presented as statistics in columns, with name, age and position of the household members together with their relationship to each other. She surprised me, this was not what I had planned or expected. I try to explain to her that there should be more words, real sentences. 'I shall try again' she says, 'on the back of the paper you gave us'. This exchange set me thinking about the meaning of written words and full sentences. What are they, what do they convey to a reader and what experience does Heywot have of any kind of prose? Can she understand what I mean with a 'full sentence'? She has been taught about sentences grammatically and should know how they are constructed, but she has most probably never read a story, a book, hardly even a schoolbook. Will she ever understand the amount of information including emotions, points of view and various perspectives that a sentence can contain if she has never come across one?

The pedagogical approach used by the teachers showed me that they understood the children's learning process to be quite additive, in close agreement with the ideas existing in the rest of society. In a workshop that I organised for the teachers of the school, I asked them to explain to me how they visualized the ways in which students matured and learned and if possible to give me some metaphors that could illustrate the process. Two of the groups gave me the following metaphors indicating in various ways how they saw the students.

Students are like a white sheet of paper. Students are like bees. Students are like a camera. Students are followers of a teacher. Students and irrigated water go where it has been prepared for them. Students are like empty vessels. What has not been sown cannot be reaped.

The goal of the teachers was then to fill the children, who were passive recipients of knowledge, with good ethics and a proper understanding of the various subjects. Thereby, the children would be made into good citizens.

We want to teach the students and make them into good citizens. We want to make the students productive. We want them to improve the expected skills in each subject. We want them to build their country and be all-round citizens in social and economic aspects. We want to change the behaviour of the students. We want to create a generation that can carry responsibility and that, as citizens will have acceptance among the people. We want to shape good citizens; therefore behavioural change is the basic objective of education; it is what the government has designed.

Statements from different groups during workshop, spring 2000

The status of Ethiopian teachers has been going down during the last ten to twenty years judged from the salaries they get today and compared with those with a similar education and work experience but working at other jobs. Teachers talked of being neglected by the Ministry of Education, which neither increased their salaries nor gave them any further paid training like workshops or seminars. The government also disregarded their knowledge since, the teachers argued, their opinions were never asked for before new educational policies were promulgated. Together with the disdain they said they encountered from students and parents their morale was hurt (**moralu yenekkal**) and many told me that if they got the opportunity to leave the profession, they would. Most felt stuck with being teachers, however, and did not think that they could get other employment unless they improved their education, which was not so easy.

PARTICIPATION

From my diary

I come early to school, I am there already at a quarter to eight. In the yard some ten to fifteen boys and somewhat fewer girls do exercises. They run in a circle, following the sports teacher's instructions 'two rounds bend-down'; 'move your hands and arms upwards' and so on. One of the grade 5 girl students is there, smiling happily to me and waving her hand. She moves her body gracefully when running. Later the children compete two and two and also run and are timed. Bellete the gardener cum student is watering the ground to reduce the dust.

Slowly, the yard fills up with other students. It is 8:30 and time to assemble the whole school in front of the flag. The students gather class by class, all of the almost 3000 students, who are there on time. Boys and girls stand separately in front of the flagpole headed by their respective homeroom teachers. Using a loudspeaker a girl reads a poem and two boys tell jokes. Some laughs and clapping of hands can be heard. All the three presenters are members of the mini-media, a school club that presents news, quizzes, and poems and jokes every morning to the school. When they have finished the lower grades are instructed to sing the national anthem and some older students join in. Far from all are singing, however. 'The melody is very difficult', I comment to one teacher. 'Not only that', he says, 'they also change it all the time. Every new government wants its own anthem and how can you develop any emotional attachment under such circumstances. Not to sing is sometimes a demonstration against the government' he concludes.

The children disappear into their classrooms, supervised by teachers with rods, who hit them more or less depending on the child's behaviour. I hurry into the administrative building to get my chair. When I reach grade 5a, Teacher Wondale, the homeroom teacher is already there, calling their numbers. Instead of calling their names, each student has been given a number to which they respond when present. Some students forget about the roll call but are quickly reminded to respond by their neighbours. When there is no answer the teacher stops a moment, calls the number again and adds the name looking at the child in question, telling her/him not to talk when names are called. 'Are you here?' he says. 'Yes sir', the child answers. And he continues. In 5a there are today only 92 students and it doesn't take the teacher long to check their presence.

The first period is Amharic, the homeroom teacher's own subject. Today he teaches Amharic grammar. Rapidly he writes a couple of sentences on the board. The noise in the classroom increases with every second. He finishes and turns around asking 'Okay, who wants a beating? Shall I get my rod out?' The noise goes down immediately but doesn't totally disappear. Then he asks the class the meaning of the first sentence on the board. Hands quickly go up, some shout 'teacher', 'teacher'. 'Be silent', he says, 'don't shout teacher, teacher'. He points to a small girl in front who gives her answer. Lots of students continue waving their hands. Then he points to a boy at the other side who presents the same answer but in a different tense. The teacher stands, reflecting upon the answer and many hands go down. 'Why?' he asks the boy. No answer. Then he gives the question to Mekonnen. All the remaining hands go down. Mekonnen answers and nodding the teacher goes back to the initial sentence and starts explaining to the students what they should be observant about. The tense is important, but there are often adverbs, which indicate what the tense should be. While explaining he puts in minor questions to the students, checking that they understand what he is trying to say. Almost all of them have stopped their private conversations and are listening attentively to the teacher. I am enjoying myself immensely testing my knowledge of Amharic grammar.

The teacher continues in the same way with the other sentences he has written on the blackboard. The children actively follow what he says and try to answer the questions. When he looks at some, as if intending to ask them a question, I can see their hands slowly come down, only to rise again when he looks elsewhere. The period ends with the teacher writing down some brief, important reminders about what he has been teaching up to now. The students are told to copy this in their exercise books. Then the teacher leaves, the period is finished. Although the noise in the classroom increases at his departure, it is only for a few minutes. Soon all the students with exercise books and pens are copying the sentences from the blackboard into their exercise books. The English language teacher, who enters after a couple of minutes, finds the students too busy writing to greet him properly. He doesn't say anything until he sees that most have stopped writing. Then he asks Mohammed to clean the board.

Participation in class

The music and the Amharic teacher showed almost opposite approaches to the students, the music teacher focusing on the notes and the Amharic teacher trying to engage the students verbally and make them understand what language is all about. This behaviour was not something specific to the periods described above, but was repeated time and again. It did not mean that the Amharic teacher gave no notes; indeed he did, facing the same situation as all the other teachers, namely students without textbooks who were to be examined on written texts. However, his notes were brief and his explanations lengthy.

In Addis Abeba and the so-called Amhara region the medium of instruction up to grade 8 is Amharic, which from grade 9 is changed into English. In other regions other languages are used as the medium of instruction. Most Birabiro children seemed to communicate in Amharic with their parents although many parents came from other parts of the country like the Gurage area and spoke that language with each other.

Teachers who wanted to engage students in a lesson needed to be very diligent in their approach because students quickly lost interest. A teacher, who tried to help a student and became involved in her/him for more than a minute, would see the rest of the class turn to other activities. Thus, a teacher had to be fast, ask sharp questions and require quick answers, to keep the students interested. Interactions between teachers and students can, partly, be categorized according to the subject matter taught. In languages and mathematics notes were usually brief and the students were prompted by the teachers to answer a variety of questions. Subjects like geography and biology on the other hand, required long notes and elaborate explanations and not much time remained for interactions with students. This pattern was strong in grade 4, where the homeroom teacher taught all but the skill-oriented subjects. The time given to interactions with students was conspicuously longer in English, Amharic and mathematics as compared to chemistry, biology etc. Despite subject similarities the ways in which teachers in school taught their students varied significantly, however, especially regarding the effort put into getting as many students as possible involved in practising and responding. The difference in involvement illustrated by the music and the Amharic teacher is one example of this variety. Another such example comes from Girma teaching physics in grade 4.

From my diary

Roll call is finished and Girma calls Amare and Birtukan forward. Looking at their shoes, he asks the class 'Which of these two would hurt you the most if he or she stands on your feet?' Amare has flat-soled shoes and Birtukan stiletto heels. All children get involved and shout, 'Birtukan, no Amare, no Birtukan'. Girma then calls 11 year old Ahmed, who sits at the front, and tells first Amare then Birtukan to stand on Ahmed's foot. He then asks Ahmed, 'Which hurt the most?' 'Birtukan', Ahmed responds. 'Why', Girma says. Ahmed is silent, the class is silent and Girma starts explaining, saying that when the movement is concentrated to one point the weight becomes stronger as compared to when it is spread out. He then tells Ermias and Teferra, two tall, broad 15 year old boys to come forward together with Hanna, thin, short and only ten. Ermias is told to lift first Hanna, who he easily lifts, then Teferra, who is more difficult. 'What is the difference', Girma asks. Nobody answers. Girma then talks to them about the relationship between weight and movement. Later he gives the class the major points of the lesson on the blackboard. There have been no private discussions, everyone has eagerly followed what Girma has been doing and the only comments relate to his demonstrations. From my experiences, Girma is an exceptionally gifted teacher.

Apart from differences due to subject, the variations between how teachers carried out their lessons could be judged from the time they set aside for note-writing, explanation and interactions respectively, and the quality of the explanations and interactions. Time given to the various tasks was, apart from being dependent on the subject taught, also a result of the teachers' motivation. Some arrived late for their lessons and left early, others might not come at all, and although most observed the time, a few might come very early and some even gave the students extra lessons. When explaining a subject some teachers made use of difficult words, often of English origin, which were written in the textbooks but for which they had no equivalent in Amharic. Many were unable to explain these concepts to the children. A few, however, like Girma had the capacity to translate abstract concepts and illustrate them with examples familiar to the children. Most interactions were characterized by requiring yes and no answers or filling in a missing word or concept that had been memorized and only the right word was accepted as an answer.

The 'why' questions of the Amharic teacher and Girma were exceptions, however. Few teachers asked this kind of 'why' question, which required that the students make their reasoning explicit. The other teachers' 'whys' were more an attempt to find out whether the student had grasped the causal mode of reasoning of the teacher or the textbook. Thus it was a matter of having learnt a causal explanation by heart rather than having thought it out independently. This can be illustrated by an experience from my own teaching. Once, when I was asked to take over the class in English the students gave me very different answers to my questions, so I started asking them why they answered the way they did. Their reactions to my why were to give me an alternative answer, and when again I asked them why, they tried yet a new answer. The teacher commented afterwards that I had asked many 'why' questions and he could not understand the reason for it. I told him I wanted the children's motivations for their answers, at which he shrugged his shoulders.

What happened during my interaction with the students was that they searched for *the* right answer to my questions. When I asked them why they answered the way they did, they interpreted my reaction as a statement that their answer was incorrect. They had no experience of arguing for their answers or of reflecting upon them. To them, and to the teacher, my why questions were out of place, either your answer was right or wrong. What was wrong could not suddenly become right because of an explanation or argument. To all of them knowledge was something delimited, it could not change, and the answers had nothing to do with the students' understanding of my questions but only with their successful or unsuccessful memorization of the words.

The experience of the why questions strengthened my impression of the school as a place where in general children were not encouraged to be active and take initiatives but rather a place where they should be filled with the right knowledge. Somehow, I had expected a little more emphasis from the teachers on children's active participation in class. In the 5-year educational policy of 2000, it is explicitly stated that 'children will be encouraged to actively participate in both learning and teaching to enhance the teaching-learning quality' (Ministry of Education 2000), and I had thought that this was a result of some re-thinking in the government with regard to education.

'People's' participation

The concept of participation has been frequently used in Ethiopian official discourse in different contexts. I had come across it when working with Swedish aid to peasants when popular participation was emphasized. The Western international community spread the concept to Ethiopia as well as to many other parts of the world through extensive use and through subjecting support to aid projects to the participation of the local people. For the major part of the 1980s and the 1990s 'participation' was considered a *sine qua non* for development. 'People's' or 'popular participation' was theoretically based on the conviction that for development to occur local people themselves should participate in government or aid projects. If the projects were developed from locally identified needs and local people themselves were given the responsibility for implementing and maintaining them, the projects were expected to be sustainable even after the departure of the aid organization or the direct involvement of the government. The 'participation' ideology thus implied a conviction that real and lasting change can only be obtained if the people concerned are involved and responsible for it from its very inception and not that it is the result of an order coming from the outside or from the government bureaucracy.

Even in the West, however, the belief in popular participation was more of an ideal than something aid organization employees were ready to implement. In an article discussing the use of 'people's participation' in Swedish aid, Evers Rosander (1992) concludes that it is a rhetoric in which many believe, but the degree of commitment decreases the further away you get from the Stockholm headquarters and the closer you get to the field of action. In Ethiopia governments have especially used the term in aid contexts but given it another interpretation. During the socialist government (1974–91) popular participation implied 'mobilization', and people were 'mobilized' to do various development activities. This meant that they were ordered out to plant trees, build roads etc. They did the work and it was in accordance with the government's plans. Under the present government (1991–) it is called 'popular participation' but, according to Vaughan and Tronvoll (2003), the participation is mainly restricted to those who are members of the party. Members are thus encouraged to discuss various issues along given guidelines but once a decision has been made, all of them have to abide by it and carry it out. Those who are not members of the party are told to implement the decisions made by the others and to fulfil their quotas, whether it concerns well-building, tree planting or whatever government plan there is. Neither members nor non-members will initiate new plans, however.

In this way, the concept 'people's participation' has a different interpretation in the official Ethiopian discourse. Rather than encouraging people to take their own initiatives for which they will be held responsible, it implies that state officials order people about and demand that they do what the bureaucrats consider good for them (Poluha 2002a). Despite this experience I was curious about how participation was thought about and used in the education sector.

Participation, a teachers' perspective

In my semi-formal interviews with the teachers I asked them to elaborate on the meaning of 'student participation' or **yetemari tesat'fo**. The teachers' answers were, as a whole, quite similar. Girma, one of the young male teachers said,

> 'Students have to be allowed participation in the learning process to answer questions'. 'How,' I asked him. 'For example', Girma said, 'after you have taught one

language item you have to practise it, so you call them forward to make a dialogue with their friend. That is one kind of participation. Another kind is to make a student a monitor...' 'Another again is that students should participate in making the rules and regulations, but I don't know to what extent they participate in our campus. Still, I think it is necessary because I think they must be made aware of what they are expected and obliged to do in school. Then if they make a mistake they are responsible. So this is what I mean by participation.'

Talking with Amaresh, a young female teacher I asked her, 'What should be included if we were to say that there is a lot of student participation?' She answered,

> *'To increase it* (student participation), *our teaching methodology is one of the means to do it. Sometimes we may be boring and they are not encouraged to participate. So it is very much up to us. If we only talk ourselves, then we cannot get their participation.'*

Lomiye, another, somewhat older female teacher said to the same question,

> *After the teacher has explained, and if there is a student who stands up and repeats some of what the teacher has said, that means the student has participated. Then, there is also asking questions and when the students raise their hands and answer and also when the students ask questions that the teacher answers.'*

Lomiye here added the idea of students asking questions. From informal talks with many teachers I understood that all appreciated the idea of students asking questions. During the entire fieldwork, however, I did not hear students ask their teachers serious questions more than maybe ten times. Apart from once, when the teacher did not take the question seriously, all the teachers tried to respond to these questions as carefully as possible. And yet no more questions came forward.

Nebiat, one of the young male teachers, commented about student participation that

> *There is too little participation. I think it is because of the curriculum. It is too difficult for them .... to promote student participation the number of students in each class should be decreased. There should be no more than 30, so that the teacher can check on each and every one of them each period...*

All in all, these comments are quite representative of how the teachers viewed student participation. To participate meant, according to them, that students listened attentively to their teachers and asked questions when they did not understand. Students were also expected to do their home- and class-work properly. Above all, however, they should respond to questions asked by the teachers. Their answering the questions was taken as proof that they had both listened and understood what the teacher had communicated. It was therefore an indication that the teacher had done the job well.

Participation, a student view

When discussing the subject of participation with the students I did not want to use the concept itself, which they might misunderstand, but asked for descriptions of 'good' and 'bad' teachers and 'good' and 'bad' students. *'A good teacher explains'*, said Maryamawit, a 15 year old girl in a group interview. *'Some even give additional examples that you do not find in the book!'* *'Yes'*, Amarech added, *'some teachers they just write and without explaining they just go out. They go out even before it rings. This is not to be expected from a teacher'*, she concluded in a condemning voice. Other students repeated the importance of explaining. Mekonnen, for example, the 15 year old monitor, said *'A good teacher is one who explains in class and gives homework. And since all the students might not have done it* (their homework)*, he shouldn't beat them. He should ask why they didn't do it, because maybe they had not understood it properly. A bad one (teacher) is one who does not explain.'*

Talking about 'good' teachers, Rebqa, 12 years old, referred to teachers as close kin, a conceptualisation often expressed by both children and teachers. Rebqa said, *'A good teacher should treat the student like his own child...'* ... *'He should be like an intellectual father'...* *'A bad teacher is someone who insults the children.'* To this her friend Judith, also 12, said *'and a good student is someone who doesn't disturb and doesn't answer the teacher, like if the teacher insults him, he will still not answer the teacher's insults'*. *'Yes,'* Rebqa said, *'just like I respect my mother and father I have to respect my teacher. What he advises me to do, I have to accept.'* *'But what if he insults you?'* I asked. *'If he insults me, so long as he is my intellectual father I have to say yes and accept his advice,'* Rebqa answered.

These characteristics were repeated again and again by students in both informal talks and semi-formal interviews. Teachers were considered to be close kin, the older ones like fathers and mothers and the younger ones like older sisters and brothers. Teachers used the same metaphor when talking about the students, implicitly meaning that as loving and responsible as a mother, father, sister or brother would be to their child or sibling, so should a teacher act towards a student. This was how things ought to be, but as illustrated above they often were not. Even if those teachers who insulted or beat them were bad, according to the students, the worst were teachers who did not explain, who 'give homework without giving examples'. Good students, on the other hand, should listen, study and answer questions. This was the agreed-upon ideal for students and teachers alike.

The meaning of participation in an Ethiopian context

What these ideals regarding 'participation' and 'good'/'bad' teachers and students show is that for students to participate and be good, they should be attentive but passive, learn the written words in textbooks or learn their summaries by heart, but not question them or come up with alternatives. Teachers, on the other hand, were supposed to be active all the time, their knowledge and their status were not to be questioned. All motion, all initiatives were expected to come from the teachers and good, participating students should *re*-act to these stimulants.

Anyone from the West familiar with the concept of participation would have expected student participation in school to mean that students were actively engaged in the activities, taking their own initiatives regarding modes of studying, being critical of texts and teachers and taking the responsibility for their own results. What actually happened was that teachers lectured to the students. Although there were wide variations between how individual teachers used time, space and teaching materials, the pedagogy implemented was based on filling the students with correct knowledge and on giving them marks for having memorized what they had copied from the blackboard and been able to re-present at examinations. What is astonishing in this situation is the wide variety of teaching approaches that the various teachers still exhibited, and that so many teachers succeeded in making the students enthusiastic about their subjects despite the fact that the students were around one hundred in the class, sitting on top of each other and lacking textbooks.

GENDER, AGE AND RELIGION IN CLASS AND PLAY

The children did not sit according to their own wishes in class but the homeroom teacher decided about the seating arrangement. In grade 4 various arrangements were tried, including sorting the children according to their rank in class. In grade 5 rearrangements were made on an individual basis to prevent the children from talking. With 100 students learning together in a small classroom the students tended to sit on top of each other, almost forced to communicate. The teacher then moved close friends away from each other and spread the older, serious students over the different benches in class. However, teachers followed an obvious pattern: girls and boys were mixed, but there was also a mixture of ages and religion at the benches. This approach differed a lot from the seating arrangements in Gojjam, where girls and boys had never been told to sit together. Once, when a teacher in Ashena told a girl to sit beside one of the boys the girl just stopped coming to school. Only a week later, after the teacher had been to her home and promised that she could sit with the girls, did she come back to school. The mixed seating, introduced by the schoolteachers in Addis Abeba was therefore a contrast with the traditional pattern as it was practised in the church compound, at funerals and at other social events.

Sitting together in class I saw students at the same bench talk, help and communicate with each other, some more frequently and with greater pleasure, others less. In grade 4 the rows also often competed with each other and I could see and hear bench- and row-mates identify with and support their representatives when competing. In these contexts, neither the children's conversation, work nor play were influenced by their age, gender or religion, nor evidently, did their bodies affect it. I saw no sign of sexual allusions in the communication between boys and girls, nor any words that would associate to such ideas. Instead the children moved around freely and exhibited very little sense of sexual bodily awareness.

When the children in grade 4 were told by their music teacher to organize themselves into groups to present a short play, they would, however, all of a sudden move across the classroom to look for their friends. Girls consulted with their girl friends and boys with their boy friends. When the groups presented their pieces, almost all were divided by gender, age and also religion. The two exceptions were one group with both Christian and Muslim boys and one group with three boys, who had been joined by their friend Messelesh, a girl.

There was also quite a lot of bodily movement in class, where girls and boys distinctly differed. Many girls would put a hand in front of their mouth when answering, making it difficult to hear what they said. Girls often acted this way since they were not supposed to be heard in public places. More boys than girls could also be seen waving their hands to respond to questions asked by the teachers, who also called more boys to work at the blackboard. When their answers were correct some of the male students often expressed their pride in visible body movements, seemingly expecting their friends to watch them. One day Ermias was called to the blackboard to do a sum. After having finished the teacher told him that it was correct. Then we could see him come dancing back between the rows to his seat, smiling all over and moving his hips in an exaggerated way. Nebiat, a 10 year old boy, made the V-sign with his fingers in front of the class when he had responded correctly. There were several other boys who expressed themselves in similar ways. But, I only saw one girl clearly show happiness at having answered correctly. This was 13 year old Amarech who held up both her hands in V-signs and smiled broadly all over her face when the teacher said that she had done her sum correctly. Her expression of happiness was received with fewer smiles and appreciation by the girls around her than those of Ermias, Nebiat and the other boys had been. As a whole, these boys and the one girl were exceptions. Most girls and boys neither smiled, nor showed any emotion to their classmates, whether when they had answered correctly or incorrectly, they just went back to their seats without looking at anyone.

During the 25-minute break it was common to see girls and boys separate to play, as in most other parts of the world, not only according to gender but also according to age. While many of the young girls skipped rope or played hopscotch during the break, the boys preferred to play ball or chase each other. A few young girls joined some of these chasing games or hide and seek, especially when there was a brother-sister bond between at least two of them. Older girls did not play in the yard; neither did older boys unless they could play volleyball. Most of them, girls and boys, preferred to spend the break chatting with their friends. In this way, the schoolyard exhibited many clear divisions of gender, age and also religion during the break, just like free group work in class. These aspects were important to the children's identities and had embedded structuring effects on their interactions and body movements.

CONTESTING EMBODIED BEHAVIOUR

From my diary

It is the fifth period and I sit on my chair at the back feeling tired and hungry. Now we only have mathematics and then lunch. The students are talking to each other, moving around the desks. Slowly the noise increases and the monitors start moving forward. In comes the mathematics teacher. He says something in a low voice that I cannot hear. The monitors are at work with their sticks and many children sit down. The teacher also sits.

Then there is commotion all over the class. Petros, a young boy of 12 first begs then pushes his female neighbours of 15 to let him pass with his exercise book. Breasts and stomachs are in the way and he jumps on top of the desk to be able to get out. 11 year old Etalem, sitting by the wall beside big Ermias and three young girls, respectfully asks him to let her pass, and when he won't, she also jumps on top of the desk and goes past them all. She wears trousers under the school uniform skirt. Even Adanech, my goodness, she is 16, on the plump side, with big breasts and long hair, walks on the desk when her friends do not move out of the way quickly enough. All their movements are hurried and I only understand why, when I see the queue forming beside the seated maths teacher. He is going to correct their exercise books and since he will not be able to do all of them during this period, and might disregard this homework when correcting later, each child tries to see to it that at least hers or his are corrected, and that they get their marks.

The students talk a lot to each other, a few move around, but the latter are told to go back to their places by the monitors. Many girls and boys also jump over their friends when returning to their seats. Others squeeze themselves in past breasts and stomachs. Bodies do not seem to matter just now, other than as possible obstacles to free passage.

What happened in class when the maths teacher entered? Although I could not hear what the teacher said, the children were evidently soon aware of the situation and prepared their books to come forward. The monitors foresaw the children's advance and were prepared with their sticks to hit them. Younger children like Petros and Etalem did what they had been taught to do, they politely asked their older neighbours to let them pass. When the latter did not react in the expected way, polite behaviour says that young children should wait, because their neighbours were older and should be respected. Etalem and Petros were in too much of a hurry for this, however. I could see a very brief hesitation on their part and then they were off, onto the bench.

With Adanech, I was a bit shocked myself. Her behaviour was just not the way a mature young girl acts. When a young Ethiopian girl sits, her knees should be kept together and her arms held close to the body. She should not make any large gestures with her hands, arms or other parts of the body. And when a girl of this age walks, her eyes should be on the floor and she should walk sedately to wherever she is going. She should not take up any space or be conspicuous in what she is doing. Preferably, she should melt into the background and become invisible. This embodiment of what it is to be a girl or young woman is part of what most Ethiopian girls, irrespective of ethnic background learn, through practice, interactions, observations and comments since birth (cf. Bourdieu 1992, Rydström 1998, Poluha 2002a). Then, to see somebody like Adanech, forget all that she has learnt about bodily behaviour, jump on to the table and walk on it to reach the teacher, that really was astounding.

During the maths period, the girls and boys thus behaved against all norms that they had been taught as proper, such as demure bodily behaviour, deference to their elders and never to walk on the desks. The context in which they did this was specific, namely the gaining or losing of marks. These marks were so important to them that after an initial, very brief moment of hesitation, they went for them even when it required what, under ordinary circumstances, would have been labelled as unacceptable ways. But their behaviour was not the result of careful deliberations or of a decision to contest accepted behaviour, rather they seemed to do it unconsciously, on the spur of the moment to get the important marks. The children's future behaviour in class did not change as a result of this incident either, because when the mathematics period was finished, they reverted to their previous behaviour. Yet, the children's reaction to the situation shows that they were prepared to adapt and behave in new ways when the rewards were attractive enough. This they did despite a rigid hierarchical pattern that they had observed since birth, had been admonished to follow and when not adhering to it, been criticized and chastised for. In this way, the children indirectly came to question a pattern that was deeply embedded in their norms, values, speech and behaviour.

CONCLUDING REMARKS

The major characteristic of Birabiro school education was that school life and life in class were closely structured by lesson plans. Teachers prepared the plans at the beginning of the school year and every week they had to report to their superiors about what they had done, in relation to the initial plan. For the school children these plans were condensed in the summaries presented to them by their teachers containing what they should know in each subject, what they had to memorize and regurgitate for the exams. The written word thus became the means through which teachers could check that the students had learnt what they were supposed to know and through which supervisors could check that teachers did their jobs. This control had two sides, however. It was not only a means through which superordinates could check on or control their subordinates but it was also a means through which adequate reporting and successful exams could become the teachers' and students' own written evidence of having actually accomplished what they were expected to.

The main mode through which teaching was conducted was through lectures where teachers tried to 'fill' the students with all that they themselves knew. Students were not expected to take their own initiatives in class, or be critical, or argue for a point of view in any subject. Student participation in school meant that students responded to rather than asked questions, and that they responded with the right word or concept; that they memorized what they had heard as well as the notes given to them; and that they reproduced all they had learnt during the lectures.[1] The general perception of knowledge was that it was limited, something that could be portioned out and transmitted to students and others in bits and pieces. Knowledge was thus perceived as stable and static rather than as dynamic. This perspective neither encouraged students nor teachers to search for new information or read papers and even less novels. The idea that new data or seeing well-known facts from a different perspective could force you to re-evaluate what you already knew and took for granted was simply not part of teacher–student communications.

The similarities between the perception of knowledge expressed in school and in the Ethiopian Orthodox Church as well as in the comments made by the Assyrian Copts and Iraqi Muslims in Sweden, are thus striking. This pedagogical approach also fitted well with local understandings of how children best learn, mature and become 'good' citizens by which the children were surrounded. In Ethiopia as a whole, new information is strictly controlled. The government, or government-directed organisations, control television, radio and most papers. Opposition journalists lead dangerous lives, always at risk of being imprisoned and even when published their work is not spread outside Addis Abeba. The internet is still accessible only to very few people, mainly teachers at the universities. Thus information about the world is held by a very small group with few means to spread it.

Despite all this, and the strength with which the old traditions influenced the teaching approach, the students' own ability to cope with new situations was remarkable. When mixed on the benches in the classroom the children, especially in Addis, had no problem working together irrespective of gender, age and religious affiliation, aspects, which in other contexts strongly influenced their choice of playmates. Not only that, however, the children were, even if only for a moment, able to shed their body language, developed since birth and through which they consciously and unconsciously expressed male and female identity, age and size. Thus, although whole epistemologies with norms, values and adult opinions as well as embodied ways of behaviour seemed to be resilient to change, they could evidently be challenged when new opportunities with attractive gains were offered.

---

1. Similar school observations have been made in among others, the following countries: Korea (Cho 1995), Bangladesh (Blanchet 1996), Tonga (Morton 1996), Ethiopia (Tekeste Negash 1996), Mozambique (Palme 2001) and Tanzania (Brock-Utne 2001).

Chapter 6

GENDER, A DISTINGUISHING AND STRATIFYING PRINCIPLE

In this chapter we shall take a closer look at how Birabiro children, girls and boys, learned to identify with and behave according to their gender. The focus is on male-female relations, as the only gender categories people in the area find relevant, and on ideas of super- and subordination. Homosexuality, whether between men or women in Ethiopia, is considered evil by Orthodox Christians and Muslims alike and thought of as 'unnatural' and is neither displayed nor talked about in public arenas. Although a subject worthy of its own research for what it can reveal about conceptualisations of gender, it will not be dealt with in the present text.

A prominent characteristic of most interactions in Ethiopia is, as previously mentioned, that they exhibit features of super- and subordination. Words of address, speech, and body behaviour all together articulate who considers her- or himself above and who below in a relationship. Between women and men, men usually have the upper hand although exceptions due to age, class and personal status abound. Not surprisingly then, the maximum female representation to the highest political institution in Ethiopia has never exceeded two per cent (Poluha 2002a) over the last 40 years despite shifts from a feudal to a socialist and then to a self-proclaimed democratic government. There were female parliamentarians under Haile Sellassie, members of the central committee of the Workers Party of Ethiopia under the Derg, and representatives of the National Council under the present EPRDF government, but these were few. Renowned historical figures and heroes were usually men, although there were exceptions such as a few wives of rulers and female rulers whose names are well known.

Peasant women's relations to the state bureaucracy are usually mediated by their husbands, apart from for a couple of years during the Derg, when women were encouraged and allowed to participate in public decision-making activities (Poluha 2000a:111–112, and 1989, 1997). Otherwise, and especially in rural areas, women are not supposed to speak in public arenas when men are present. Men in the countryside have the right to, and often do, make major economic decisions alone, although there is an ideal that decisions should be made together by husband and wife. Exceptions may occur as for example when the wife has some kind of side income, parts of which she may control (Pankhurst 1992). The Civil Code of 1960, however, still sees the husband as the head of the family to

whom the wife owes obedience. Women's dependence on their husbands is further strengthened by the fact that family and religious laws give a much lower
marriage age for girls as compared to boys, who then have more experience and
greater maturity when they marry (Daniel Haile 1979). What is surprising in this
context is the high rate of divorce in Amarinja-speaking areas, often initiated by
women (Poluha 1989, Pankhurst 1992). Even more astonishing may be the
acceptance of and lack of stigma attached to prostitution, especially among
Amharas, to the point where earlier prostitutes do get married to men in official
positions (Laketch Dirasse 1978). However, prostitution is also considered to be
low on the hierarchical ladder and today, with HIV-AIDS rampant in Ethiopia,
a life-risking affair as well. Nevertheless, all of the above is part of the make-up of
male-female interactions and of the scenery that the Birabiro children encountered through lectures in school and TV but which they above all observed in
their everyday lives and learned to take for granted.

The debate about male-female hierarchies and differences has travelled a long
way since the end of the 60s and the beginning of the 70s when it gathered
momentum in the social sciences. First there was a questioning of whether male
dominance was a cross-cultural universal, then began the enquiry into the homo-
geneity of the categories 'male' and 'female' in diverse societies. This in turn resulted in an investigation into the 'difference' between men and women, whether
relations are everywhere structured on the basis of sexual reproductive capacities
and if they look similar cross culturally.[1] More recent approaches have argued
that even biological differences are culturally constructed and that there is as such
no distinction between biological sex and gender since both of them are culturally
constructed.[2] Today's research also focuses on differences within the categories
women and men and how aspects of class, ethnicity, sexual identity and religion
affect these.[3]

In my approach to Birabiro children I shall investigate how difference
between girls and boys is socially and culturally constructed and will use the concept gender difference for what the children perceived as such. My emphasis will
be on the children's practices (Connell 1987, Ortner 1996), how they conceptualised what they did and what their ideas about how they ought to act were. I am
also inspired by Ortner's discussion on how female agency can be differently constructed from male agency, something that she concludes from a comparison
between heroines and heroes in the Grimms' Fairy Tales (1996:9–10). I shall
make a similar comparison between statements about 'good' and 'bad' girls and
boys to discuss Birabiro children's conceptualisations of female and male agency.

---

1. See e.g. Rosaldo and Lamphere 1974, Ortner and Whitehead 1981 and Yanagisako and Collier
   1987.
2. See Connell 1987, Butler 1990 and Broch-Due et al. 1993.
3. See e.g. hooks bell 1981, Mascia-Lees and Cohen 1989–90.

STEREOTYPES, IDEALS AND PRACTICE

To create order in a complex world individuals usually use stereotypes. These refer to simplified, homogenising and bounded models of a category or group of people, depicting what are thought to be their specific characteristics. Stereotypes are often used to establish borders and facilitate inclusion and exclusion of individuals and groups from a signifying us. Of major importance is that the very existence of stereotypes often acts as a filter and influences the way we perceive and categorise the people we meet, often without checking whether the categorisation we made was correct. In this way, stereotypes, like any practice, are both constructed out of our experiences and structure our perceptions of those whom we encounter and the interpretations of the events in which we participate.

Ideals stand for that which is desired and wished for and which is often unobtainable. Ideals are often normative and act as models for how things 'ought to be'. In their statements about 'good' and 'bad' boys and girls the children often mixed stereotypes and ideals which frequently depended on the context in which the topic was discussed. In the following I shall not distinguish between the two but focus on what the children through their various statements told us about their gender system and how it worked.

The children often reflected upon what was right and wrong, good and bad, on how they ought to conduct themselves and often compared this with actual behaviour. The way they expected themselves and felt that others expected them to behave and act was frequently condensed in the categories of a 'good' and a 'bad' girl or boy, epithets they used about each other and themselves. While providing the major normative characteristics, the 'good' and 'bad' categories also often came to function as models for the children's behaviour.

Mekonnen, a 'good' boy

Mekonnen was a serious young man who did not often laugh. Initially he was not easy to interview. He gave brief answers to my questions and seldom elaborated on any of the issues. My third interview with him was more informative. On that occasion Mekonnen was with two school friends who seemed to make him relax and develop some of his ideas further.

Mekonnen was fifteen and lived with his mother, two older brothers and two older sisters. He had great respect for his mother and was very close to her and to one of his brothers, who took a close interest in Mekonnen and always checked his exercise books. Neither his mother nor any of his siblings was employed but his brothers now and then got an income from daily labour and trade. Mekonnen's father was dead. In school Mekonnen got good results. He ranked second in grade 4 and was elected monitor by his classmates in grade 5. He was not absent from school unless there had been a serious accident or death in the family.

Every morning, before school, Mekonnen went to church, not only during the fasting periods but also on other days. He was serious about his religion and tried to follow the precepts of the church. When it was not the fasting season, he went home to eat breakfast after church, and from home to school. Mekonnen liked school, and his first priority was to learn as much as possible and get as high grades as he could in class. To this end, he studied very hard.

> *Mekonnen: After school I go to my friend's house, three days a week, and we study together.*
>
> *Eva: Is he also in grade 4?*
>
> *Mekonnen: Yes, so we use the same books. We ask each other questions from the books.*
>
> *Eva: What else do you do after school?*
>
> *Mekonnen: On two afternoons a week I play football. I am in a team.*
>
> *Eva: And what about your homework?*
>
> *Mekonnen: If there is homework I ask permission from our trainer and do the homework first, otherwise I may be excluded from the team.*
>
> *Eva: Then what do you do?*
>
> *Mekonnen: Well, when I have studied or played football I eat dinner at home.*
>
> *Eva: Do you eat alone?*
>
> *Mekonnen: No, I often eat with my brother*
>
> *Eva: Then what do you do?*
>
> *Mekonnen: Then I go to a friend's to watch television and then I go home and sleep.*
>
> spring 2000

Teachers and students alike respected Mekonnen. I never saw a teacher punish him, instead they always asked him questions, especially when they had given up on the other students after these had repeatedly presented the wrong answers. Mekonnen's name was the only one that came up when I asked his classmates what characterized a good, helpful student and if they had any in their class. Girls and boys alike referred to him when I asked them to give me a name. Prompting them to give me more names they would mention some and then withdraw them saying, '*but he* (or she) *does not share his knowledge with us*'. By this they meant that they had given the names of clever students, but these did not really help others. Berhanu, a thirteen year old student said in an interview together with Mekonnen and Teku, while giving Mekonnen a hug:

> *Berhanu: A good student is like Mekonnen. When the teacher doesn't come, he helps us. He acts like a teacher and stands up and when we just continue talking, then he gets tired and hits us. But he does it for our sake. But we will not understand that. But a good one is like Mekonnen.*

(.....)

Teku: Yes, who will explain when we do not understand.

Berhanu, Teku and Mekonnen, 13, 14 and 15, boys, autumn 2000

Often when teachers were absent I observed Mekonnen come forward with a textbook, stand in front of the class, where the teacher usually stood, and start giving examples in English, mathematics or geography. Then he asked the students to respond to his questions. Since it was difficult for him to keep the others silent while he taught the class, the two deputy monitors would unasked join him to keep order. No other student in class commanded the same respect as Mekonnen. Not only the classmates, even the neighbours appreciated him, as Mekonnen mentioned in the same interview:

> *Eva: Do you have any memory of when an adult praised you?* (....)
>
> *Mekonnen: For me, when I had studied hard and came home from school with good results the people in the neighbourhood, in my area there are lots of different sports games like tennis and they* (adults and other children) *push them* (children) *into that. And since I do something different and come home with good results, then they praise me.*
>
> (Ibid.)

With regard to gender roles, Mekonnen had very strong views. These came up when we discussed how he and his two friends would treat their own sons and daughters when they had them.

> *Eva: What about boys' work and girls' work?*
>
> *Mekonnen: Boys' work is to get water, run errands and girls' work is to make stew, coffee, clean the house, wash the house, wash household utensils. That is her job.*
>
> .....
>
> *Eva: Not one of you* (three boys) *have found it possible for a boy to e.g. make stew?* (Lots of laughter from the boys.)
>
> *Mekonnen: I didn't think of that for him. After all, he is a boy, he must do boys' work.*
>
> *Eva: What happens if you mix the different kinds of work?*
>
> *Mekonnen: I don't know but he* (the future son) *will have a bad feeling about lack of respect.*
>
> *Eva: How?*
>
> *Mekonnen: Well, he will think, how come, when there is a woman, that I should do this? That is why I will divide the work for them.*
>
> ......
>
> *Eva: Even married men in Sweden cook, because both husband and wife work and there are no servants* (laughter).

Mekonnen: Here there is no such thing. This is not the Ethiopian tradition. There is no woman who will say I am not going to do the work. She has to work.

....

Eva: If she doesn't work, are you going to beat her?

Mekonnen: If she doesn't work it is better to be silent. He will eat outside and come home, if she says she is not going to work. If nothing is prepared, how can you eat? If nobody works, then you cannot eat.

Eva: But isn't it possible to change your idea about this?

Mekonnen: No, that is not possible.

(Ibid.)

Mekonnen has a very strong feeling of responsibility towards the rest of society. In the interviews I asked all the students what they would do for their country if they were given the possibility and Mekonnen answered as follows:

Eva: I make you the Prime Minister of Ethiopia for one day. During this day, you can make three decisions, not more, what would you decide?

Mekonnen: If I had power I would make the people work; see to it that those who have not studied will study.

Eva: This is one decision; those who have not studied shall study.

Mekonnen: Okay and secondly, to collect the old people who cannot manage on their own and take care of them. And thirdly, to improve the country's economy through creating different jobs.

(Ibid.)

Old people, many of who cannot manage on their own, surround Mekonnen and his classmates. When the poor, 'sponsorship' children are served their free lunch in the auditorium they eat together with poor, old people who are served free lunch together with them. Some may sit and beg in the streets on holy days and they also congregate at the church, which many of the children attend. Mekonnen is also concerned about unemployment. Living in one of the poorest areas in Addis he is surrounded by unemployed people both in his own family and among neighbours and friends.

'Good' and 'bad' boys – some definitions

The children's comments about Mekonnen put him into the category of a 'good' boy. This categorisation was further vindicated through the children's definitions of 'good' and 'bad' boys.

Maryamawit: A good boy should study, not stay out late, meet with nice people. As a student he should study and when he works he should work. He should only do good things.

Maryamawit, 15, girl, spring 2000

Rebqa: (A good boy is) *one who is not a* **doriye**, *who obeys his mother, and who keeps his clothes proper and does not tear the clothes.*

Judith: Who helps his mother properly, who shares with his mother what he has earned; saying so and so much I have earned, here take this, live from this and work on this. From whatever he earns, whether as a shoeshiner or something else, who will tell her, here this is for sugar and for your coffee.

Manassebesh: For example in our compound they are poor. One child went to South Africa. He sends them (money) *now and then. And when he doesn't send them they eat pea stew. Then when he* (the bad boy in the house) *says to his mother, pea stew is this what you offer me, and then he throws it on the wall. So this is a bad boy.*

Rebqa, Judit and Manassebesh, 12, 12, and 10, girls, autumn 2000

Yenur: A good boy, he has to study properly, he shouldn't go with bad boys.

Eva: How should he behave towards his father?

Yenur: Whatever his father has told him to do, he should do it, and whatever are his duties, he should do them.

Yenur, 12, boy, autumn 2000

I discussed with Ermias, a sixteen year old boy how he would treat his future children, he wanted to have a son and a daughter, and the following conversation ensued:

Eva: Can the boy learn to make stew?

Ermias: If he has the interest, but a boy doesn't make stew.

Eva: He doesn't, does it have to remain that way?

Ermias: Yes.

Eva: Is it good if it remains that way?

Ermias: I don't know but in our country a boy does not make stew.

Eva: And he doesn't bake **injera**?

Ermias: No he doesn't bake, but there are those who do it.

Eva: How do people consider them, those men who bake injera and make stew?

Ermias: Well it is their own personal affair, it is fine with me if they do it.

Eva: And what about doing it yourself?

Ermias: That would not make me happy.

Eva: Why is that?

Ermias: Men do not do women's work now. Men have their own work.

Eva: And it worries you? Will neighbours and friends laugh at you?

Ermias: If they see it yes. That is how it is.

Eva: Aha, if they see you doing it they will laugh at you?

Ermias: Yes.

Eva: And that makes it frightening?

Ermias: Yes.

Ermias, 16, boy, autumn 2000

Ermias was difficult to interview and to get some personal reactions from him I felt I had to provoke him, as can be seen from the interview. Ermias's comments indicate that although he himself will not condemn a boy or man who cooks, something he might say to humour me, he still prefers men to do men's work and women to do women's work. His comments also illustrate how hard it would be for a man to cook even if he wanted to because a man who cooks might be laughed at and looked upon as somebody who does not know his gender and therefore is not quite part of a society so strictly divided by gender.

The main characteristics of an ideal good boy are that he is obedient to his parents, especially his mother, that he runs errands, does not do girls' work and that he studies hard. The opposite of this is a bad boy, a boy who is like Fatima's cousin, whom we encountered in a previous chapter and who was always ordering her about and beating her. It can also be someone like Maryamawit's brother,

> *Maryamawit: My brother, he can come and ask me something and before I have a chance to answer, he hits me. Now we have fought and have not talked to each other for a very long time. He even tried to hit my mother, and she cried. Now he insults her and she only cries. He doesn't give us any money and he doesn't eat at home. We live from what my 18 year old brother earns in Mercato. He is like a mother and a father to us. We even asked a relative to give advice to my brother. He talked to him but my brother did not want to listen. We are afraid of him.*
>
> Maryamawit, 15, girl

The above description also fitted well with what Judith and Manassebesh defined as a 'bad' boy:

> *Judith:* (A bad boy is someone) *who doesn't obey his mother. Who is a **doriye**. Who goes from one area to another. Who bothers his mother daily with having the teacher tell him to bring her* (the mother to school because the boy has been disturbing class). *Who is a thief.*
>
> *Manassebesh: Now for example a girl has to be inside at 7 o'clock, and a boy, I don't know. But there are those who stay out until 11 in the evening before they come home. This is what I call a bad character for a boy.*
>
> Judith, 12, Manassebesh, 10, girls, autumn 2000

Thus we can see that 'bad boys' were, at least partly, defined in opposition to the 'good boy'. The main characteristics of a bad boy, as the children enunciated them, were that he disobeys, does not run errands, does not share his income, stays out late, may even steal, and the worst of all, does not respect his mother.

Messelesh, a 'bad' girl

Another person, who unlike Mekonnen was categorized as 'bad' by adults and some of the children, was Messelesh, a young girl of 14. Messelesh told me that both her parents were dead and that she had grown up with an unmarried aunt, a sister of her mother's. According to a person from the school administration, however, Messelesh's father died before she was born. When the mother found another husband the baby Messelesh was given to the grandmother and grew up with her, her aunts and an uncle. The person who told me this said that it was better to grow up with a grandmother than with a mother. That was her own experience and it was part of the Ethiopian tradition, she told me. I do not know which story was correct. On some occasions I noticed that Messelesh lied both to some of the teachers and to me but it was usually easy for me to find out, and when I asked her about a statement she had made, she could always explain why she had said what she did. Still, she seemed to have spent many years with her aunt in the Birabiro area.

The aunt studied until grade 6, and used to have a job in a factory. She lost it however, and her experiences of unemployment and very little education had made her eager for Messelesh to take her studies seriously. But Messelesh did not do her homework and had poor school results. Sometimes Messelesh talked of her aunt as her mother, sometimes as her sister and sometimes she categorized her as her aunt. Towards the end of the fieldwork Messelesh stayed with another aunt, who was married and had a couple of children. Messelesh said that she did not know how many. She stayed there, she said, because this aunt did not ask her any questions. When she came from school she could do her homework and sleep. When I returned in the autumn of 2001 Messelesh was again back and living with her first aunt.

While Messelesh lived with her first aunt she helped her wash dishes and clean the house. She did not like to cook or make injera, she told me. She liked none of the female tasks in the house. In grade 4, Messelesh also used to work for cash, folding papers into cones. I asked her about this work.

Eva: Why do you work? To get your own money or what?

Messelesh: I don't get money for myself, it is for them.

Eva: Is it for them?

Messelesh: It is for her.

Eva: It is for her. Do you always give it to her?

Messelesh: I give it to her.

Eva: All of it?

Messelesh: No, I may take 50 cents for myself (out of 6 Birr).

......

Eva: Working this much is to help her?

Messelesh: Yes it is to help her. First of all, if she had had a job she would have helped me, but since she doesn't have any it is up to me.

Later in the interview, which was conducted while Messelesh was still with the first aunt, I tried to find out if, how and for what Messelesh was punished at home, saying:

Eva: If you come home later than 7 p.m. does your aunt worry?

Messelesh: She expects me at 6 p.m. and I only stay until 7 if I have not been able to sell the papers before.

Eva: Aha, so you stay until you have sold what you have?

Messelesh: Yes.

Eva: And if you do not come home on time, what does she do?

Messelesh: Sometimes she gets angry with me and says, you why don't you come home on time, is it because you did not sell? And sometimes, well she is just silent.

Eva: Aha, when she gets angry, does she hit you?

Messelesh: But I am not late now.

Eva: But when she gets angry does she hit you?

Messelesh: A stick is not bad.

Eva: Does she hit you with a stick?

Messelesh: No, but if somebody hits you with a stick it doesn't help. But if you get advice, you learn.

Eva: So she uses advice?

Messelesh: Yes.

Later again in the interview I wanted to know if and how Messelesh was praised and asked her, what her aunt said when she praised her.

Messelesh: Well she says, may you grow up well, of course.

Eva: May you grow up well?

Messelesh: Yes

Eva: What can be the reason for her to praise you?

Messelesh: Well it happens that she goes some place and thinks I am not at home. For example, one person goes one place, when she goes, nobody knows when she is going to be back. Only God knows. She can even die on her way.

Eva: You worry about her?

Messelesh: Yes, or she can come home ill. And then I clean the house very well and make it shine and wait for her. Then when she sees the house, it looks nice. But if everything is in disorder when she comes, it is bad.

Messelesh called herself a Punk, and was quite conspicuous in school. Her hair was cut very short, in a fashion that resembled that of boys. She also wore a big jacket, balloon trousers and boots, just like some of the boys.[1] Once I asked her about her choice of haircut and clothes and she responded:

> *Messelesh: From when I was born I have been having trousers. I never wore a dress. From when I was born they bought me trousers and since, I never, I don't like dresses. And the reason why I became a Punk, is that there are some people who believe in **Buda** (the evil eye). My hair used to be very long, in the whole family, my mother, everyone had long hair, and mine was long too. And when I went out to wash it and to comb it, then someone must have seen me, I think, because beginning from then I started to have wounds on the neck. And when the wounds came up, I shaved my hair. And again when it grew long, I got the wounds, then again I shaved it, and since then I started to cut it and from then on I had no problems.*
>
> *Eva: Aha, and when the teacher becomes angry, what do you do?*
>
> *Messelesh: Then I tell them that I want to be like this.*
>
> *Eva: Some become very angry.*
>
> *Messelesh: Yes it is Teacher* (her homeroom teacher in grade 5), *if he suddenly gets angry with me that is why. I didn't use to wear a dress, but it is to show him respect* (that she wears a dress now, for the first time, on top of her trousers) *because on other occasions I didn't put on a dress. With Teacher Girma he asked me to put on a dress, and I would tell him that it doesn't suit me today. But Teacher, since I like him so much, and he looks at everyone as his own children.*

Messelesh was very much aware that adults were suspicious of her. She had no girl or adult friends, she told me, but she had a strong belief in God. In the school adults often insulted her, without her having done anything, just because of her hair or dress. She told me of one such incident with a female administrator.

> *Messelesh: I have cut my hair very short and for some I appear to be a **doriye**, but the one who knows me is God. And sometimes when we come, there is the administrator, and she insults, she insults you! When she sees me with children, she insults me, she uses really bad insults.*
>
> *Eva: Is that because you are different?*
>
> *Messelesh: That is she insults with very, very bad words* (Messelesh is almost crying).
>
> *Eva: Really, what does she say, for example?*
>
> *Messelesh: 'You, and they call you a girl'! Oh really, there is no insult that she doesn't use.*

Messelesh felt hurt by the administrator's insults, especially when she implied that Messelesh was not really a girl. At the same time, some of her classmates com-

---

1. This is very unusual in Ethiopia and although I tried to ask her about it, I did not get any clarifying information about how and from where she learned about being a Punk.

mented that Messelesh was the only girl who used as ugly insults as the worst boys.

The story of her hair continued, however. One day when I came out from an interview with a teacher, I saw a lot of people talking to each other excitedly in a corner of the administrative building. Among those were Messelesh and her female companion dressed in similar clothes and with the same haircut. I tried to hear what was being said but there were too many voices filled with emotion, and I could not understand what it was about. I asked two adults, what had happened.' *Messelesh and her friend have shaved their hair at the back and look like boys'*, one answered. '*They are both wild, (doriyes), and only have boys as friends'*, said another person. '*And look at her'*, she added, '*look at her trousers and jacket, dressed like a boy'*. Messelesh and her friend were standing there with a sheepish grin on their faces, looking rather embarrassed. Then they were told to go home and come back the next day with a parent, and they left.

I went into class and asked the children close to me what had happened to Messelesh. '*She has shaved her hair'*, said Ermias. He also implied that she behaved more like a boy and that was not good. '*The teacher then told her to shave all her hair and then let it grow'*, he added.

The next day I asked the two adults I had talked to why there was such an indignant ambiance with regard to Messelesh. One of the adults said*: 'The school has rules about haircuts. Girls are not allowed to shave their hair the way Messelesh has done, and she has to follow the rules of the school'*. I do not know what kind of face I showed him, but he asked: '*Do you think it is good what she has done?' 'I do find it extremely interesting'*, I said. '*What she has done goes against all traditional Ethiopian rules about how girls ought to behave. She is a rebel and I do find that interesting. It needs a lot of courage to do what she has done. That is why I want to talk to her and hear her version of what has happened'*. They looked at me with surprise, but left the issue. Messelesh did not come to school the following day, but a couple of days later I found her at the auditorium where she had had her lunch, and asked what had happened.

Messelesh: I usually cut my hair this way. Last year, Teacher Girma did not get angry with me because of it.

Eva: Didn't you think that maybe Teacher Wondale would become angry?

Messelesh: No I never thought of that.

Eva: What happened?

Messelesh: Well he called my name and then he became angry when he saw me. He asked why I had cut my hair like that, but I became so scared that I couldn't answer. (Messelesh usually gets silent when adults scold her and ask her rhetorical questions.) *He said that either I had to shorten the hair at the top or shave it all off, if I wanted to come back. I told him I would, and then I left.*

Eva: So what do you plan to do now, are you going to continue your studies?

Messelesh: Yes I am going to go to school.

Eva: And what are you going to do with your hair?

Messelesh: I am going to cut it, but I don't have the money yet.

Eva: How much is it?

Messelesh: 1–2 Birr.

I told Messelesh to wait, but not wanting the other children present to see what I was doing I went into a side room, took out the money and came back.

Eva: All right, here is the money. You can use it for cutting your hair if you want to or for something else if you prefer to do that.

Messelesh: No, I want to go to school. I shall use it for cutting my hair.

Messelesh cut her hair, but did not bring her aunt, as her homeroom teacher had told her to. When I asked her where the aunt was, she told me that she had gone to France, which was quite imaginative but not true. I think Messelesh was afraid to tell her aunt that she had to come to school because of her hair. She tried to pretend that she had never been asked to bring a parent, but Teacher Wondale reminded her of it. About a week later, Messelesh brought a young man to talk to Wondale. Afterwards Wondale told Teacher Girma and me that this was her brother. She has no parents but lives with an older and a younger brother, Wondale told us. Girma, who had been Messelesh's homeroom teacher the previous year then informed Wondale that Messelesh had no brothers, she lived with an aunt. He also said that Messelesh had been a problem in grade 4, but that she had improved a lot now, after she had been separated from her friend. Later I asked Messelesh why she had lied.

Eva: Why did you lie last time?

Messelesh: Last time he (Teacher Wondale, her homeroom teacher) *was really giving me worries. And I didn't want her* (the aunt) *to come and see it. I didn't want him to meet with her. He might have asked her why did she become a Punk and say, tell her to stop being a Punk and so on. Since she shouts at me and gets angry with me it is better if she doesn't know, I mean.*

Eva: So you are afraid of her?

Messelesh: Yes.

*Eva: And for that reason you brought this young strong man (**goromsa**)?*

Messelesh: But he is a relative. He also knows my aunt. He is her friend. And since he knows about her, he calls her his sister. And he (Teacher) got angry when he came. Whose so-called brother are you bringing, Teacher said. And when he said like that I told him that he was my friend. So how can you bring him, he said and he became very angry.

Eva: When you get scared, you become silent, but when you explain to people they will not be angry with you.

Messelesh: Oh, but she (the aunt) *is something, she is something and she will be angry when she hears about it. She is some kind of Satan. She hits me really bad. She will find something and use it to beat you with. She doesn't think about it, she just acts. And she gets angry so quickly.*

It was after this incident that Messelesh moved to her other aunt. Somehow, Messelesh was later allowed into class. When I came back from a trip of two weeks to the north, I found her there, busy with her schoolwork.

'Good' and 'bad' girls – some definitions

Messelesh seemed, in many ways, to fit into the category of a bad girl as the students below defined such a person. They were asked to define both 'good' and 'bad' girls and boys, and some of their definitions were as follows:

Naema: Most who play after school are the boys, they play ball. But if girls don't go home after school their parents will worry. But since they know that the boys are playing outside they don't worry about them. Last time when teacher Nardos said that we should come for lessons for girls only, many girls told her that their parents would not allow them to attend. But boys are boys, they can do what they want.

Tekia: I always go home after school. I am never outside playing. When I come home they tell me what work I am to do. In our area it is dangerous to play outside because there are so many cars, that is why they tell us to stay at home.

Eva: So you can work at home and you are good at that, but you are not able to stay in the street because of the cars. And the boys are not able to work, it is too hard for them (they had told me earlier that boys were unable to cook and clean, it was too difficult for them) *but at the same time they are capable of playing in the street with all the cars. Is that correct?*

Tekia: But boys, even if they are told to stay at home, they will not accept it, they rush out anyway. ...... But in Ethiopia, if a girl leaves her work and goes out, it is said of her, this one, what kind of a girl is she? Doesn't she do her work before going out?

Naema: For example if girls play, now they will say, how come they are out playing? Why don't they go in and do their work? But boys.

Eva: Who is saying this, is it the boys or?

Naema, Rekik and Tekia (almost shouting): *It is the women, women mothers.*

Naema: When they pass us.

Rekik: And when they (girls) *play and jump with their legs high, they* (the women) *get angry and shout insults. So instead of being insulted it is better to play in the compound.*

Naema, Tekia, Rekik, 11, 10, 10, girls, autumn 2000

Viewing Messelesh in the light of these girls' definitions of a 'bad' girl, it is possible to see that she in many respects fits in with such a description. She is boyish, and insults her classmates with insults that are only used by boys. She hits somebody whom she understands to be insulting her. She moves to another home when she has quarrelled with or is afraid of her aunt. What is surprising is that while doing all these rebellious acts, Messelesh still seems to feel that she has to adapt to the rules telling girls how they should be. Thus Messelesh told me, when I asked how she expected her own daughter to behave.

> *Messelesh: Some old women, when I put on trousers, they say, are you a woman, how come you look like a man. If I don't want her* (we talked of Messelesh having a daughter in the future) *to be called names like that, she will have to have a dress.*

Continuing the discussion about how she would treat her prospective daughter and son, I asked whether she would treat them differently, to which she said:

> *Messelesh: Well, the boy, he will play football outside. He will stay out in the evening. He will do what the neighbourhood does. But the girl, since she has nowhere to go, she will sit down with me and relax.*
>
> *Eva: What if guests come to your house?*
>
> *Messelesh: The girl, I will tell her to stay at home.*
>
> *Eva: Is that to help you?*
>
> *Messelesh: Yes, to help me. Stay at home to wash their hands and such.*
>
> *Eva: Can't a boy wash hands?*
>
> *Messelesh: He can of course do it, but, there is play and things and when someone calls him he will run away, so for that reason the girl, there is nobody who will call her, so she can sit down at home.*

In several respects then, Messelesh seems to agree with many of the criteria about how girls and boys should behave. Even though she herself does not fit into it, she wants her imagined daughter to do so in the future not to be insulted, and she still thinks that she herself is a good girl and actually, it is only God who knows who is good and bad.

Another aspect of what characterizes a good girl was expressed in definitions put forward by some of the boys, who introduced the issue of female sexuality, something the girls had never referred to, apart maybe from Rekik's 'girls who jump high' by which she might have meant that they showed too much of their bodies which ought to be covered.

> *Yenur: A good girl, she shouldn't do bad things outside with boys, go with them. Girls should play with girls. She should study properly. And she has to help her mother and father, she should run errands.*
> Yenur, 12, boy, autumn 2000

Ermias: A good girl, it means that in the neighbourhood her voice will not be heard. That is, there are those adults who insult others but to be respected she should not be insulted by them. She should run errands for them.

Ermias, 16, boy, autumn 2000

Berhanu: A bad girl is one who goes from one man to another. Then she shows what kind of a character she has and people will insult her and talk badly about her.

Berhanu, 13, boy, autumn 2000.

Mekonnen: One who obeys her mother, her neighbour, the people in the neighbourhood. Who stays with one man, that is what I call a good woman.

Mekonnen, 15, boy, autumn 2000

As a whole, we can see that what characterizes bad girls is that they disobey, they do not respect their elders, they do not help, but go out in the street, go with boys and do not study. For good girls it is the opposite, although similar to good boys, they obey, help, show elders respect, stay at home, work and study. A common reason for why girls are said to become bad and disobey is that they are not circumcised, according to my interviews with the girls.

*Tekia: Girls, who do not do what their mothers tell them to, and who have not been circumcised, about them it is said that it is because they were not circumcised. She dries up, and she doesn't obey but becomes a **doriye**. But if they are circumcised, they do not become anything* (bad). *There is one big woman in our neighbourhood, very big, who has not been circumcised, she is really mannish, a **doriye**. Everybody in our neighbourhood knows her.*

Rekik: In our neighbourhood there is one girl of my age who has not been circumcised, she is really boyish, a boyish kind of thing. She gets up in the middle of the night to do sports, she plays football with the boys ......

Tekia, 10, Rekik, 10, girls, autumn 2000

Messelesh told me that she had been circumcised. She even remembered when it had been done. Usually Ethiopian girls are circumcised as infants, but for Messelesh to remember it the circumcision must have been carried out late in her life. From Messelesh's way of telling me about it I think she was telling the truth.

THE DIFFERENCE THAT GENDER MAKES

Similarities between children

From the above quotes, by both girls and boys and even further, from what was discussed above in Chapters 3, 4 and 5 we can see that there are many similarities in how girls and boys think that children should behave according to the norms.

In relation to adults they should subordinate themselves. 'Good' girls as well as 'good' boys should show adults respect, be obedient to them, run errands, come home on time, not misbehave in the streets, which will make their parents ashamed of them, and never insult their parents, especially not the mother. In school, children should do what the teachers tell them to, be obedient, come prepared, and not interrupt the teaching.

When the children talked about what was expected of them, they usually spoke in general terms and did not seem to make any distinction between girls and boys. They thereby gave the impression that both categories were expected to fulfil the same demands and that the same rules, norms and ideas applied to all children. Children as well as adults also mostly used the collective term, children (**ledjoch**), and more seldom referred to girls (**set ledjoch**) and boys (**wond ledjoch**) when they talked about the norms that should regulate the behaviour of human beings of a young age. Yet, male children were not necessarily categorized by the male gender. The word, children, **ledjoch**, often referred to boys exclusively, while the female category was always added when girls were referred to.

When talking about girls and boys separately, it became obvious that expectations on each category varied quite a lot, both in the opinions of adults and in the eyes of the children. These ideas about 'children' and 'girls' and 'boys' respectively seemed to exist at different levels of consciousness. When talking about 'children' one rather homogeneous kind of understanding and a similar set of rules and ideas were expressed by all categories. Very often these ideas seemed to apply to what was expected from boys, as the norm for behaviour. When talking about girls and boys separately, much more specific, sometimes contradictory, ideas were voiced, especially regarding the girls. No one seemed to be aware of or make any reference to this contradiction, which evidently could co-exist in people's minds, maybe because it was voiced in different contexts (cf. also Strauss and Quinn 1997:210–252).

Differences between girls and boys

What then were the differences in rules and norms that children and adults thought should apply to girls' and boys' behaviour? In the following I shall discuss girls' and boys' use of space and time, references to female sexuality, expectations of obedience and deference and the gendered division of work as important themes that recurred in the children's definitions and discussions indicating that different norms and values were part of the sets of ideas held about what characterised girls and boys.

Space inhabited by human beings has rules, which define by whom it can be used and how. Shirley Ardener argues that '(S)ocieties have generated their own rules, culturally determined for making boundaries on the ground...'(1993:1–2). Thus, the use of space becomes an effect of the social construction of relations of equality and inequality stamped on the ground and the occupancy of some spaces can give prestige to some categories of people while they at the same time may degrade or even confer impurity on others. Various spaces also have their own gate-keepers who can change during the course of a day or a season depending on who the occupants are. These gate-keepers also have the power of exclusion and inclusion of various members of society in the space they control (cf. Ardener 1993).

The main arenas used by Birabiro girls and boys were their homes with the compound, the school including the classroom and the yard, the religious institution and the roads in between these places. When referring to these places among themselves and in talks with me the young boys and young and older girls usually expressed the idea that each place in itself was quite safe for them but that the roads they had to walk to get there could be very dangerous. Older boys did not show such fear. But even though places like home and school were considered safe, girls and boys still used them differently due to both gender and age. Girls were expected to be inside their homes, easily accessible when parents or other family members wanted their services; boys were more often outside in the compound or in the street. In school older girls and boys usually stayed very close to the wall of the school building talking to each other or remained in the classroom working on various subjects. Young boys, however, spread their games over the whole school compound, some running after each other, others playing ball, teasing and fighting each other; young girls played less lively games and stayed close to the walls. In the street several of the boys spent time talking to their friends or playing while some also practised with their football team in a field further away. No girls played in the streets and the few I saw talking to each other seemed to come together from school only stopping outside a friend's home to conclude a conversation before returning home. There was thus no explicit separation of space according to gender, but the ways in which girls and boys tended to use it differed.

There was also a greater permissiveness towards boys and it was somehow considered natural, as many girls expressed it, for boys to be out in the streets with their friends while girls were expected to be in their homes, or at least to play within their own compounds. It was more of an exception than a rule for girls to be in the street other than on their way to or from a specific place. Girls who stayed or played in the streets were considered bad; boys who did so were thought of as mischievous. Women who saw girls in the street without a purpose therefore felt they had a right to scold them.

Another difference in the behaviour of girls and boys emerges if we take a closer look at what the children have said about time. Girls' use of time was strictly regulated in relation to space. At home, much of their time was spent on work and if they went out, they should be home before it was dark. Although the norms were the same for boys, they were still not expected to follow them. Thus, some boys just stayed in the streets and thereby got more time for play since it was difficult to send them on errands when they were not around the house. This was also accepted as 'boys are boys and nothing can be done to change them'. Many boys also stayed out later than girls of a similar age, although some of the very young ones worried about being in the streets after dark.[1]

Sexuality is another aspect, mentioned by boys as something that could categorize a girl as bad. Girls talked of public places in the dark, as areas of danger; you could be assaulted there, robbed of what you had and maybe some thought of, but did not find it fit to mention, as a possible place for rape or intercourse. Thus, for the girls interviewed, 'bad' girls could seek out such places but it is difficult to say whether they thought that girls went there for the sake of sex. It is also difficult to draw any conclusion about what boys' and girls' different ways of talking about sex could be due to. Maybe both thought of 'bad' girls in relation to sex meaning girls that 'went with one man after another'. Still it appears as if that thought was more preponderant among boys than girls. This does not mean that boys thought that men could have several girl friends. According to them, men too should stay with one partner and not change. This was expressed when I asked them directly about it, but not what they spontaneously told me in relation to 'good' boys. Still, somehow, they seemed to think that it was more 'natural' for men to have many female friends than for girls to have many male friends. A boy with many girl friends was not 'bad' in the way a girl with many boy friends would be considered so. Sex in itself is a subject hardly ever touched upon in most Ethiopian homes. It is so personal and intimate that neither mothers nor fathers discuss it with their children.

Another area where we can discern a difference is with regard to obedience. The norm, again, is the same for girls and boys, but expected behaviour or what would be accepted, differed between them. Both 'good' girls and boys were expected to be obedient to adults, yet time and again the children's utterances revealed that less obedience was expected from boys as compared to girls. Girls were, in other words, not allowed much disobedience. They were even, in certain contexts, expected to sense what parents and adults wanted, and execute their wishes even before they had been verbally expressed.

Deference through speech and body language is another area where norms for boys and girls were said to be the same, but expectations differed. 'Good' girls should not speak in a loud voice; preferably their voices should not be heard at all; while those of boys were always dark, loud and carried far. Girls should not use insults, but nobody was surprised when boys used them. Girls were supposed to hide their bodies in cloth, not use big movements when they played and not participate in sports activities in school that could reveal intimate parts of their bodies; boys encouraged each other to expose their bodies, not in the nude, but to show muscles and strength. Girls would often shrink physically in the street and in front of adults, while boys more often, especially in public places when no adults they knew were present, allowed their bodies to expand.

---

1. For similar experiences in Cuba, see Rosendahl 1997.

That work should be divided by gender was taken for granted, and accepted as a dominant discourse in society. Thus, when I presented it as a topic for discussion, and something that could be questioned most Birabiro students showed surprise. Initially they were hesitant when talking about it and only slowly did they formulate stronger opinions on the matter. Some girls, however, as mentioned above, found it unfair that they should work so hard and for such long hours, when boys only had to share the work and then only carry out a few of the tasks. Others thought that although housework took too much of their time, they found cooking to be a special female area of knowledge, which they very much doubted that men could master.

Most boys seemed to view the division of labour in the same way as Mekonnen, as something established that was not to be questioned. A few, however, were like Ibrahim, who wanted his own imagined future son and daughter to share the tasks and help each other, the way he himself did with his sister. Apart from Ibrahim, who was unusually reflective, no boy talked of the present division of labour as unfair, the way some girls expressed it. The fact that the work shares, as they were distributed, occupied much more of the girls' time was something that did not seem to be part of the boys' awareness. The Birabiro boys as well as most of the girls had gradually learnt to take the gender distribution of work for granted and think of it as 'natural'. Since the boys had neither been made to reflect upon and evaluate it nor shared the experiences of the girls it did not occur to them that things could be done differently, but neither did it occur to many girls.

The six girls in the countryside in Gojjam, seemed to have reflected more on what they considered an unfair distribution of work. They all had the experience that it was almost impossible for them to study since they were – and had to be – inside the house, and thereby accessible to everyone who needed some task done. They always worked and as soon as they took out their books they were interrupted. Their brothers, on the other hand, always took their books when they herded the cattle and were not interrupted unless a cow strayed into somebody's field. The brothers could therefore always answer the teachers' questions on the homework, while the girls, who had never had time to prepare themselves, made the teachers angry with them. Girls and boys should therefore, according to these girls, help each other with all tasks. In the future, the girls argued, there should be no division of labour according to gender. All the interviewed girls imagined that they would get a salaried job and live in town, which would preclude any division of farm work between their children.

Half the boys in Gojjam wanted their imagined future son and daughter to help each other with all the work in the house. They also envisaged a future with a job in town for themselves. Otherwise, I think, they might have reasoned differently, due to the exigencies of farm work. The other boys wanted the gender division of labour to continue, more for sentimental reasons it seemed. They wanted their son to help them in the various tasks, while the daughter could help her mother, 'that would be nice', they said.

All those girls who had tasks to do at home, in Gojjam and in Addis, were quite aware that they worked longer hours than their brothers. A few were adamant that this must change, but a majority did not want any radical change in the gendered division of work.

One of the major reasons for the unwillingness to change is, I think, that there are also other, evaluative aspects to gendered work, which make the issue more complicated. Girls, who did their work at home well, were positively talked about and allowed to feel proud of what they had done. There was a positive reward for them however much or little value they attached to it. But for boys, there was nothing they could be proud about or boast of, if they assisted at home. No one would praise them for it. If they were to tell their male friends that they could not play football because they had to make a stew, the friends would be flabbergasted. The idea was absurd. Furthermore, the boys' mothers or sisters did not want them in the kitchen. Some women even worried that a neighbour would see her son in the kitchen and make her feel ashamed because he behaved like a girl. Thus, even before a son or brother could start to enjoy cooking, those women who were closest to him, the mother and sisters, often shamed him through laughing at his initial, crude attempts into leaving the kitchen. In this way, women actively kept the boys away from so-called female jobs. Boys learned that they could only be proud if they had carried out manly feats, like being good at football or some other sport or for having done well in school. Girls as well, could be proud of good school results, but even if they were good students, they needed to be able to cook.

Male work also had a higher status than female and girls who managed boys' work would be praised rather than shamed. I once heard a 2 year old daughter who had managed to lift and turn an ox whip be addressed as '**wond**' or 'man' by a proud father, while a little boy of three who took the coffee tray to a guest was snarled at with the word '**set**', or 'woman', by another man without any comments from those present. The unequal value attached to girls' and boys' work was an integral part of the cultural schema and such reactions did not prompt any opposition. The whole value system was thus intricately constructed and both girls and boys had something to lose but only girls something to gain, if it was questioned.

Implications of gender differences

The capacity to see the self as a duality, the I, the subject, who due to my reflexive ability can also see a me, an object, makes it possible for the subject also to categorise her- himself as for example a girl or boy. This capacity of self-awareness not only makes it possible to categorise the self but it also permits the subject, the I, to evaluate the actions of the self and see whether they fit in with what is expected from such persons as 'agents-in-society who live in a moral order' (Harris 1989: 603) or not. Furthermore, situating one's self within a certain category of persons (ibid.:605) also implies awareness of the framework or lenses used by society to view and evaluate such persons, whether the self chooses to question this cultural framework or accept and adapt to it. In the case of Messelesh for example, she chose to question the framework in certain respects, like in dress, haircut, use of insults, way of walking etc. while in others, especially regarding her imagined daughter, she accepted the exigencies placed on 'good' girls, or at least showed awareness of the harm that might befall somebody contesting the relevance of such categorisations.

Taking this capacity for self-awareness into account I find it relevant to assume that the worldview espoused by Birabiro girls and boys and their perceptions of their selves within it were deeply influenced by their daily activities, observations and experiences. They learned about differing expectations on female and male agency. Good girls were active agents at home for the family and also in school but became bad if found to be too active especially with matters that were not thought of as female. They were taught modesty, to use a subdued voice and not to speak unless being spoken to. Good boys were active in school and encouraged to take the initiative, speak out, and voice their opinions. When girls and boys followed these different rules and admonishments they could also be expected to develop differently since there is a close relationship between awareness and participation where awareness positively affects participation which in turn affects awareness (Gaventa 1987:40ff). Thus boys who were encouraged to be outgoing could be expected to encounter lots of different people, be exposed to a variety of different arenas and hear about a number of different topics. In the process they would learn to read, understand and know how to behave in such contexts and with different people. Girls, on the other hand, were told not to take part in outside activities or interact with strangers or be conspicuous and could as a result be expected to gather less knowledge, experience and awareness of how to behave in public.

The point of view that it was improper for girls to make themselves seen was also translated into a visible difference in how girls and boys comported themselves bodily. Compared to the bodily behaviour of Swedish youngsters both girls and boys in Ethiopia behaved modestly; they were withdrawn, even inconspicuous; but compared with each other the Birabiro girls and boys behaved quite differently. Boys would hold their back and head straight, some would even look you in the eyes or almost, there were degrees; while girls would physically shrink and their eyes often not reach higher than your feet. Furthermore, the fact that girls had less time to study, were not encouraged to do so as much as boys and were less exposed to public arenas most probably also had an impact on their school results. In class boys had better results than girls even though there were many boys with poor grades and a few girls who came out with very good results.

Furthermore, I would argue that the differential treatment of boys and girls had an overall impact on them, especially their self-awareness since it set them up with different frameworks for perceiving the world, structuring their imagination about what roles they could play in it according to male and female opportunities.

PERPETUATING THE GENDER SYSTEM

All Birabiro girls and boys were aware of the gender system as it impinged on the way they were supposed to act and behave in most arenas in life. The perpetuation of the system seemed more to be a preoccupation with the behaviour of girls, however, while much less attention was paid to what boys did. Adults did not interfere in or follow up on the boys to the degree they did with girls. Furthermore, the perpetuation or re-enactment of the system was more a result of female than male gate-keeping and of an implicit understanding of the man as the norm.

Female gate-keeping of arenas and norms

The major gate-keepers as we have learned in the preceding pages were the adult women, the mothers and neighbours of the girls. Through questions, insults and comments about the girls' behaviour these women played an active role in constructing the girls' reputations and influencing their behaviour. They sometimes asked the girls directly why they were in the street, implying that they should be at home working, but they also talked about them indirectly, with neighbours, the girls' mothers and the girls' friends thereby creating images of some girls as 'good' and others as 'bad'. Some women also took it upon themselves to supervise and admonish those girls who deviated from accepted norms and make them adapt.

Fathers, other adult men and boys were much less involved in such practices. Only occasionally would a father be made aware of a son's or daughter's negligence and asked to punish him or her while an older brother would be more harsh on his sister than on his brother and might even pull the sister off the street if he found her playing where she should not be. Girls were often much stricter in their follow up and criticism of other girls and when the latter deviated from the norms, they even spoke badly about them. Although the behaviour of boys was also supervised, outright interference in their activities was much more limited.

I did not discuss with the girls' mothers or other adult women in the Birabiro area why they found it so important for the girls to follow the rules for female behaviour, like staying off the streets, working at home, acting withdrawn, not talking to adults etc. but have gathered information on the subject from other Ethiopian women through conversations in towns and in the countryside. The reason why women may act as their own gate-keepers limiting their activities and spheres of influence is also a topic, which has been dealt with in other contexts and I shall present some of these discussions, to which I shall add my own understanding of why it was important for mothers to safe-guard the reputation of their daughters.

In a now classic paper Edwin Ardener (1977 [1972]) coined the expression about women being a 'muted' group. His argument was that women have been little studied and less written about by anthropologists because they were often less articulate than men. The reason for their silence was that they had not been exposed to the public arenas where men had been able to develop a male discourse with male codes. Having neither learnt nor practised this discourse, women have had difficulties expressing themselves in accepted rhetoric; they had become mute. However, women as well as other muted groups, like gypsies, often developed their own internal models which were not shared, or only partially so, with the dominant group. And, Ardener suggested, women perhaps also expressed their ideas or models of the world through other forms than expository speech (ibid.). Developing these ideas in an introduction to a series of articles on women Shirley Ardener suggests that muted groups like women may be exhausted after having spent their lives investing *'a great deal of disciplined mental energy'* into *'conjoining the deep models of a muted group with the surface model of the dominant group'* (1977:xvii). This investment may be one reason why muted groups often appear to be conservative and even 'cling to' models, which disadvantage them, Shirley Ardener argues. Another possible explanation for women's conservatism working against their own interests is according to her (ibid.), that what is valued or considered as social success by the muted group can differ from what it is in the dominant group. In this perspective, the insistence by some of the girls in school that they knew how to cook, while the boys did not have the ability to do it, can be seen as a defence of their own female model of merit, in which there was no place for boys.

Another reason why women were such strict gate-keepers of the girls could be the anxiety they may have felt when confronted with blurred boundaries between girls and boys. Most Ethiopians understand the division and distinction between the sexes as natural, a biological given, which they take for granted. To question such a fact of life is dangerous since we do not know where it may lead us.

The gate-keeping, especially when carried out by girls vis-à-vis their friends, may also be interpreted as a request for solidarity; that those of 'your own kind' fall in line, if not, the reputation of all would be endangered.

A topic which has been too little discussed in connection with female gate-keeping and which I think may be of overriding importance to understand the continuance of many of the practices, including the subordination of women, is the role and responsibility of women as mothers. In Ethiopia, as elsewhere, it is the responsibility of women, usually the mothers, to bring the children up. The relationship between the mother and the child, girl or boy, is very close and when asked which person was closest to them, almost all the Birabiro children answered 'my mother'. The children's close bond with the mother was also reflected in how they insulted each other.

One boy wrote about how much he disliked the insults that the students threw at each other because they always targeted the other person's mother. However, he wrote, she has nothing to do with the disagreement between these two, and yet, he commented, she is the one who is insulted. Before reading this essay I had observed and been surprised at the frequency with which an antagonist's mother was insulted during disputes, and although I asked many students, nobody could explain why they insulted the other person's mother. I was surprised since this kind of insult has no precedence in Swedish even though I know that it is common in many other countries. Reflecting upon it, most of them also found it wrong. Yet, I would suggest, that since the person closest to most children was the mother, they used her name to get at the one they wanted to hurt since they knew that an insult of the mother would be most deeply felt.

This intricate and close relationship between mother and child also has another side. If a daughter or son misbehaves, especially in public, they will bring disgrace upon the mother. Other women will talk about the lack of respect her children have for her and that she has not brought them up well. The mother's honour is jeopardized since it has become publicly known that she was not capable of doing what was expected of her, she had not been a proper mother. There is an extensive literature discussing aspects of honour and shame especially in the Mediterranean area, which, however, almost exclusively deals with the honour of the father, seemingly taking it for granted that he, as head of household, is the one who suffers if his children, especially his daughters misbehave. I feel that these discussions have neglected the role of the mother and the fact that it is she who is responsible for bringing up both daughters and sons into respected citizens. This task closely impinges on the mother's honour and status in society, especially among other women and can be understood as part of a model that women share. Because not only are mothers equally incriminated with their daughters if the girls do not follow the norms of proper behaviour but in the Birabiro school the female personnel also felt that they would be held responsible by parents and teachers from other schools if improperly dressed girl students were allowed to attend class. I would therefore argue that if we want to understand the intense female gate-keeping and the ramifications it has for the girls' opportunities to study and to get to know a larger public world, it is as important to study the honour and status of mothers and adult women and how they are bound up with daughters' and girls' behaviour as it is to study the honour and status of fathers and adult men.

The treatment of Messelesh epitomizes, I feel, the Ethiopian focus on girls and the fear that they might behave as boys. Messelesh's way of dressing, her hair cut, boyish bodily behaviour and talk, all challenged and threatened established gender configurations. Adults more than children, and women more than men, found her appearance outrageous and reacted strongly against it, insulting her in vehement terms and punishing her as hard as they could. As marginal in society she was a clear sign of danger that also threatened to contaminate others if she were allowed to continue (Douglas 1992). The treatment of Messelesh was further emphasized by the Ethiopian conception of **yelugnta**, which means that you not only heed what other people will say about you and your family, but that you perpetually worry about it. To have **yelugnta** means always to act with an eye to the possible reactions of the people who surround you (Poluha 1994:962). This is what we can see in the behaviour of the adults when Messelesh had had her hair cut like a boy's.

Man as the norm

Another way to approach the perpetuation of the gender system is to try to understand the reasons for men's and boys' limited involvement in the socialisation practices. Adult men were hardly ever involved in the bringing up of their daughters and were asked, by wives and female relatives, to talk to sons only in exceptional cases, as when the latter had committed some very serious mistake and would not listen to the women of the house. Boys did not interfere much in girls' gender behaviour either, but showed somewhat more vigilance in the peer group. Similarly to the experiences described by Thorne in the USA (1993:111–135) the Birabiro boys supervised and prevented each other from crossing gender and age categories. Boys who played with much younger boys could thus lose the respect of their peers if they were found out. Yet, Birabiro schoolboys' preoccupation with gendered behaviour was weak as compared to that exhibited by girls and adult women.

One reason for the apparent lack of male interest in safeguarding gender borders may be that men and boys never felt the hegemonic gender model, with man as superior and woman as inferior, to be threatened. There were no boys that dressed, behaved or played like girls, apart from very young brothers, who were soon taught to stop. It could also be that the boys were satisfied with being and becoming part of a dominant male discourse, knowing that one day, by their right of being born boys, they would accede to the adult male position. Women as well as men not only accepted this discourse but women were also instrumental in constructing it. Through comments, admonishments and invectives to sons and brothers, women and girls emphasized existing ideas of what it was to be a 'real' man, thereby strengthening and enforcing a male hegemonic model from which both boys and men benefited. In their interactions with men and boys in Addis, girls and women would, similarly to what Shire describes for the Shona (1994:147–156), affirm some forms of masculinity while they questioned others, thereby often supporting established patterns and undermining alternatives.

Another reason why men and boys did not try to change existing gender relations may be what Connell calls the 'patriarchal dividend' (1996:172–173) attached to the gender order. Connell argues that the advantages accruing to men due to current gender arrangements have mainly been studied through the disadvantages they give to women and not from the perspective of the benefits obtained by men as a result of them (ibid.). If we take the perspective of the Birabiro boys it is obvious that the present gender order gives them much more time both to study and play compared to girls. Fewer people in the household can order boys about and boys can give orders to more people than girls. Boys also experience public places and learn how to behave in them, something that gives them more security when they later have to act in such arenas. In school clever boys get more respect than clever girls from teachers and students alike. Relations are asymmetrical as in the case of the selection and election of monitors where teachers and children deferred to boys as those who would be able to keep order.

Against the background of all these processes the persistence of the gender system is really not surprising. There were, however, some counter-discourses.

COUNTER-DISCOURSES

The one sphere within the gender order that some of the children questioned, was the division of work. In Addis, Fatima was most outspoken about how unfair she found it, and some of the other girls in Addis thought it would be good if boys helped more. All the rural girls in Gojjam had experiences similar to Fatima's and were very critical about what they thought was an unfair division of labour. They expressed these ideas in very strong words despite being young, between 11 and 13, and shy, thereby giving expression to a counter discourse which went against all dominant thoughts and ideas about the gendered division of labour and based exclusively on their own experiences. Ibrahim and a few boys in Addis and half the boys in Gojjam were also open to a change in established norms and thought it would be proper for boys to 'help' girls with household tasks and they also said that they wanted their sons to do so in the future. There is an important distinction between these girls and boys. While the girls had shared the responsibility for many, if not most, household tasks, most of the boys had only assisted at home and had not really experienced how time-consuming the tasks could be. Their understanding of the girls' plight was therefore limited and not really embodied. Not much else in the gender order was questioned by the children, apart from Messelesh's deviating way of dressing and comporting herself and the way both girls and boys forgot gender as well as age when they could gain some marks.

Although the children were aware of and partly questioned some of the norms, they were in no position really to contest them. As dependents in their households and young children they could not change anything, since to behave differently might have implied that they would be ostracised from the peer group.

What the boys and girls, whose opinions differed from the established pattern, remind us of is that there are variations in how girls and boys conceptualise and personally interpret the hegemonic gender discourses (cf. Thorne 1993). Focussing on masculinities Cornwall and Lindisfarne (1994) remind us that gender differences are often presented and perceived as absolute and dichotomous. Discussing the concept of 'hegemonic masculinities' they argue that it is an ideology which privileges some ways of being a man and defines other masculine states as inferior or subordinate. Such descriptions, they argue, often rest on essentialist interpretations and do not refer to the parties concerned, or the context and time when an interaction takes place. But in actual fact, they argue, notions of masculinity are fluid and situational and it is only by studying the processes in which varying masculinities are developed that we shall be able to dislocate notions of hegemonic masculinity (ibid.:4, 9–10). Similarly, I would suggest, there are also notions of 'hegemonic femininity', which privilege some ways of being a woman and give a lower status to alternatives. In everyday interactions the varieties are, however, numerous and complex.

Ambiguities and multiple interpretations of how to act in different situations could be found among both girls and boys in the Birabiro school. Thus, two boys without sisters or brothers told me that they sometimes went into the kitchen and cooked food or made coffee for their mother when she came home late at night from work. The circumstances and their feelings for their mother made them do this although they talked about it in very subdued voices and, I guess, they would not brag to their friends about it. There were also some boys who played with younger boys and even played with girls mostly because they had a special relationship to the person. She or he could be the sister or brother of a friend or neighbour, someone whom they liked.

There were also girls who were less interested in cooking and cleaning than they were supposed to be. Girls who preferred to study rather than wash clothes and cook and girls who wanted to play more. Even Amarech, the only daughter of five children and responsible for all the work in her home, could as mentioned earlier, act in a quite 'un-girlish' way in school. She often spoke loudly, took up space and never hesitated to work at the blackboard in class. While Messelesh, so 'boyish' in many other contexts, was extremely shy and subdued in the classroom. If we were to look for arenas where gender had more limited consequences for boys' and girls' behaviour (Thurén 1996) I would suggest the school and the neighbourhood volleyball ground, when such a field existed. However, I cannot imagine any arena where gender would have no consequences whatsoever.

These variations within the established normative gender patterns are, however, important both because they can be viewed as part of a counter-discourse to the hegemonic patterns and because they illuminate the weaknesses and actual varieties of the discourses and how the gender order might change.

CONCLUDING REMARKS

Although some of the girls and boys found the gender system unfair, especially with regard to the division of labour, it was still being perpetuated through their everyday interactions with each other and with adults. The strength of the system had many facets; lack of awareness that girls and boys were treated and thought of differently, and that this had important implications for their self-awareness; an implicit understanding of man as the norm, implying among other things that a greater value was attached to male work as compared to female. Furthermore, adult women were important gate-keepers, who saw to it that trespassers were punished. These women had invested a lot in the continuance of the system and could lose their honour if daughters or girls, for whom they were responsible, did not abide by it. They therefore supervised the girls and tried to maintain the borders. Those who were displeased with the gender order had little to gain from questioning the whole or parts of it but could be ostracized instead. There was also a 'patriarchal dividend' in the system for boys, according to which they had a lot to gain from its perpetuation. The fact that the gender discourse had also been both mentally and physically embodied by the children who experienced it as natural and often took it for granted, also made it difficult for them to question it.

Chapter 7

THE IMPORTANCE OF 'US', CATEGORIES OF BELONGING

INTRODUCTION

This chapter describes and analyses Birabiro children's perceptions of three categories of people who formed part of their everyday life: their friends, adherents of the same religion and fellow citizens or Ethiopians. Ethnicity was not an important category for the Birabiro children for reasons which will be discussed below. The children's family of origin with one or both parents, their sisters and brothers, a grandmother or grandfather, aunt or uncle and a cousin or two, provided the basic group around which their identity was constructed. As discussed in Chapter 4, the people who lived together also constituted a primary collective from which the children expected protection, control and care, and towards which they had respect and responsibility, especially regarding the redistribution of various resources.

The self-awareness and ability of the 'I' to reflect upon the 'me' and categorise me together with people of the same characteristics, which the children exhibited, and as was discussed in Chapter 6 with regard to gender and age, illustrates the children's knowledge and awareness of the cultural models in use in their society. The major criteria applied for developing a shared sense of belonging to which the children referred were also those which adults in the neighbourhood considered important. To the children, friends were people with whom they shared their secrets, who were close to them, of their own choice, while religion and citizenship which were ascribed from birth, emphasized the importance and meaning of co-religionists and co-citizens but made it vary due to the context and the people present.

The children repeatedly mentioned all these people as some kind of self-referral, consciously, it seemed, invoking categories larger than themselves but to which they felt they belonged. Although the properties of these three categories and the ways in which they influenced the children's everyday lives varied, they were still part of the daily pattern, like searching out your friend every morning, praying at home or in the church or mosque, and parading in front of the flag in school to sing the national anthem. In this way, friendship, religion and citizenship formed a backdrop to their lives or a framework within which the children conceptualised themselves, not only as subjects and actors, but also in their relations with other children and adults, who either exhibited similar traits or were different and stood out as contrasts, or significant others.

The purpose of this chapter is both to illustrate the importance of these categories for the children's sometimes conscious and sometimes unconscious identity building, and to show how they actively negotiated, re-interpreted and changed the meanings of both religion and Ethiopianness to fit in with their own picture of what it ought to be. I shall also discuss how some of the Addis Abeba children's experiences of the Ethiopian state differed from those of rural children in Gojjam and what possible impact this may have for future conceptualisations of the state in Ethiopia.

FRIENDS

Friends were important to the Birabiro children and the bond between friends was close with frequent meetings and many secrets exchanged; yet the bond was tenuous. Friends could suddenly stop talking to each other or become enemies and needed mediation to reunite. When describing their choice of friends girls and boys emphasized how similar they and their friends were, both in personality and interests, rather than how their friends stood out as special or were different from themselves. The similarity was also what came out in the children's descriptions as that which made equality between friends possible.

Choice and meaning

Gender was an important distinguishing characteristic when children played together, as discussed in Chapters 5 and 6. This point was further emphasized when I asked Batnori, the 11 year old girl and Mohammed, the 13 year old boy, with whom they played and how they made their choice of playmates.

Eva: But you (girls, we had discussed about boys before) *do not play in the road?*

Batnori: We do not play in the road, really we have a little one for ourselves. We do not need much space when we play the way they (boys) *do. And there is always disturbance when they play. They hit each other and insult each other. There is no order. When there is no order that is how they play. But we, there is no insult, there is nothing. Since we play in a place we have chosen, we do not quarrel with each other. If I make a mistake, I accept it, and if she makes one, she accepts it when I say so.*

Eva: Aha. But when do boys play with girls?

Batnori: Boys, when they cannot find a ball, when they cannot find playthings, then they come to us. Then we let them join us. We cannot say no or argue against it.

Eva: You can't? You let them join you?

Batnori: If we argue against it, they will beat us.

Eva: Really? Is it always by beating?

Batnori: Yes they beat us if we say no or something, they beat us.

Eva: That sounds hard.

Batnori: It is hard. That is how the boys are. But when we are alone, we play peace-fully together and then we go (home) *to study.*

......

Batnori was the eleven year old girl who lived with her mother, grandmother and five year old brother in the school's neighbourhood and whom we met in Chapter 3. Neither her mother nor her grandmother was employed. I do not know on what they survived. Her father was remarried and lived elsewhere in Addis Abeba. Batnori's elder sister lived with him. The father liked the sister very much but cared less for her, Batnori said. For the big holidays Batnori never received any gifts from him, although he had the money and her sister always got presents from him. Still, since he was her father, she loved him, she said, but that was all there was to it. Batnori started school relatively late since her mother had no money to pay for her. After she had joined the school, she stayed away for one year due to heart problems. In grade 4 her results were not good and she had to repeat the grade. Batnori was easy to interview, and talked a lot without my prompting her to develop her ideas.

Batnori had three close friends, who lived in her neighbourhood. They were all girls, one a year younger, one of the same age and one a year older than her, all attending different classes. To all of them gender was important when they selected their friends, both in school and in the neighbourhood.

Eva: In the cafeteria, do girls talk by themselves or with boys ...?

Batnori: With girls.

Eva: You don't often mix?

Batnori: Often we do not mix, because they are very big, they are not our peers (e'kuja). Even with the small ones, when we say, let's play, we don't understand each other. Unless it is children from the neighbourhood, we don't understand each other. Why, because they don't want to agree with us.

Eva: Is it because they don't want to?

Batnori: Yes.

Eva: When you want order they don't want it?

Batnori: Yes, when we want order and play together like friends, then insults, they insult and they fight, so we often do not play together, together with students we don't know.

Here Batnori made a distinction not only between girls and boys but also between students and friends from the neighbourhood. According to her it was easier to play with children of different ages when you were from the same neighbourhood because then you knew each other better and followed the same rules.

Mohammed echoed Batnori's ideas. He was the 13 year old boy who in grade 4 had told me that he lived with his mother, father and father's brother, and in grade 5 mentioned that he lived alone with his mother. The father used to be un-employed, but helped his brother who was engaged in trade. The mother was also unemployed, but sold small items in the market. Being an only child Mohammed had told me that he helped his mother a lot in the house. He therefore had little time for play. Yet, Mohammed had a few very good friends with whom he played occasionally. All of these also lived in the neighbourhood.

> *Eva: With whom do you play, when you play ball or tell riddles or stories* (what he had mentioned earlier in the interview as play)?
> *Mohammed: Always with a friend, with children from the neighbourhood.*
> *Eva: How big are they?*
> *Mohammed: They are like me, my size, my age, the ones I play with.*
> *Eva: Your elders or those much younger than you are not your playmates?*
> *Mohammed: Yes, they must be your e'kuja* (peer group, same age, size and some-times status), *if not, it does not work.*
> *Eva: Why is that?*
> *Mohammed: Really, we don't understand each other properly. When we are e'kuja, we don't fight, we don't do anything, we understand each other and play. Whatever happens we agree, but if we play with another e'kuja, there will be use of force and one will say, it is mine. That is why it is best to play with your own e'kuja.*

Thus like Batnori, Mohammed emphasized how important it was that friends were of a similar age and size to be able to play together smoothly. He did not mention gender, but somehow seemed to have taken gender for granted since it became clear from the rest of the interview that boys played with boys and girls with girls.

Actually all the children reiterated the statement that girls and boys do not mix. Yet as Batnori said, boys sometimes forced themselves upon girls' play. It also happened that a brother and his male friend joined a sister and her girl friends in their play and, although the general tendency was not to mix, there were ex-ceptions. These observations partly agree with Thorne's (1993:89–110) argu-ment that there is over-reporting about the differences between girls and boys and too little reporting of when they play together. According to her, even when re-sults show that there are boys and girls who play together or that only a minority of the girls or the boys usually perform what is called typical girls' or boys' play, this is somehow forgotten when reports are written. On the other hand, Thorne also observed that there is more separation between girls and boys in school as compared to in the neighbourhood, giving the figures that 80 per cent of play-ground groups were either all-girl or all-boy in those American schools where she herself did fieldwork (ibid.:49).

Age was another such dividing factor, where large gaps prevented children from mixing. However, a couple of years' difference between playmates in the neighbourhood was more frequent than in the school. This corresponds to what has been reported from Sweden and other Western countries. Norman (1996:127, 128), for example, mentions that beginning from the age of 4–8 and above, age and gender become ever more important for the children's play and their friendships.

Friendship implied doing things together. Young girls and boys played games, boys of all ages played football, some older boys and girls played volleyball, if and when they had access to a field and a ball. Apart from play, friendship also implied that you could study together or that you could watch television in the friend's house. Above all, however, friends were important because it was only with them that you could share your problems and tell your secrets. This was especially relevant to the older children, who did not want to worry their parents with their own problems while young children still tended to tell their problems to their parents.

One of the most important characteristics of the children's friendship relations was their egalitarian character. The children formulated this in different ways. Batnori mentioned that she 'accepts' when her friends tell her that she has made a mistake, and Mohammed talked of the importance of playing with your peers to avoid strife. In the classroom, friendship, equality and hierarchy were expressed in how children borrowed and lent things to each other as can be understood from Mohammed.

> *Eva: Why does your teacher get angry with the students?*
>
> *Mohammed: (When we) lend each other (things). To lend each other is actually good. But the reason why he doesn't want it is after they have lent to each other, one will not return it. And, furthermore, they will fight and quarrel with each other. That is why he says, do not borrow from or lend things to each other. Everyone should have his own, he says. But actually to lend each other is good.*
>
> *Eva: To help each other?*
>
> *Mohammed: Yes, but what our teacher doesn't like is what comes after.*
>
> *Eva: When they fight with each other?*
>
> *Mohammed: Yes, when they fight with each other. When one person borrows and says he doesn't want to return it.*
>
> *Eva: Do they do this with you?*
>
> *Mohammed: When I lend to my friends, they return it. Why, because we are equal. Our age and our what (thinking), but what they do, they take from the small children. When they (the small ones) give them, they take and they don't return it. They are just silent and don't return it.*

Thus, when lending things to friends in class, Mohammed always expected to get back what they had borrowed from him because he was their equal. Those who due to age or size were in an inferior position could not expect such reciprocity, however, and time and again I heard young children plead with their older male classmates to return a pen or an exercise book. Sometimes they were told that they would get it later but often their requests only met with silence. Their subordinate position was thus explicitly expressed in their things not being returned.

Fragility of friendship

Although equality was such a key feature of friendship, equality among friends proved to be a precarious phenomenon to Birabiro children, similarly to what has been described for children from other parts of the world. James (1999:98–120), for example, discusses two types of tensions in children's lives based on her field-work with young English school children. The first tension, according to James, results from the fact that children have to live with both hierarchy and equality simultaneously. In school and in many other arenas they are supposed to compete with one another, for the best marks, behaviour, sportsmanship and so on and thereby advance hierarchically. At the same time, they are expected and expect themselves to have egalitarian relations with their friends with whom they compete (ibid.:111). The other tension children must learn to manage, James argues, revolves around conformity and individuality. Not to be left out of the group, the children must conform, adhere to the 'rules of the game' and show that they know the norms and can be considered as one of the crowd. At the same time, those who want to become prominent, or leaders, must excel in individuality, master the masculine or feminine accomplishments, which children favour and strive for, but do it within the accepted normative framework (ibid.:115–116).

Mohammed can be seen as a person successful in negotiating such tensions in school. He often acted as monitor in grade 4 and 5 helping Mulat and Mekonnen, the selected and elected monitors, keep order in the classroom. In grade 4 Mohammed was also often told by the homeroom teacher to read to the class, both in Amharic and English, when the teacher was called outside to talk to administrative personnel or parents. Like most of his classmates, Mohammed was deeply aware of the rules that the teachers wanted to uphold in class, one of which stated that students were not supposed to chat with each other. With 100 students talking, the noise became unbearable and it was impossible to teach unless they were silent. Sitting behind Mohammed in class I often saw him busy chatting with his classmates, however. Once I asked him how it came about that he was not punished for his talking. He told me that the teachers never saw him. I watched him even closer after that and saw that although Mohammed was talkative, he was at the same time very alert and half his mind always seemed to attend to what the teacher was doing. As soon as there was a lot of noise, or the blackboard needed cleaning, he would be there to assist and uphold order. In this way, his alertness seemed to help him negotiate a good relationship with the teachers and escape punishment from them while he also kept in good contact with his friends in class.

Mohammed's schoolmates respected him and many asked for his help. Both older boys and some girls sitting around him often turned to him and asked that he explain some schoolwork, which he usually could and did. Asaferew, a younger boy with better results, was never approached in this way. The students said that Asaferew was the cleverest boy in class, but he would never help you. *'He prefers to keep his knowledge to himself so that he alone gets the good marks'*, one of the boys commented. Mohammed's readiness to help and also his good standing with the teachers were, I think, important factors that gave him security in his relations with older and bigger class mates, like the mutual respect between him and Mekonnen. Being respected by teachers and classmates also allowed him to nego-tiate a position in class somewhat above both his age and size. This climb in the hierarchy could have made Mohammed drop old friends but he stuck to his best friend Ibrahim with whom he also associated outside school.

A common reason for the disruption of friendship was that a secret told to a friend had been, or was said to have been, passed on to a third person. The habit of sharing secrets made the children vulnerable to each other. Repeatedly I heard of disputes, especially among girls, that originated in a secret having been told to a third party. When the one whose secret had been told heard of this, she would stop communicating with her previous friend and avoid her. Among boys, friend-ship was more often disrupted through disputes over how the rules of the game being played should be interpreted. Diverging interpretations led to heated dis-cussions involving insults and physical fights, whereby friends were made into enemies.

Both children and teachers were quite aware that even a small dispute could develop into a feud with relatives involved. Batnori told me that when she was six, she had had a fight with her five year old friend, Mekdes, who had scratched her in the face. It was not clear how Batnori had hurt Mekdes. Because of the fight, Mekdes' relatives threatened to harm Batnori, her mother and even her grandmother. Both the mother and grandmother became scared and took the matter to Batnori's and Mekdes' schoolteacher. He understood that the issue was serious and made both children and parents sign a paper saying that if either of the girls started to fight with the other, she would be banned from school. Both girls signed together with a parent and since then Batnori had never had another fight. Mekdes' relatives also left Batnori and her family alone.

The fear that feuds would easily spread was also the reason why the homeroom teacher, Girma, in grade 4 did not want the students to borrow things from each other, or to insult each other. According to Mohammed:

> *Mohammed: Yes, it is often with insults, that they start* (fighting) *in our school. After they have insulted each other, they start fighting each other. And then when they fight each other, then they will hurt each other. And when they hurt each other then the families start fighting. You see one* (child) *being hurt, and tomorrow he will bring parents, and they ask who hit him, and find out, and they may start fighting with his family. That is why Teacher doesn't like it when they fight each other. It can reach far. An eye can be ruined, teeth flung out when they fight.*

Friendship implied a deep emotional involvement in another person, an attachment that made children vulnerable to each other especially since some friends could be 'bad'. Such so-called 'bad' friends could be smart and use the friendship to entice you to absent yourself from school and to roam around with them. These 'bad' friends could make you smoke cigarettes and stop caring for your family and school. Therefore, children said, they had to beware of such friends. Another kind of friend, still dangerous, but not so bad were those who stole things, hit old people, disturbed adults in the street or made fun of the disabled. Some in this category engaged in fights or made their friends fight. All friends were thus, according to the children's way of reasoning, potentially dangerous since your emotions for them could prevent you from distinguishing right from wrong and make you do things you otherwise would not have done. Since it was difficult for children to know who was 'bad' and who 'good' parents should check their children and find out whom they befriended. This was especially important since there were also 'good' friends who could make you study harder and become more helpful at home.

Mediation

Often when disputes arose, the children tried to mediate between the friends who had fallen out with each other. Actually, all the children I talked to in class had in one situation or another acted as mediators. There were strict rules for mediation, however, as I learned when I asked Mohammed about his experiences.

> Eva: Do you sometimes intervene if two of your friends fight?
>
> Mohammed: Yes, I have to, they might be hurt and in our neighbourhood they fight a lot and when they do, we try to mediate. And then they make peace and we can play.
>
> Eva: Is it only among boys that you mediate?
>
> Mohammed: Me, if they fight, even the girls. One has to intervene.
>
> Eva: You do. Aha. Is it only your age-mates (e'kuja) that you assist or … ?
>
> Mohammed? Yes. My age-mates. The big ones I cannot manage them you see.
>
> Eva: What do they say if you intervene between them?
>
> Mohammed: If I mediate between them now when they fight they may hit me since they are big.
>
> Eva: That means they don't want it.
>
> Mohammed: Yes, the big mediate between the big, but if you do it with our age-mates, if you mediate between them, they will stop because they respect me.
>
> Eva: And if the young ones fight?
>
> Mohammed: Them also I help.

Three of the most basic rules in any mediation process, according to Bailey (1978:194–214), are that the mediator has to disconnect himself from being understood as partisan, that he must show or claim to represent a larger group than each of the two contestants, and that he either represents a group to which both contestants belong or a value to which both subscribe. When these criteria are not fulfilled, it is well nigh impossible to take on a successful mediation process. A lower age, size or status than the combatants themselves thus makes it impossible for anyone to take on a mediation process between them. This was also the children's experience. Repeatedly they made comments such as: *'I cannot take them on, they are bigger than me'*, and also *'when I asked if I could help them, they laughed at me, saying, who do you think you are?'* Rahel's words summarize their experiences; *'you can only mediate between people of your own e'kuja* (peer group) *or between those who are younger or smaller, but never between those above you in age or size.'*

The purpose of most mediation I had observed earlier in Ethiopia (Poluha 1994, compare also Lewis 1989) and those described by the children was to reconcile the contestants, and not to look for a culprit or to obtain some kind of absolute justice. The reason was not to put all the blame on one party because then the other could easily feel slighted and future cooperation between them be put in jeopardy. To this end, successful mediation implied that both parties had to come together and each had to make some amends and show a willingness to start anew.

Major characteristics of friendship

As a whole, friends were equal, open and confiding in each other. Children trusted their friends with their assets as well as with their problems and secrets. They expected a 'generalized' form of reciprocity (Sahlins 1972) from friends, which they did not have in other relationships. In a society where most relations were explicitly hierarchical, a hierarchy expressed verbally, in body language and in the general treatment of the other, friendship stood out as different, something which had mutuality and was dependent on your choice. This did not mean that friends always kept their good relations. As is well-known friends fall out of favour with each other, make new friends and may even want to forget old ones. But when Birabiro children stayed friends or re-established their friendship, they also stayed equal.

The children's friendship was fragile, however. There were so many activities going on around the girls and boys all of which might have disruptive effects on their friendships. However, even the vulnerability may have differed between boys and girls. Boys appeared less vulnerable since they often played in bigger groups and seemed to deal with their problems as soon as they arose, while girls more often played in two's and became lonely when they fell out with one another.

RELEVANCE OF RELIGION

Religion as part of the identity

The children in grade 4 and subsequently grade 5 were either Muslims or members of the Ethiopian Orthodox Church (EOC), or categorized themselves as such. There was a third category, 'Pente' in which the children included members of all protestant religions as well as the Catholic Church. Nobody talked of her- or himself as a Pente, however, since as we shall see below it was not advisable to do so.

In their daily interactions with people in their surroundings the children came to express their religious adherence in many different ways. Often they did not seem to think of what they said and did as pertaining to their religion but took their own practices as a 'natural' part of their lives. Yet, when asked about certain deeds and utterances, and thereby made to reflect upon them, they would refer these to their religion and show awareness that they had religious aspects (see Chapter 3). Mostly, however, as when discussing ethical issues (ibid.), the children's opinions came spontaneously, without reflection. The feelings, ideas and judgements that they expressed in different contexts can therefore be said to be part of their identity and cultural schema.

First of all, the Birabiro children took it for granted that everybody had a religion. In one of the interviews 12 year old Judith asked me '*Excuse me, please Eva, but what is your religion?*' I told her that actually I had been baptised a Christian but that I no longer believed in any of the religious systems. I had seen so many people commit harmful acts towards their fellow human beings and yet, they not only called themselves but were also thought of by others, as being very religious. So, I said, '*I respect those who in their acts show respect for other people, what they say is less important*'. Both Judith and her friends Rebqa (12) and Manassebesh (10) were shocked. Not so much at what I had said about respect for others in your deeds, as at my no longer believing in any religion. '*But Eva, you must have a religion*', all three of them told me together. '*If you have no religion you don't have friends*', said Rebqa. '*You won't know how to behave*', said Manassebesh. '*Many people will come and try to forcefully pull you into their religion*', said Judith. I tried to calm them, saying that I had lived like this for many decades without problems. They did not look convinced, however.

The 'naturalness' of religion partly seems to come from the fact that the children's days were regulated by the precepts of their religion. The food they ate and when, depended on whether it was a fast or not. During fasts Christians did not eat any animal products and usually no breakfast, and Muslims abstained from food and drink from sunrise to sunset. Some of the children went to the mosque or church regularly, sometimes every day. Prayers were also conducted in the homes especially by Muslim children, and religious teachers taught the children how to conduct themselves properly at home, in the street and in the place of worship, sometimes going into minute details as when showing and explaining how they should give alms with due respect to beggars.

Religious holidays were celebrated with good food and, if people could afford it, with meat from a properly slaughtered animal. Just before Easter some Christian children showed their extreme unhappiness at not having enough money even to buy a hen. One girl told me that after some of her classmates had discussed the size of the hen their mother had bought, they turned to her to inquire about the size of their hen. Bitterly she said to me:

> '… *even though they knew that we had not bought any'. 'It is not only the hen', she added, 'I don't think my mother can afford all the butter, the onions and the eggs that have to go with the hen'. 'But maybe my brother will bring one when he comes',* (she added hopefully).

According to her, to ask about food was one of the worst ways of shaming another person because for Easter everybody would have chicken stew, only extremely poor people would be without.

Girls sometimes also used their clothes to indicate whether they were Muslim or Christian. Some Muslim girls wore scarves over their heads so that all their hair was covered, while others wore the scarves the same way Christian girls did with much of the hair showing. Often, both Christian and Muslim girls went without a scarf, however, with their hair beautifully made up. Naema, the 11 year old girl, pointed out to me that there were some other differences in the way Muslim and Christian girls dressed and moved. Christian girls, she told me, can have trousers but if a Muslim girl has trousers she has to have a dress or skirt on top so as not to show the lower part of her body. To show the body was not part of the Muslim tradition, she added. According to my observations, however, most of the older Christian girls who wore trousers also had a dress or skirt to cover the lower part of their bodies.

Sports and games indicated some other arenas where Muslim and Christian children could differ, according to Naema. Muslim girls were not supposed to jump or run since their skirts might lift and expose their legs. Such behaviour could make them the laughing stock of their peers, and their mothers would scold them. In such ways, religion could influence how girls, but not boys, dressed and comported themselves in school and in the neighbourhood.

The area from which the children were recruited to the school is religiously mixed. Christians were in a majority but lived together with Muslims, often as close neighbours sharing a compound. This geographical proximity promoted social exchange between children and parents of different religions. For religious holidays neighbours would congratulate each other and even invite each other to various non-meat dishes, since animals are slaughtered differently according to the religion. However, although proximity and circumstances could make children of different religions into playmates, I did not see any religiously mixed friendships in class. The children talked, laughed and joked with each other but close friendship, as defined by the children themselves, seemed to depend on religion and gender. Yet, girls and boys of both denominations repeatedly told me that belonging to a different religion was not something they saw as an obstacle to friendship. They talked about each other as human beings saying that in essence there was no difference between them. In class I saw no aggressiveness and no derogatory remarks or religious insults were passed between Christians and Muslims. Both talked, however, of Pente in very negative terms.

Religion in the Ethiopian society

For more than a millennium Christians and Muslims have lived together in the geographical areas that today are called Ethiopia and Eritrea. Christianity became the state religion of Axum as early as at the end of the fourth century, when king Ezana and his followers saw to its expansion into the surrounding areas.

The first contacts between Christians and Muslims took place in the 7th century when followers of the prophet sought and gained refuge in Ethiopia. Later, Islam spread partly through conquests, but the main impetus was the trade carried out by Muslim merchants. Small Muslim principalities were set up in the south and southeast and from there trade was conducted. Islam then followed the trade routes and spread to merchants in towns and to nomads living in the lowlands (Tadesse Tamrat 1972). Over the centuries there were several clashes between the Christian kingdom ruled by more or less strong kings and various Muslim kingdoms and sultanates that sometimes paid tribute to the Christian kings and sometimes conquered them.

In very general terms, the distribution of religious adherents remained the same as the initial pattern. Christians in the countryside live in the highlands and often have administrative posts in towns. Muslims in the countryside live in the lowlands and tend to work as merchants in towns (Trimingham 1965). In the reign of Haile Sellassie the state had close bonds with the church and there were few Muslims in government or administrative positions (Clapham 1969). To go in for an administrative career you were, with few exceptions, expected to speak Amharic fluently and be an Orthodox Christian. In Haile Sellassie's time all official holidays were Christian and only with the Derg were Muslim celebrations made into national holidays. Muslims entered state education only late in Haile Sellassie's reign, afraid, according to Markakis, that their sons would lose their religious traditions in state schools, where everything was taught in Amarinja and Arabic was banned (Markakis 1975:156–9).

A major change in the Orthodox Church that I have been able to observe over the past 20 to 30 years has been a steady increase in the attempts of the Church to teach people about the Orthodox ideology and to involve the adherents more in the Church's various activities. As a result of these internal missionary activities, probably combined with the political upheavals and insecurity in the country for the last three decades, many Orthodox Christians have become more conscious of their religion and more intellectually and emotionally involved in its future. Some of these changes imply that over the last twenty years it has become more common for adults and children to fast, and the fasting has become more rigid. Fasts that were previously categorized as 'priests'' fasts are today also observed by educated adults and young children in Addis. Fish, which used to be considered fasting food no longer is. Some even abstain from the traditional coffee ceremony since rumours say that it is against the Christian religion. There have also been disputes over burial grounds between people from different Christian denominations. Previously all Christians could be buried in Ethiopian Orthodox Church (EOC) cemeteries, but recently members of the Protestant religions have been forbidden to bury their dead in ground consecrated to members of the EOC. Some individual priests were even said to fine members of their flock who had been known to consort with Protestants or Catholics. Even children are enrolled by the clergy of the Orthodox Church in the fight against foreign Christian churches. Some of the children mentioned that they had been told by their priests 'to lead those back to their own religion that had been led astray' and to do it carefully so that they would not be lost on the way.

Those who were most active in trying to 'take souls away from the Orthodox Church' were pointed out by the children as members of the various Protestant religions and sometimes even individual members of the Catholic Church. The children had learnt that all these foreign religions came from the USA with lots of money and that foreigners lured people into leaving their own religion to become what they called 'Pente'. One of the most important differences that these foreign religions exhibited, children said, was that they did not venerate Mary, the mother of Jesus, properly. One of the boys argued that the fact that 'Pente' was so similar to Orthodox Christianity and yet so different showed that it was Satan that had sent it to Ethiopia. There were also children who expressed a reluctant admiration for members of the 'Pente' religion '*since*', they said, '*they behave correctly, and do not drink or use blasphemous words the way our priests often do*'.

The reference to Pente probably originates in events at the end of the 1970s when the Evangelical Churches experienced a strong growth in their numbers in the west and southwest of Ethiopia where Islam and the EOC were weak (Eide 2000:201–209). Due to their growing membership and people's strong adherence to them, Eide (ibid.) argues that the Derg saw the Evangelical Churches as a threat to its own power. Labelling them 'Pente' and categorizing them as 'imported religions with anti-revolutionary objectives' the Derg severely persecuted its members. The children were unaware of this background and did not make any distinction between various Protestant religions or between Protestantism and Catholicism. What was interesting was that even the Muslim children experienced the advances of the 'Pente' as something negative. Both Orthodox and Muslim children saw their own religions as an integral part of Ethiopia and its history while 'Pente', which came from the USA was an alien religion and posed a threat to the children's own Ethiopianness.

In their negative opinions of Pente both Coptic and Muslim children were thus remarkably united. This could make life difficult for any child adhering to a Protestant religion, as revealed to me by 11 year old Alemu, one of the boys in class. In an interview Alemu had told me about the religious situation in his home. Originally his father had been Orthodox Christian and his mother Muslim. Then both had become 'Pente'. But in connection with the death of the mother's mother, the mother had been convinced by relatives and a Muslim priest to return to Islam. This had happened some years previously. The father and the children tried to persuade her to come back to her Protestant religion but up to now she had refused. Alemu was categorized as Muslim by his classmates and his two closest friends were two young Muslim boys. One day, after I had started with my group interviews, Alemu found me alone in the compound and asked that I should not reveal to anyone in class what he had told me, namely that he was 'Pente'. Since all his classmates thought he was Muslim, he preferred it that way, he said. I promised him to keep silent.

Religion and children

The revitalization of the Orthodox religion affected both children and adults in Addis Abeba since religion had a strong impact on the lives of children in their everyday practices, their worldviews and their conceptualisations of good and bad. There was a big difference between town and countryside, though. During my 30 years in the same Orthodox village in northwest Ethiopia I had seen no sign of similar changes in the religious practices of the people living there. Children in this village had only limited contact with the church. It was only when they had married, had had children and reached the age of 25 or above that they went to church and participated in its various activities. Some village children who studied in the nearby town of Dangla, mentioned being invited to new discussion groups at the Orthodox Church, but although they went there a couple of times, they were not attracted by it and did not continue. By the year 2000 the Orthodox Church's internal missionary activities had thus as yet not reached the heartland of Christian Ethiopia, the Gojjam countryside. Peasants living there were very firm in their Orthodox beliefs, though. Thus I was told that the Ashena Peasant Association had voted against agricultural aid offered by a Protestant NGO, because they did not want any interference in their religion.

Whether the revitalization of the Church was due to more Protestant missionaries coming from abroad or to the fact that major political upheavals had taken place during the past 30 years, is difficult to say. Most probably it was due to both, as well as a number of other factors like economic stagnation and new ideas brought forward within the Orthodox Church itself. It has similarly been observed that Islam has also been revitalized and strengthened in Ethiopia over the past ten to fifteen years, with more missionary activities and mosques being built partly as a result of money contributed by Saudi Arabia (Erlich 2003).

ETHIOPIA, ETHNICITY AND BEING ETHIOPIAN
Ethnicity and the Ethiopian past

In its fight for power against the Derg regime, the EPRDF had been allied to both the Eritrean and the Oromo People's Liberation Front all of which had used ethnicity as the basis for their attack on the central government. As a consequence ethnicity became the major political issue and was on top of the political agenda. After the take-over in 1991, the country was divided into ethnically defined federal states, each formally given the right to self-rule. In the states, the majority language was used for both administrative and educational purposes. The constitution allowed the states to secede from Ethiopia if a majority of the population so wished and Eritrea soon seceded. A major difference between the present and all previous Ethiopian governments is that while Ethiopian nationalism used to be of overriding importance to the previous regimes, including that of the Derg, regionalisation and ethnic nationalism have been at the top of the present government's agenda. Despite this change the regions or states are still controlled from the centre, as will be discussed in the next chapter.

Historically there have been many large-scale population movements in Ethiopia, especially during the 16th and the 17th centuries. The reasons for these have been many, with conquest, religion, suppression of insubordinate groups and people searching for improved living conditions, among the most prominent. The result has been a mixing of ethnic groups. People with different ethnic backgrounds live side by side; sometimes one group has dissolved into another, sometimes new groups have appeared. As neighbours, people have learned from each other and cooperated. Frequent intermarriages have also resulted in mixed offspring. In this way, an ethnic permeability with loose borders between the respective groups has come to characterise the Ethiopian 'ethnoscape'. The flexible relationship between ethnic groups was also promoted by the fact that the Ethiopian state was quite loosely organised until the end of the 19th and the beginning of the 20th century.

Despite the flexible borders between groups the rulers over recent centuries have mainly been of a highland Christian stock, supported by farmers dependent on plough-agriculture, and using Amarinja as the *lingua franca* in the whole country. This does not mean that all highlanders or all Christians or even all Amarinja-speakers belonged to the ruling class. Although the rulers came from an Amhara, Tigray, Oromo, Gurage etc. background, the large majority of the people from these language groups were far from power. They were peasants or pastoralists of whatever linguistic group, whose work and surplus could be

165

appropriated by the elite. Those speaking other languages and having other ways of 'doing things' than the Orthodox highland elite were more oppressed than those speaking the same languages, since they had to fend for themselves in a foreign language. Yet, over the centuries class interests seem to have predominated over ethnic belonging as the major factor determining political alliances and a '*lateral ethnie*' (Smith 1994:73), as I have argued elsewhere (Poluha 1998:36–37), developed through inter-ethnic marriages between members of the upper class. This class system was flexible in the sense that a man, rarely woman, who had mastered Amarinja, adhered to Orthodox Christianity and had developed a good client-relationship with a powerful patron could advance to the top from lowly origins, if he worked at it and if his luck (**edelo**) was with him ((Messay Kebede 1999). Even if not many men did rise and attain positions of influence the perception that it was possible was part of people's cultural schema, as mentioned above.

The fluid upper class had been strongly supported by the Ethiopian Orthodox Church, indeed the two had been interdependent and had ruled the Ethiopian state for centuries. As will be discussed in greater detail in the next chapter my argument is that the mode of rule that was developed had also set the pattern for how the state continues to be governed. Contrary to a general tendency to label this ruling class Amhara or Abyssinian, I prefer to call it Ethiopian for two major reasons. The first is that Ethiopia has never been ruled by one ethnic group, but as I have said, by a class from a mixed ethnic setting. The second is that this class has ruled large parts of present-day Ethiopia for so long that it has allowed a distinct mode of interaction to develop between state officials and citizens. This mode is characterized by a pattern of patron–client relations where state officials act as patrons and peasants or poor townspeople as clients. The pattern thus exhibits strict super- and subordination with officials showing haughtiness and arrogance while the poor bow and scrape their feet. The mode of interaction may have been and may continue to be completely different when conducted within local groups. However, when local people have dealt with state officials the hierarchical pattern has been similar according to my observations in Hararge, Arsi, Shoa, Wollega, Tigray, Wollo or Gojjam and irrespective of whether the government has been feudal, 'socialist' or 'democratic'.

Birabiro school children and self-referral

The children in grade 4 came from a large variety of ethnic backgrounds, maybe because they lived in the market area, but perhaps also because most parts of Addis Abeba are both ethnically and religiously mixed. Some of the children, who were born in Addis, told me that their parents came from the countryside when they were young because they had had a fight with their father or just because they went to Addis looking for a job. Other children, born and brought up in the countryside, were only taken to Addis by their parents when it was time to start school. Many of those born in Addis used Amarinja as their first language and some did not speak the language of their parents. Others used the language of their parents at home and Amarinja outside the home. Those who were brought from the countryside when it was time to start school seemed to have learned Amarinja quickly, during their first school year. The pronunciation of Amarinja words was not an issue in school, teachers did not talk about it and I heard no children throw insults at those whose Amarinja pronunciation was influenced by another language.

In class there was no mention of ethnicity when children interacted, neither did they use it when they were angry and wanted to insult each other. The children were surprisingly unaware of the ethnic stereotypes I had come across in different rural and urban contexts, which were used by people who wanted to make jokes about themselves. It was mainly when we discussed who the children were, what they did and what they and their parents wanted them to become that they sometimes referred to their own ethnic background, and then in terms of the language spoken at home.

There may be many reasons why the children appeared to be so unaware of ethnicity and ethnic stereotypes in Addis Abeba. There is the obvious fact that the city encompasses many ethnic groups who live together without geographical boundaries dividing them. Addis Abeba is, in this sense, a melting pot because people in the city live in mixed neighbourhoods, work together and marry across ethnic boundaries. Another reason for the seeming unawareness of ethnicity can be that those who came to Addis went there in search of jobs, open to learning something new, including a new language. It can also be that the children were too young to have experienced ethnic prejudice. Or it may be that contrary to government politics Birabiro children did not care about ethnicity. What was important to them was their being Ethiopian. This was a topic on which some had firm ideas. Yenur for example stated that 'educated Ethiopians should not go abroad to work and if they go abroad, they should not be allowed to change their citizenship into that of the other country'. I do not know from where he got these ideas and I heard no other child mention anything similar although being Ethiopian was important to all of them.

Mekonnen, the 15 year old 'good' boy told me that his association, when I mentioned the word Ethiopian, was, *'Someone who works for the country, for the people'*. And his friend, 13 year old Berhanu added, *'since they come from all ethnic groups* (nationalities) *they work for all'*.

An important means that was used by the school to communicate a sense of being Ethiopian to the children was the hoisting of the national flag and the singing of the national anthem every morning before classes started. I asked the children what associations they had with the words 'national anthem' and 'national flag'. About the anthem 16 year old Fatima said: *'I think of our country and about what is happening, and that I want to reach a high position. I feel very strongly about*

167

it.' And when I mentioned the flag, 15 year old Mekonnen said, *'that is the sign of us, it is green, yellow and red. Green for development, yellow for religion and red for the sacrifice, the Patriots' blood* (when defending Ethiopia against the Italians), *that is what we think.'* And Fatima said, *'I think of something special, like Haile* (Gebre Sellassie, a male gold medal winner at the 2000 Olympics), *who has competed in another country and then the flag comes up for him, and when Derartu* (a female gold medal winner at the same Olympics) *cried, it was not for herself but for respect for her country. So it is nice with our flag.'*

As we can see from the reference to the winners of gold medals, who were mentioned by many children, they associated their national anthem and flag with what was depicted on the television screen and transferred from international sports arenas where Ethiopian athletes competed with success. On television they could see their own sportsmen and women stand up in front of the world while the Ethiopian national anthem was played and the flag hoisted. The 11 year old girl Naema and her 10 year old friend Rekik expressed it thus:

> *Naema: Me I am very glad to be an Ethiopian. I want my country to become very rich.*
>
> *Eva: Yes, so do I, but it seems hard to get there.*
>
> *Naema: Yes, she is the poorest in the world, isn't she?*
>
> *Eva: Yes, that is right.*
>
> *Rekik: But Derartu and the others make the country known.*
>
> *Naema: Even if we are poor, those who competed in Sydney were countries that are well off, and still we succeeded in winning over them.*

Naema's observation that despite being so poor Ethiopia could produce sportsmen and women who could win over those from very rich countries again emphasized the idea that you can become anything, irrespective of background, if only you work at it and your luck is with you. Later that week, when the Ethiopian Olympic team returned to Addis Abeba from Australia most schools and offices closed and people were told over the radio and television to go out into the streets and welcome the team home in order to show them their pride and gratitude for what they had accomplished. The people of Addis filled the streets and gave the team a triumphal homecoming.

Access to television, which many Addis Abeba children had, thus boosted their sense of being Ethiopian, especially when the TV brought pictures from far-off countries, which showed successful Ethiopians hailing the flag while the national anthem was played. The television had enabled the children to visualize Ethiopia as something people in other parts of the world related to and admired. This made it more gratifying to them to consider themselves Ethiopian. Ethnicity, on the other hand, had no symbols, at least not at the time, that could reinforce the children's sense of identity as forcefully as nationalism. Even when the children talked of what they wanted to do and to become in the future, they always referred to their responsibilities as members of a family and as Ethiopians. They had to study hard to be able to help their parents with their younger sisters and brothers. But they also had to study hard and get good jobs in order to take responsibility for the community, Ethiopia, which allowed them to study. Stambach reports a similar attachment to home and family in Tanzania where the children wanted 'upwardly mobile and successful people to retain connections with their natal families' (2000:151).

This can be compared with the rural children in Gojjam for whom the situation was different. They hoisted their regional, Amhara flag daily and sang the regional anthem. They had no access to television, which could make them feel part of the success of Ethiopians in international competitions in the way Birabiro children could. These Amarinja-speaking children did not have any strong sense of being Amharas either, since there were no significant others to whom they could relate. In the long run the fact that children in the different regions sing their regional anthems and hail their regional flags may result in a stronger sense of local belonging and a weakening of the bonds with an Ethiopia, which for them may be a place that is difficult to imagine.

A major reason why being Ethiopian was important to Birabiro children may be that they shared some of those attributes considered essential to any nation-building project. The basic precondition for developing a sense of belonging with a nation state is, according to Benedict Anderson (1991), the printed word. Anderson argues that a population that can read and write in their own language can also communicate ideas and visions in words and phrases that are mutually recognizable, and which promote feelings of a shared community. Schools are a key factor in any nation-building project and have historically promoted the homogenisation and spread of languages all over the world through the printed word. Schools, as could be seen at Birabiro, are also a major medium for emphasizing significant national symbols like the flag, the national anthem and the map of the country. The latter is important since it depicts the borders and thereby teaches the students who 'they' are and helps them distinguish themselves from 'others', who live outside those borders. These symbols were prominent in the Birabiro school and the children were aware of them even though many were the first generation in their families to go to school.

There are other aspects to the state than shared national symbols, especially those adhering to a state which calls itself democratic, and to which the children had been less exposed. Newbury (1994) summarises the main criteria of democracy, including Dahl's (1982) minimal definition, as 'the presence of institutionalised mechanisms by which citizens may change the personnel holding power, respect for the rule of law, accountable governance and protection of human and civil rights' (ibid.:2). Elections have taken place in Ethiopia but have not been so free and fair as to allow for a change of personnel holding power. For as long as is known in Ethiopian history rulers have always come to power by the use of force. The laws, as discussed earlier, are in place, but are not impartially applied.

Depending on who you are laws can be bent and it is impossible to predict how they are going to be used. Human and civil rights are consequently differently interpreted and applied depending on who does the interpretation and to whom it is going to be applied. Children complained about some of these practices, especially the nepotism used when jobs were distributed and the misuse of public resources by government employees. They also showed an awareness of how things 'ought' to be, such as impartial treatment before the law and equal opportunities irrespective of background. Their observations of government officials and their normative ideas about how things 'ought' to be were never expressed together or at the same time, however, and they did not seem to have a problem with this apparent contradiction.

What is less often mentioned in texts on the state, maybe because it is somehow taken for granted in the West, is the expectation that the state should act as a fair re-distributor of resources. Work, education, pensions, infrastructure, food, all are taken for granted as part of the duties of the state towards its citizens and they also seem to be an important ingredient in the glue that makes people and states stick together. These obligations are little recognized and spread in Ethiopia, although peasants' expectations of food and work from their government is steadily increasing. The absence of such obligations in Somalia, where the state was run by and in the interests of clans (Simons 1995), may have contributed to the disintegration of a state with which few identified, despite sharing both language and religion.

Although Birabiro children have not had access to all these 'taken-for-granted' obligations of the state, apart from going to school, they were still developing national feelings, both expressed as a sense of belonging to the state and as feelings of responsibility towards 'their' country. What feelings of belonging and what 'imagined' communities take their form in the minds of school children in the regions who lack the presence of the major national symbols is more difficult to know, however.

CONCLUDING REMARKS

The group of friends, the religious group and being Ethiopian were the three main categories of 'us', apart from the household with which the Birabiro children identified. The religious group and being Ethiopian were collectives into which the children were born while friends were the result of their own choice. Friends were equal and functioned as such; constituting a relationship that provided a strong counter-discourse to all the hierarchical relations surrounding the children. This same equality, however, had important limits since the selection of friends was restricted to the peer group thereby reducing the actual choice to children of the same sex, age, neighbourhood and often also to the same religion. Even mediation was in this way limited to the peer group or to those of an inferior status who were either younger or weaker. Thus, although friends were equal the very implementation of the principle of equality underlined the presence of hierarchical layers since there was no recruitment beyond the peer group.

Hierarchical relations were even more conspicuous within the Ethiopian state and in the religious institutions. Children could often see influential men surrounded by various insignia of power like weapons, soldiers and imposing cars in the streets and on TV. Women were usually excluded from such arenas and held no key positions in either church or mosque. Children were aware that positions in both religious and state institutions were strictly ranked. The hierarchy itself did not seem to bother them though. The idea that they could reach any position was shared by all, girls and boys.

The ascriptive quality of religion and Ethiopianness as something you are born into and cannot change made the children take these aspects of their collective identities for granted. They gave them security and helped them know how to live their daily lives. At the same time, children re-interpreted the meaning of both religion and citizenship. To some religion was important and they even took it as a mission 'to bring back the lost sheep'. To others, although religion was part of their everyday life, it was not something they reflected much upon. Ethiopianness was also under perpetual negotiation. Ethiopia being a poor country but with gold medal winners and the national flag on televisions all over the world inspired some of the Birabiro children to feel responsibility for its future, others instead longed to go abroad, to get an education or to become professional football players.

Due to both local and global events the children consequently had changing conceptualisations of what religion and Ethiopianness meant. In their ways of speaking about these phenomena it was possible to discern how traditions were re-created but also how they were being negotiated and changed. What should be remembered is that through taking membership in the religious community and being Ethiopian citizens as their birthright the children also became part of much of what these collectives stood for, such as patron–client relations with explicit rights and duties, where they as children were at the bottom, but where the hierarchy was fluid; and a knowledge system where knowledge was perceived as limited and unchangeable. They also identified their respective religion with being Ethiopian thereby creating a bond that united Christians and Muslims against agents of 'imported religions', which threatened the unity of Ethiopia.

Chapter 8

STATE–PEOPLE RELATIONS IN ETHIOPIA

The Ethiopian leadership has been seriously engaged in trying to change the country for the last 150 years. The intended, or unintended, result of all their efforts has, however, been a strengthening of the state apparatus and a consequent prevention of change of the dominant cultural schema in society. In this chapter I shall examine how reproduction of continuity has been promoted at the level of the state despite rulers', intellectuals' and students' fervent preoccupation with change. My inquiry will be made through a closer investigation into descriptions of the history of the state as it has been interpreted by political scientists, historians, economists and anthropologists. Focus will be on how the state has been formed historically and what its major characteristics are. In the last chapter I shall relate the major features of the state to what in the previous chapters has emerged as the distinctive cultural pattern of the Birabiro children expressed in, among other things, their interactions, thoughts and practices.

My historical review about the present Ethiopian state will focus on the period from 1855 until today which I shall divide into three parts: The 'Modern' Imperial period from 1855–1974, the years of the Derg, 1974–1991 and the reign of the EPRDF from 1991 until the time of writing in the autumn of 2003. Interpretations and analyses made by various writers will be used as points of reference to describe the consolidation of the Ethiopian state. Emphasis will be given to five areas that have been instrumental in the control of the state apparatus and have contributed to its continuity: the political sphere with the administration of the state and its institutions; the police and army; the economy, including technological innovations and adaptations; the educational system; and the overall ideology which has been used to legitimise the way power has been exercised. Focus will be on what has been done in practice rather than on what was intended or stated.

MAJOR TRENDS IN STATE DEVELOPMENT, ECONOMY, TECHNOLOGY AND EDUCATION IN THE MODERN IMPERIAL PERIOD

The historical entity called Ethiopia is one of the oldest state formations still existing in the world. Its early history, including the period before and during the state centred around the city of Aksum, and extending up to the end of the thirteenth century, is rather obscure. But at least two legacies from this period, the Geez script and the Monophysite Orthodox Christian faith, are still important elements of the Ethiopian society. Side by side with this Christian state, there were various independent kingdoms, sultanates and societies with less hierarchical modes of decision-making. The peoples living in the geographical area of what is today called Ethiopia spoke different languages and professed different religions. Some adhered to Christianity, others to Islam and perhaps most had their own animistic religions. Warfare, conquests, payments of tribute, as well as periods of peaceful co-existence and trade characterised the interactions between the various groups.

From the end of the thirteenth century AD, the Christian state, which eventually achieved hegemony in the region, was led by a dynasty of monarchs (the so-called Solomonid dynasty), who claimed descent from a liaison between King Solomon of Israel and the biblical Queen of Sheba. What characterised the monarchs of this period was that they were warrior kings who constantly moved around with their huge armies to conquer new territories or punish recalcitrant old tributaries. From 1632 onwards, however, the monarchs began to settle in a fixed capital (Gondar) and power gradually shifted from the monarchs into the hands of regional warlords. This lasted until 1769, when the strongest of the regional warlords took control of the state in the name of puppet emperors whom they promoted and deposed at their will. This continued until 1855, when the emergent supreme warlord dispensed with the need for a puppet emperor and crowned himself as Emperor Tewodros. Throughout the preceding centuries, the development of the state apparatus or organised government was circumscribed (except perhaps in the Northern Shoan region of the early 19th century).

From 1855, however, it is possible to see a gradual but almost uninterrupted attempt to build a strong state-apparatus within the Christian highlands; an apparatus that slowly expanded both in space and depth to cover what is today known as Ethiopia. My interest here is not what has happened historically in different parts of the country but in the contents of this state-building project, distinctive aspects of which I shall try to trace within the major arenas discussed above, of politics, police and army, administration, economy, education and ideology.

The explicit goal of Tewodros was to unify the country under a single central government. He therefore set out to rid himself of other centres of power and concentrate authority in his own hands. Tewodros' approach was to place his own officials as governors in the new administrative units. In order not to lose the officials to other kings or lords Tewodros paid them salaries. Similarly, when Tewodros started to create a national army he made the soldiers economically dependent upon him directly and cut the links to their previous lords. Tewodros also wanted to limit the influence of the church and 'stressed the construction of roads rather than churches and palaces' (Rubenson 1991:172). As a whole, Rubenson argues, Tewodros wanted 'to limit spiritual authority to spiritual matters and drastically reduced the land holdings of the church'(ibid.:172). He also wanted to manufacture his own arms but until this was possible he bought modern weapons from Europe.

Tewodros did not have much success in his unifying and centralizing attempts because the forces against him were strong. Opposition came from the most varied quarters, not least from the clergy, that did its best to undermine his authority among the peasantry. The warlords of the various regions also wanted their power back and rebelled whenever the opportunity presented itself (Markakis 1975:21). Tewodros' dealings with foreigners were also unsuccessful. To demonstrate his dissatisfaction with the European powers and particularly Britain, he imprisoned some 'diplomats' and refused to release them until a dispatch of a troop of British soldiers, who, supported by opposing Ethiopian warlords, managed to encircle his stronghold at Maqdala. Faced with the prospect of being captured by the British troops, he committed suicide in 1867.

After a protracted struggle, which lasted until 1871, Yohannes, a lord from Tigray, became the next warlord to be crowned emperor. Yohannes had little time, and maybe also less interest than Tewodros to consolidate the state (Markakis 1975:21, 22) but he took it upon himself to safeguard the independence of Ethiopia from intruders that approached both from the north and from the west. While defending the country against Mahdist forces coming from the Sudan, Yohannes died in battle in 1889.

The most powerful of the warlords vying for the throne after Yohannes was Menelik. Before becoming emperor, Menelik had already greatly expanded the territory of his Christian kingdom to the southwest thereby moving the centre of the state southwards. The region was rich in crops, animals and land and came to be used as a treasury for all of Menelik's further activities. One of Menelik's major aims, much like those of Tewodros and Yohannes, was to keep Ethiopia's independence. To this end he defended the country against repeated imperialist attacks from Italy, France and Britain. In the process he used the income from the southwest to invest both in strategic weapons and as payment to officers and soldiers. He also appropriated land in the south, which he distributed to his followers as well as to the church and to peasants who fled starvation and disease in the north (Marcus 1995:135, McCann 1987:200).

During the reign of Menelik an outline of Ethiopia as a 'nation-state' was designed; international treaties defined the boundaries of the realm, which have stayed much the same until today; there was a semblance of modern government through the establishment of ministries, provincial administration, embassies, etc. The centralization of the state also continued. Local rulers were forbidden to have modern arms, taxation was further developed and imperial courts were established all over the country (Marcus 1995:3). To promote trade Menelik developed internal communications such as the Addis Abeba–Djibouti railway, inland routes, post and telecommunications, all radiating out of and into Addis Abeba. Thereby he also reduced the importance of provincial centres. With all these innovations 'Menelik's reign represented the triumph of the centralizing idea' according to Marcus (1995:3), who argues that a model developed whereby 'the sovereign has increasingly dominated every facet of national existence. All allegiance is owed to him and to the apparatus of royal power. Only by accommodation to the official culture of the state can the individual hope to succeed' (ibid.:4).

Apart from the investments in infrastructure, there was little industrial or technological development under Menelik and only limited investment in education. The first Ethiopian school, the Menelik School, was opened in 1908 despite opposition from the Church that feared the influence of foreigners and foreign ideas. Various Protestant missions which started their own schools represented other educational investments.

As Menelik became incapacitated by illness in 1909 and eventually died in 1913 there was an intense power struggle which reached its zenith in 1916, at which time Teferi Makonnen, later crowned as Haile Sellassie I, emerged as crown prince and regent under Menelik's daughter who was crowned empress. No important developments took place with regard to the centralization of the state, economic investments or new technological or educational advances during these years of struggles for power. In fact, the struggle continued during the early years of Teferi's regency. Only after having secured his pretensions to the throne in 1930 could Teferi Makonnen continue the centralization process, a process which was interrupted during the Italian occupation between 1935 and 1941, but was resumed when Haile Sellassie returned to the throne. Like his predecessors he kept control of the army, of tax collection and of appointments in his own hands. Haile Sellassie introduced a standing army, had laws codified, regularized tax collections and standardized administrative procedures. All these measures were necessary to ensure an orderly and efficient government. Grafted onto an age-old system of patron–client relations, the whole apparatus became an edifice in the service of the crown. Control, as previously, was exercised through the use of rewards or punishments. What counted was loyalty to the pinnacle of power who, in this case, was the emperor.

To increase government revenues to pay for, among other things, the standing army, the peasants became the ones most heavily taxed. Yet, since their productivity was low, the taxes from the peasants had only a marginal impact on the treasury (Schwab 1972; Ståhl 1974) and most government income came from customs duties on trade. Through international aid, such as agricultural package projects, attempts were made to improve the productivity of the peasants. These attempts were not successful, however, and did not bring about an improved productivity or a better standard of living. A major reason for the lack of success according to many sources (Ståhl 1974, Cohen and Weintraub 1975, Bengtsson 1983, Negusse Woldemicael 1984) was the landholding system, which lacked incentives for peasants and tenants. Despite suggestions for land reform, even from the emperor, the two chambers of the Parliament could not agree on any new land laws probably because land was the main basis for power and survival for the members of the Senate as well as a good majority of the others. The reason why the lords themselves did not develop their areas has been debated. Donham

(1986) argues that the lack of economic development in Ethiopia during the feudal era is due to the fact that the lords were not interested in investing in their domains since they had no hereditary rights. According to Tsegaye Tegenu (1996:51) this argument is not valid, however, since, among others, Crummey's articles (1983, 1988) show that private ownership and trans-generational continuity of the landowning class was a fact in Gondar. It seems possible though that the lords like the emperors focussed on obtaining power and tributes, which made them engage in their armies and neglect their land.

Some limited changes have occurred in the economy in the 20th century. Thus, beginning in the 1920s, a slow shift from subsistence to semi-commercial agriculture could be observed, especially in the south (Marcus 1995:43). Later economic investments under Haile Sellassie made the state dominant in transportation, communication, power, textiles, hotels, construction materials etc., in total about fifty-eight enterprises. In almost half, the state held 50 per cent or more of the shares and it was the sole owner of fourteen (Markakis 1975:336 and footnote 15). Major exports were coffee (70 per cent), hides and skins, meat and live animals (ibid.). The basic technology used in peasant agriculture remained the same, however, from the 12th to the 19th century (Donham 1986:15) and even until today (McCann 1987:203).

The educational sector developed slowly despite diminished church opposition after the 1920s (Tekeste Negash 1990:12). As regent, Teferi Makonnen opened a school in his own name in 1925. A special educational tax was introduced in 1926, a date which according to Tekeste Negash (ibid.), can be seen as the beginning of a national educational system. The Italian occupation disrupted this system, which had to be rebuilt after the war. Between 1942 and 1966 Haile Sellassie himself kept the post of Minister of Education indicating the importance he attached to education for Ethiopia's development. However, a UNESCO-sponsored conference of African states on the development of education in Africa in 1961 observed that Ethiopia lagged far behind other African states in education. Until the mid-40s education was the second highest post in the budget. Then it slowly declined and after 1963 only about 10 per cent of the budget went to education. On the eve of the 1974 revolution primary education was accessible to only 12 per cent of the school age population.

To summarize the main trends of the 'Modern' Imperial period, we can say that centralization and a strong state were the key concerns under the successive emperors. They fought to keep the country's independence and not be colonized like much of the rest of Africa. They had, however, realized that to carry out what they wanted as emperors, especially against a recalcitrant clergy and nobility, they needed to control the state-apparatus themselves. This they did according to a patron–client relationship the model of which was continuously being refined.

The centralization process of the period focussed on five areas: control of the army as well as the police, realized through personal appointments, special training and salaries, all done from the centre; control of the administration of the state through personal appointments of bureaucrats and officials; control of the fiscal system through the establishment of general rules, personal appointments and salaries from the centre; a unification of the legal system through the establishment of a court system and the codification of laws; and control of the economy through the promotion and taxation of trade to pay for all the innovations. A key concept in all this was 'control' implying both knowledge at the centre of what was happening and personal loyalty of employees or appointees to the emperor on whom they depended. The system was sustained by means of rewards, favours and punishments of all degrees.

The economy was mainly based on peasant subsistence agriculture from which taxes were extracted. Very little investment was made in agriculture from the centre, either in security of tenure, land improvement, new technology or in teaching peasants about alternative techniques, crops etc. One exception was the introduction of the eucalyptus tree from Australia under Menelik. Some semi-commercial independent land and technological investments were allowed in the south. The few other investments that were made were mostly deployed in infrastructure, the service sector and the food industry. Very little was invested in industrial development or the development or adaptation of new technologies. Investments in manpower were also limited. At the end of Haile Sellassie's reign, 96 per cent of the population was illiterate.

The legitimising ideology for this rule was a close linkage between the state and the Orthodox Christian Church, which, by the act of anointing the Emperor, declared him the 'elect of God'. Most, but not all, of the emperors may have claimed descent from the so-called Solomonid dynasty. In actual fact, however, at every transition the would-be leader needed to fight militarily or politically to subdue other contenders and only then would he be designated as 'elect of God' by the Church (Messay Kebede 1999). The authoritarian structure thereby became not only valid and considered as legitimate but was also generally accepted. There was little questioning of the autocrat or his ideas and few alternative policies were proposed.

Throughout the Imperial era, there did not seem to be much intellectual political opposition critical of the respective emperors. Beginning with the 20th century, however, some new ideas appeared to be simmering. Critical voices were being raised by a small group of intellectuals, among whom was found the famous Gebrehiwot Baykedagn. In a 1912 essay on Ethiopia, he pointed out and criticized the strong anti-modernization views expressed by both Church and nobility (Tekeste Negash 1990:2, 13, footnote 6). In Haile Sellassie's time the early opposition to his rule was more personal than political. It was only after the abortive coup d'état of 1960 that the simmering opposition came to the surface. From then on, students began to articulate vociferous opposition and to stage repeated political demonstrations demanding change primarily through land reform. The criticisms continued at an accelerated speed until the final overthrow of the Imperial regime in 1974.

THE PERIOD OF THE DERG 1974–1991

With the advent of the so-called Derg and the way it assumed control over the country, the centralization process made a big leap forward. This said, there were large variations in the way the state and the people were conceptualised by the Derg before and after the years 1976–77.

The take-over of the state was initially a very slow process closely related to the gradual realization that Haile Sellassie was no longer the strong emperor he used to be. In actual fact power eroded from within the empire, from what had been thought to be the most secure stronghold of the state, namely the army. In 1974 mutinies broke out in the south, north and centre with complaints from the soldiers about their living and working conditions. These were inefficiently dealt with and students, teachers, taxi-drivers and priests further encroached upon the government's power through strikes in Addis. While unrest continued a small group with representatives from the army, air force, navy and police was able to form a committee, the Derg, which started to act separately from the official government. Testing its power with imprisonments of members of the regime and with the issuing of policy statements without encountering any resistance, the Derg started to act officially in September 1974 by deposing Haile Sellassie and declaring itself the Provisional Military Administrative Council.

During the ensuing months, the orientation of the Derg shifted from the vague slogan of '**Etiopia Tikdem**' (Ethiopia First) to 'Ethiopian socialism', which was declared in December 1974. The socialist inclination was further developed through the nationalization of banks, insurance companies, and other financial institutions and of private industrial and commercial companies. Proclamations ordering the nationalization of all rural land and later also of urban land and extra houses followed.

The nationalization of rural lands implied a redistribution of land and the setting up of new institutions to implement the law. This extraordinary task was given to the rural population itself, to the adult men who were heads of their households and organised into Peasant Associations (PAs). It was a delegation of responsibility from the centre, which went against all previous traditions, against all formal and informal rules according to which the state kept its control over people. It did, however, not break with the traditions of male power in major decision-making bodies (Poluha 2002b). Women and youth were organized in separate organizations under the PAs.

To develop the countryside, implement the land reform and to promote literacy the National Development Through Cooperation Campaign, or Zemecha, was launched sending university and secondary school teachers and students from all over the country into the rural areas. An enormous amount of energy was thereby released with very little control from the centre (see also Halliday and Molyneux 1981:111). A similar although somewhat more controlled process was initiated in the towns with the nationalization of urban lands and extra houses.

In this way all sources of individual wealth held by the landholding class had, over a couple of months, been obliterated. Even the dominance of the Coptic Ortho-dox Church was eroded when major Islamic celebrations were made into national holidays.

Whether the Ethiopian revolution really was a revolution or not, and if it was a revolution then of what kind, are questions that have been the focus for much debate (see e.g. Markakis and Nega Ayele 1978, M. and D. Ottaway 1978, Lefort 1983, Halliday and Molyneux 1981). Discussing the subject of revolutions Christopher Clapham (1990) puts what happened in Ethiopia during these years on a par with experiences from China, North Korea, Cuba and other countries categorizing them all as 'real' revolutions. What is distinct about such revolu-tions, he argues, is that 'two basic conditions must be met. First, a set of circum-stances must be present which prompt the collapse of the existing institutional order, and which amount in sum to a 'revolutionary situation'. Secondly, meas-ures must be implemented to construct a new institutional order.' (1990:2). These changes have according to Clapham, and with which my own experiences concur, taken place in Ethiopia. Clapham also argues that revolutions do not lead to mass participation or equality but to 'the creation of a powerful state' (ibid.:7). Although I disagree with this statement regarding the first years of the revolution, because they, in my opinion, were characterized by little state control and much encouragement of mass participation, this changed in 1976–77 when the control apparatus became not only strengthened but also hugely enlarged especially com-pared to how it was under Haile Sellassie.

The initial tightening of control over the state apparatus may well have been prompted by the resistance, which met the Derg. In its efforts to consolidate its power, the Derg had to contend with armed political groupings like the monar-chist Ethiopian Democratic Union (EDU) and leftist groupings like the Ethio-pian People's Revolutionary Party (EPRP), fight insurgents in the north (Eritrea and Tigray) and face attacks from Somalia in the southeast. Even within the Derg, there was an intense power struggle and a series of bloody purges. In 1977, however, Mengistu Haile Mariam emerged as the undisputed leader of the Derg after eliminating all other contenders to the central power, re-enacting more viv-idly and brutally all the power struggles of the previous centuries.

From 1976–77 the administration of the state became even more centralized than during the Imperial regime, not only through the control of the bureaucracy and the military but also through the control of the population via Urban and Peasant Dwellers Associations. The whole of the local bureaucracy was exchanged and new persons were appointed to important positions at the centre. A key to all appointments was not merit but loyalty to the politics conducted by those in power and above that loyalty to the chairman, Mengistu Haile Mariam. Violence through killings, executions and imprisonments was a major ingredient in the rule as it was used to get rid of oppositional individuals and groups and put fear into others. The violence was facilitated by amendments to existing legislation, new penal and criminal procedure codes and special courts (Clapham 1990:108). The military apparatus was enormously expanded, Halliday and Molyneux give the figure of 44,000 men in the armed forces in 1974 and as many as 230,000 employed in 1980 (1981:148). During this period people in the countryside and in towns also became subject to control. From having been independent Peasant and Urban Dwellers Associations dealing with their own administration, all peasant, urban, women and youth associations were now organized at the central, national level from which control was easier. This control was apparently not felt to be enough, however, because at the local level procedures also changed. While those previously elected to executive committees had been people known and respected by the local peasant and urban community and chosen by them, the new leaders began to be selected by the political cadres for being loyal to the chairman and to the 'socialist' goals. Bureaucrats, peasants and urban dwellers were furthermore controlled through the use of national plans and 'directives', which via budgets, price regulations, routines and rhetoric structured their lives and work. Certain types of farming, like state farms and cooperatives were promoted to the disadvantage of individual farms. Town dwellers were further controlled via rationing of food and other indispensable products.

The economy under the Derg was characterized by its socialist approach and attempts at central planning. Land had been nationalized and although a major part of it was cultivated by independent farm households state investments were directed to state farms and producers' cooperatives rather than to individuals. There was a strong ideological belief that collective forms of production were more rational and efficient and would result in higher yields than any individual or private cultivation. These expectations proved sadly wrong, however. Even if state farms showed higher yields per hectare the investments in machinery and labour were so high that they worked at a loss. Producers' cooperatives in turn had lower yields per ha than individual farmers (Alula Abate 1983, Fassil Kiros 1984, Mengistu Woube 1986, Mekonnen Getu 1987, Cohen and Isaksson 1987, Ståhl 1988, Poluha 1989, 1990).

Investments directed to non-collectivised farmers were often made through programmes and campaigns aimed at improving soil conservation and afforestation. In a study investigating the possible lasting impact such inputs could have had on farming techniques Yeraswork Admassie (1995) found that with the change of government in 1991, all inputs and new techniques introduced by the Derg just evaporated from the farmers' practices. In his dissertation Yeraswork Admassie attributes the lack of change to the top-down approach used by government officials. The officials had often forced people to apply new modes of farming even though they did not find them beneficial. Two major reasons why the innovations were not attractive to the farmers were that on one hand, the new techniques were not locally institutionalised and, on the other, the peasants lacked security of tenure. Since they could lose the land they farmed in the next re-distribution they were not interested in a long-term goal of promoting the quality of the land. Thus the top-down approach of the government and the insecurity of tenure combined with price regulations according to which individual peasants and cooperatives were forced to sell a certain quota of their grains at highly reduced prices, were all strong disincentives to more efficient forms of production.

After the nationalization of banks and larger industries, most of which had foreign ownership, very little investment was made in industrial production. The little that was invested was, according to Clapham (1990), put into textiles, cement, oilseeds and beverages, and had a specific socialist economic stamp since these industries were established as joint ventures with socialist countries. They were few in number but absorbed an enormous amount of capital per hired worker constituting what Clapham calls 'showpiece projects' (1990:148). Urban unemployment steadily rose and the increase would have been much larger had land not been nationalized so that people stayed in the countryside. About 95 per cent of the industrial investments were made by the state. The slowly emerging national bourgeoisie from the time of Haile Sellassie I was thus radically weakened through the proclamations, apart from a small group engaged in retail trade.

For the period of 1974–1990 the growth rate was 1.9 per cent, while population growth was 2.7 per cent (Eshetu Chole 1994:311). Instead of an improvement in the standard of living the situation thus worsened for a large majority of the Ethiopian population during the reign of the Derg.

The new technological innovations under the Derg were mainly of an organizational character intended to promote collective work. People worked as employees on state farms and in state industries or in producers' cooperatives. These were promoted and supported both in rural and urban areas. There was little success with either form or organization, however, and the productivity per capita did not rise as compared with what was produced by non-collectivised workers and private farmers.

Under the Derg there was a gigantic attempt to expand education. Literacy campaigns were conducted in 15 languages all over the country and by the end of 1985 about 12 million people had passed the literacy exam. These campaigns were carried out with a lot of enthusiasm but there were also many who disagreed with their coercive character. People who failed to attend or did not come on time were severely punished. Worse than that was that there was little follow up, such as new training or accessible reading material, which meant that a return to illiteracy for a large group of people was inevitable.

Literacy campaigns were combined with the building of new schools in all the regions including in the rural areas. The intake increased fourfold from 73/74 to 83/84 in primary, secondary as well as in higher education (Clapham 1990:150). The increase in quantity resulted, however, in a decrease in quality. This was partly due to the fact that the expansion increased the number of children per teacher and partly because schools had to be made better use of and children had shorter school days, mostly learning in two or three shifts per day. The curriculum itself was not considered adequate and as mentioned above, Tekeste Negash (1990, 1996) argues that a major reason for students being unemployed after 12 years of schooling was that their education was not relevant to the conditions in which they found themselves. As Clapham (1990) notes and which I observed as a teacher in Bahar Dar, a fairly good education for a relatively small number of children had under the Derg been transformed into quite a poor education for a much larger number of children.

The Derg's and especially Mengistu Haile Mariam's rule of Ethiopia was supported by a new mythology and a new ideology. A socialist rhetoric was developed telling people and officials how to distinguish between friends and foes and between good and bad deeds. Although the major objective of the various policies was allegedly to improve people's living conditions and to develop an egalitarian society, the ideology was in practice used as a pretext to stifle any difference in outlook. Appointments were obtained through political loyalty, preferably combined with some kind of patronage. The higher up in the hierarchy a person was positioned, the more he was expected and expected himself to be able to repeat the right rhetoric, to be knowledgeable about the ideas of the chairman and enforce their implementation at any cost.

When those in higher positions encountered opposition or ideas deviating from what they defined as the 'right' way to solve problems, the use of ever more violent repression against those who disagreed with them gained acceptance and legitimacy in party quarters and among their clients. This was a gradual process, which on the one hand emphasized obedience and accountability to those above you in the hierarchy and on the other allowed arrogance and even the use of brute force towards those below you. Not everyone acted in this way but there was very little open criticism of those who did. Independent opinion was stifled because everyone was afraid of possible reprisals if they spoke out on a subject on which the chairman might have another opinion. Mengistu Haile Mariam had himself used violence and killed people on his way to power and through his own behaviour he promoted the concept of 'might is right'. Among peasants, workers and all those not involved in the party, the behaviour of the power-holders fostered insecurity, fear of speaking out, of losing a job, of being imprisoned and even of being killed. They found it better to keep silent and do only what they were explicitly told to (Poluha 2002a). The rigid economic socialist policy similarly inhibited all personal and private initiatives since these by definition were not in conformity with the government's policy.

The period of the Derg became in this way a regime where old traditions were not only continued but also given ever more emphasis. The state and its control apparatus were expanded and further developed. Control from the centre was strengthened via new patron–client relations and expanded into many new spheres of life, and people kept silent. The main opposition came from the organised liberation movements in Eritrea, Tigray and some Oromo areas. These movements ushered in the downfall of the Derg not only by forcing it into costly wars but also by indirectly eroding its internal fabric. The protracted wars with many casualties on all sides made conscription necessary and quotas of soldiers were requested from each peasant and urban dwellers' association. The forced conscription and rising number of casualties caused a lot of resentment not only among those remaining at home but also within the army. Criticism, dissent and for many a feeling of the uselessness of all the fighting spread to both rank and file. Attempted coups against Mengistu Haile Mariam failed and his own violent reaction towards the coup leaders further sapped the morale of the soldiers. Slowly, what was probably Africa's largest army crumbled from within and was easily overrun by the opposition forces that could enter Addis Abeba without major fight in May 1991.

THE PERIOD OF THE EPRDF, 1991–

When the EPRDF took power in 1991 in close cooperation with the Eritrean People's Liberation Front (EPLF) and the Oromo Liberation Front (OLF) many expected the centralization process not only to be halted but also to be reversed. For the two fronts which initially shared power in Addis Abeba (EPRDF and OLF), ethnicity was a central point in mobilizing the population against the Derg and the expectation after the take-over of power was that the country would now be decentralized along ethnic lines. This partly happened. The new transitional government established ethnic federalism under ethnically defined states, each with its own parliament and far-reaching powers over development activities. Each also used the majority language for both administrative and educational purposes. According to the constitution the states even have the right to secede from Ethiopia.

Despite such efforts towards decentralization through a new legal framework the implementation of the laws has not had a decentralising effect. Several reasons seem to be behind the lack of such achievement. One is inherent in the EPRDF view of ethnicity. The official conceptualisation of ethnicity is that it is an objective criterion easy to distinguish from the outside. The re-mapping of the country into so-called ethnic states emphasized the understanding that ethnic groups have at least the followings characteristics: they are static, geographically distinct, all its members have similar interests and they are cohesive groups rather than categories of people. The TPLF conceptualised their own experiences from mobilizing people in Tigray against the Derg in this way and now expected ethnicity to fulfil the same function but for development activities.

This understanding of ethnicity fits in with a mechanical view of human beings but pays no heed to people's own experiences and feelings. Contrary to this view, recent social constructivist research argues that a person's identity is constructed in interaction with others of the same and of other kinds and is defined in the process of interaction by those party to it. Thus, what people themselves feel about their belonging and identity and how others categorize them are,

183

according to this research, the major organizing principles of ethnicity. Belonging will thus be influenced by both context and people involved and rather than being fixed it will be part of a process with changing interpretations.

The consequences of the government's rigid conceptualisation of ethnicity transferred onto the map of Ethiopia were mixed. For those who previously had not been allowed to use their own language in schools and offices the change was a long-awaited recognition of their culture. For many others, the map misrepresented their experiences; parents and grandparents had migrated and could not be identified with one fixed place of origin; others who considered their mothers as well as their fathers to be part of their roots and who were of mixed parenthood were also at a loss when having to identify with one place. Depending on the circumstances people felt they belonged to one, several and sometimes no ethnic group at all. Neighbours could have different language backgrounds and there were instances when individuals or families did not agree even though they came from the same background. Sharing a culture and a language thus did not necessarily mean that opinions and ideas had to be the same.

The issue of representation further complicated this divergence of opinions. Democracy vested in an ethnic group implied that rights were collective and not individual, but the question was who could represent the collective, especially when groups of people were in opposition to each other? In many areas where the experiences of the inhabitants differed from those in Tigray, communities were not so easy to mobilize even when they spoke the same language. People's experiences with the Derg seemed to have made them reluctant to voluntarily engage in activities with government officials.

What has proved even more resistant to decentralization is the delegation of planning and the transfer of executive and administrative power to the respective states. According to the constitution the National Regional States (NRSs) were given the duty and responsibility to carry out their own plans and policies. At the same time their dependence on the federal state was retained since while their policies were to follow the norms established by the federal government they lacked their own professional staff to develop such policies. Above all, however, the national states are economically dependent on the federal state because only about 10 per cent of the revenue is generated within the states and as much as 90 per cent comes from the federal government (Vaughan and Tronvoll 2003:86, 87). These conditions have made it necessary for the states to adapt to the federal government and would have made it difficult for them to follow any predilections of their own, even if they had had any.

Decentralisation efforts have met with another problem, which according to Vaughan and Tronvoll (ibid.) resulted from the EPRDF conceptualisation of democracy. As mentioned above, democracy has been understood by the EPRDF as the collective rights of ethnic groups vis-à-vis each other and the state. Collective rights are also understood to be vested in the party whether in the TPLF or in its various affiliates in and outside the EPRDF. Members of the party have, according to TPLF ideology, the right and the duty to discuss all topics presented by the party. Once the discussions are finished, consensus proclaimed and decisions made, these have to be followed by all its members. This process of 'democratic centralism' in the vein of Lenin has, however, its disadvantages with respect to decentralisation and the possibility to influence the discussion. Firstly, because a majority of the population in the respective National Regional States are not party members, even though they have the right to apply for membership. Secondly, those who are weak in the public arena, like women, children or minority groups, also constitute a majority of the population but have great difficulties making their voices heard, whether they are members of the party or not. Their experiences and opinions are therefore not used to inform collective opinions and decisions. Thirdly, in a hierarchical society it is difficult to say whether consensus has really been reached, because it is usually the opinions of those high up in the hierarchy that are interpreted as the consensus and translated as the general decision. Rule through collective democracy therefore often means that the approach is as authoritarian and hierarchical as that of any socialist or feudal form of governance. This has, among other things, been reflected in appointments in the bureaucracy, which, even under the EPRDF, have continued to be personal, with accountability to those who appointed the person rather than to the fulfilment of clearly defined duties. Loyalty to the party is, as expressed by Prime Minister Meles Zenawi on television, more important than competence. The separation of positions into politically appointed officials and administrative officials, which followed the split in the TPLF in 2001, seems to have had no impact on the decentralisation of the state.

Although the judiciary is constitutionally independent of the executive, practice shows that there are close links between the two. With the take-over of power in 1991 a large number of judges that had been working under the Derg were dismissed. New judges, supportive of the EPRDF party were appointed, but their number was not enough to fill all positions. Lack of personnel did not result in fewer imprisonments, though. There have been many political arrests with their cases pending due to lack of prosecutors and judges. Today there is a general distrust of the judiciary. Experiences have shown according to both peasants and representatives of the middle classes that what one person can do with impunity others cannot. Such observations and comments are made about political as well as economic transactions both in private conversations and in the press and these experiences seem to add to a general climate of insecurity and distrust of the judicial system. Although new judges are recruited and trained the dependence of the judiciary on the executive has as yet not changed (see also Vaughan and Tronvoll 2003:98–100).

In the economic sphere, the 1999/2000 report by the Ethiopian Economic Association indicates that the Ethiopian economy "did reasonably well ... between 1991 and 1998" (EEA 1999/2000:12). This judgement is partly contradicted by the data presented later in the report, where it is said that agriculture, (upon which a majority of the population is dependent) 'performed better during the last ten years of the Derg at an average rate of growth of two per cent than during the post-reform period at 1.6 per cent' (ibid.:17). This is related to a population growth of about three per cent per annum implying that there has rather been deterioration in the standard of living. The liberalising measures in agriculture such as the elimination of price controls, the abolition of quotas and the ability to hire labour (ibid.:196) are commended in the EEA. But the land policy is criticized for discouraging investments in land. While the GDP share for agriculture has been about 55 per cent for the last 18 years, the share for industry has remained static averaging about 10.6 per cent (ibid.:16).

Although the EPRDF officially subscribes to the support of private capital within the economy the EEA study mentions that there are still serious limits to free investment, entrepreneurship and free competition. All land is also government controlled and can neither be bought nor sold. The possible impact this may have on the farmers' concern for, interest and investment in their land is today a hotly debated issue outside the party. Inside the party it does not seem to be an issue since government control of land has been inscribed in the constitution.

What is called the private sector is actually mainly made up of two core groups, the Midroc business empire, owned by Sheik Mohammed Alamoudi and the party-associated enterprises, the so-called EFFORT. The Midroc enterprise accounted for almost 70 per cent of the foreign investment (EEA 1999/2000:41). EFFORT stands for the Endowment Fund for the Rehabilitation of Tigray and was established in 1995 by the TPLF. Their activities range from agriculture to trade, textiles, livestock, mining, transport and the finance sector. Members of the party manage the Fund. This dominance in the private sector of especially party-owned enterprises has made the emergence of new private entrepreneurs close to impossible.

There has furthermore been little investment and consequently little development in technology, either to improve agriculture or industry. According to the EEA 'Ethiopia's agricultural labour productivity is one of the lowest in the world' (ibid.:197), counted in value added per agricultural worker. On top of this the contribution of the manufacturing industry is not only low, but the trend has also declined or stagnated (ibid.:240). As a whole it seems as if despite radical liberalising laws with regard to private investment not much has really happened and the ruling party continues to direct much of the economy through the state machinery and through the party enterprises, EFFORT.

The war with Eritrea in 1998 appears to be another factor that strained the overall economic performance. Following the EPRDF take-over in 1991, the number of people employed in the army had been drastically reduced. As a result of the crisis, the military sphere has again increased dramatically. Thus the expenses involved in equipping a large army as well as the expenses of waging a major war are considered to be one of the most important reasons for the poor economic performance since 1998 (Vaughan and Tronvoll 2003:102, 103).

With regard to education the EPRDF has as its objective to reach universal primary enrolment in schools by the year 2015. Education opportunities have expanded since the Derg and the net enrolment ratio has almost reached 50 per cent (Educational Statistics Annual Abstract 2001:5). This has been achieved through increasing the number of children per class but also through an increase in the number of teachers. New schools and institutions to train teachers are being built all over the country, local languages are used as media of instruction in the primary grades and books in the various languages are produced. The shortages to overcome are, however, enormous. There are budgetary deficiencies, a shortage of teachers, of schools and of books. The share of education in total expenditure decreased from 16.1 per cent in 1995/96 to 9.6 per cent in 1999/2000 (EEA 2000/01:205) and between the years 1993 and 1997 education was only four per cent of the GNP indicating the limited government interest in the subject despite its grand visions.

What has been obvious up to now is that despite a liberal rhetoric, and maybe also good intentions to promote a market economy and decentralize the state, the present Ethiopian government has not really broken with its historical past but continues to follow a tradition according to which all political and economic activities are controlled by the centre. The government's inability or unwillingness to change may be closely bound up with its Tigray experiences and its ideology. In Tigray the peasantry had been successfully mobilised because, the TPLF argued, they constituted a homogeneous group with similar needs, interests and political outlook (see Vaughan and Tronvoll 2003:117). According to the party history all major decisions were first discussed at various levels in the party before conclusions about what to do were agreed upon. The party followed the principle of democratic centralism and, it is said, gained legitimacy because they were able to 'deliver the goods', such as freedom from the Derg, food aid etc. The strength of the party was thus bound up first with its internal discussions and then its capacity to deliver economic and political success. As a consequence, Vaughan and Tronvoll argue, this process 'generates "all the right language": it emphasises all of the factors thought desirable by most liberal democrats (decentralisation, participation, inclusiveness of discussion, etc.). It also invests each with a markedly different meaning…' (ibid.:117). The implications of this approach have thus been the opposite, control has been kept at the centre, the established hierarchy has been respected, and the collective, in the form of the ethnic group has been understood to be more important than the individual. Consequently people-state relations under the EPRDF do not differ much from those under previous governments. Similar patterns have over time been re-enacted in discourses and through interactions between leaders of the state and its various citizens resulting in the recreation of similar cultural schemas. Summarizing the characteristics of successive Ethiopian regimes Kassahun Berhanu (2000:210) states:

In a way it could therefore be argued that the basic foundations of the authoritarian mode of governance in Ethiopia remained basically unaltered with the ever-present omnipotence of the state towering over society. The common trait that can be attributed to the successive Ethiopian political regimes as to their behaviour is that all were keen to appropriate the lion's share of available political and economic space. This was mostly to the detriment of the welfare and autonomous development of society, and at the expense of popular participation in government.

A CULTURAL MODEL OF PATRON–CLIENT RELATIONS

The centralisation of the state, which characterised Ethiopia's history between 1855 and 1974, has continued until today. Emphasis has been, and continues to be, on a strong state, which can control both its borders and its citizens. The distinctive pattern of relations that has developed between emperor or head of state and various employees in the government offices, the military or the police and between these, especially officials in the bureaucracy at various levels, and the Ethiopian people can be characterised as patron–client relations.

The patrons at the top have based their positions on a number of different criteria like inheritance, being the elect of God, having economic resources and, being men. The decisive factor has always been that they have had command over an army with which they have succeeded in eliminating all competitors to the position. The major means through which the Ethiopian heads of state have risen to power and kept the position once they have achieved it has been through establishing links with other 'strong men' whom they have wanted as followers. The intention has been to make clients fulfil their wishes and to eliminate all competition to the patronage. The close patron–client relationship has been necessary for the ruler to be able to control his clients.

The patron–client relationship has had its own rules regulating expectations and interactions between the parties. All have been based on some kind of mutuality of interests since even clients expect to get something out of their positions that they otherwise would not obtain. Patrons expected and ideally received the undiluted loyalty of their clients who should work hard in their service. Clients, on the other hand, could be given land, jobs, salaries and other economic advantages they were in need of. There was also prestige attached to the various positions and it was a reward in itself to be in the favour of a strong ruler with whom emotional bonds were often established.

The rules were clear and patrons had to protect their clients, show them benevolence but also know them personally. Clients, in turn, should show deference, obedience and respect for their patron, but above all, be loyal to him. In the case of the bureaucracy this loyalty and need to obey has often seemed to imply not to take any initiatives on your own, not even act unless somebody in a superior position has told you to. In as much as rulers could dismiss their clients the latter could also criticize their patrons for not living up to their expectations or not following the rules. In the Amhara tradition for example there is still the use of **sam enna werk**, or wax and gold, a verse according to Levine (1972:5) with 'two semantic layers. The apparent, figurative meaning of the words is called the "wax"; their more or less hidden actual significance is the "gold"'. The client's criticism could thereby be hidden as the gold in the verse. Yet, although a certain amount of criticism was possible, a client could do very little if the patron wanted to get rid of or dismiss him. The right of appointment and dismissal, the **shum shir**, was the prerogative of the patron.

The strength of the system was emphasized by the fact that everybody knew how to behave and could read and interpret each other's acts. Since the rules were so clear within the collective where patrons and clients found themselves, it also gave members a certain sense of security. At the same time everyone was convinced that the hierarchy was flexible and that anyone, or at least any man, could reach the top of it. This flexibility of the hierarchical system and the knowledge that patrons usually reached their positions through devious schemes may be what gives the pattern its opposite characteristic feature, namely a general sense of insecurity about whom you can really trust. Patrons expect loyalty but can never be sure if they are getting it. They know that any client, just like they themselves previously, will try to improve his condition and if he finds a better patron his loyalty will be lost. Clients also know that there is usually an end to their patron's good will so they must make alternative plans. This insecurity has made it legitimate for clients 'to eat' while they have the position and the opportunity to do so, meaning that they and those surrounding them expect them to take bribes or dues to make up for the time when they will lose their job and be out of favour with their patron. This is expressed as 'he who did not 'eat' while in power will regret it when demoted' (**teshomo yalbella sishar yeqochewal**).

The collective to which the heads of state historically felt allegiance was to an Ethiopia not always clearly defined but often understood as in opposition to the various European countries, while under the present regime the most important collective is the ethnic group. Associated with the collectives are the moral responsibilities that rulers have to the population. As rulers they should keep law and order in the country without which people cannot live. Today, however, peace is no longer enough, instead peasants and workers also expect the government to bring them an improved livelihood consisting of schools, food, agricultural inputs and a higher standard of living.

There are problems with the economy, though. Similar to the period 1855–1974 the major preoccupation of the later rulers of the Ethiopian state has been the defence of the country from all perceived internal and external opponents. This has implied that all major investments have focussed on obtaining a strong military and police force. As a consequence there has been little growth in the economy over the past 150 years. The country is poor in natural resources and the soil, from which the large majority of the population still has to survive, is, due to outmoded techniques, depleted of nutrients. There have been few investments in new technology or basic industries. Support has been limited to food, beverages and light industry. Infrastructure like roads, electricity, hospitals, tele-communication are at an extremely low level. Institutional capital (de Vylder 2002) such as faith in public institutions like the legal system and the press is lack-ing and the social capital or confidence and trust in the government and its insti-tutions as fair and predictable seems to be at an ebb. The only exception is the non-government local level organisations, which are characterized by human decency and horizontal relationships.

The educational standard in Ethiopia is, furthermore, one of the lowest in the world. Not only that, however, the contents of the education and the way knowl-edge is perceived and transmitted does not promote critical thinking or people who formulate new questions or look for new answers; neither is this required within the state bureaucracy today. The educational system instead helps produce passive officials who can agree to do only what they are told to and thereby main-tain the state apparatus as it is.

The ideology, which initially supported the patron–client model for the Ethiopian state consisted of cooperation between church and state where emper-ors were anointed as the elected of God and considered as father figures for the population. The Derg's legitimating discourse was made up of a socialist rhetoric where everything was done in the name of the people. Today's rhetoric is similar, although other concepts more in line with a democratic discourse have replaced those connected with socialism.

To sum up it seems as if one of the major weaknesses of the cultural schema of patron–client relations, which has dominated interactions between the leaders of the Ethiopian state and the people for the last 150 years, is the insecurity on which it is built. All the leaders have sooner or later worried that their clients were, maybe, not loyal. This concern has forced them to expend both energy and funds in an ever stricter control over an increasingly larger number of the popu-lation, giving priority to investments promoting control, rather than to the devel-opment of the country.

Chapter 9

CONTINUITY AND PRECONDITIONS FOR CHANGE

The question which initiated my research about Ethiopian children was 'Why do hierarchical modes of government have such durable forms?' In this last chapter I shall try to answer the question by reviewing some of the factors discussed earlier which, I argue, have had a great impact on the continuity or durability of cultural schemas. I shall start by summarizing some of the mechanisms through which Birabiro children learned how to communicate with others 'properly', according to local understandings, and how they learned to interpret events in similar ways. Next I want to review some of the crucial aspects of what they learned, considered important and with which they identified. I shall then bring the *how* and the *what* the children learned together and discuss how their interactions came to structure their cultural schemas and promote their durability.

Cultural schemas show many similarities with the work of organisations and bureaucracies that also have a tendency to perpetuate their patterned system of rules. A closer look at the mechanisms that tend to strengthen and reconstitute existing modes of work in organisations sheds further light on the reproduction of cultural schemas in state bureaucracies too. A key ingredient in the analysis of organisations and how they function is the concept of power. Experiences of how power works in organisations can, if applied to the dominant cultural schema in Ethiopia, also help us better understand its durability despite revolutions and an exchange of people in power.

There is not only continuity, however. Change happens, although it is an ambiguous phenomenon with both negative and positive implications. Change always implies a loss of that which was, that which will be altered as a result of the change. Individuals frequently adapt and change, even though system or cultural schema change seems to be more difficult to bring about. In conclusion, I shall here not dwell on what may cause change in the dominant cultural schema in Ethiopia, or what may be considered as desired change by various interest groups, since such a discussion would obviously have required another book than the one I have written. Instead I want to conclude with some preliminary ideas about what seem to be preconditions for system change, conditions that may be necessary for change to appear mentally and physically possible to people anywhere, not only in Ethiopia. In my argument I shall lean on our previous discussion about how continuity is reproduced and apply the insights we have gained to a number of anthropological cases dealing with change.

CONTINUITY OF CULTURAL SCHEMAS AND ORGANIZATIONS
Birabiro school children and cultural continuity

To manage in society children learn how to communicate, understand and deal with the systems of rules and regulations, which dominate in their environment and are considered as proper modes of communication. Children learn about these forms, their raison d'être and emotions attached to them through observing, interacting and negotiating with other children and adults. The experiences children get from these activities teach them what it is possible to do, what works and what they cannot do. Not only words are used to communicate norms, values or emotions, children also express themselves through body movements, postures, gestures and facial expressions. We could see how the Birabiro children showed respect for adults through bowed heads, eyes on the floor and shrinking bodies and how they accepted punishments when not having done their homework, even saying that a beating was good for them. Practising and testing how things worked were other key ingredients in their learning process and Ahmed's and Batnori's explanations about their diary notes illustrate how Ahmed learned that erasers and exercise books could vary in quality and Batnori understood what should be included to make a social event successful. Many children also saw some of their teachers as role models and tried to copy their behaviour.

What the Birabiro children learned was that most relations in their surroundings were hierarchical where one person was super- and another subordinate. Their way of reasoning has shown that they took it for granted that each party to a relationship, like a parent or adult relative and a child, should provide something the other needed but also that those in higher positions were considered more important than those in lower. Children's subordination thus implied that they needed to ingratiate themselves with adults, show them deference and execute their wishes.

The children referred to the hierarchical system as relationships carried out within a collective, usually the extended family, the religious group or even Ethiopia. The collective was important because it provided children with security, love and control for which they were expected to reciprocate and show loyalty, respect and dutifulness. There were rights as well as obligations within the collective and it was your right to be taken care of and to be part of the redistribution of assets but it was also your duty to take on adult responsibilities when your turn came.

The hierarchy within the children's various collectives was strict in the sense that a person with a higher rank or position should always be shown the right degree of deference. Yet, the system was flexible and always in a process of change. Children and their parents strongly believed that if they worked hard and their luck (**edel**) was with them there was no end to what they could become. There was an incredible optimism in the children's ideas about the future. No one expressed the thought that background or position could influence school results, and apart from those girls who criticised their workload at home there was no reference to unequal opportunities. There was, however, a great awareness of the importance of having connections (**zemed allew** – he has a relative) if you wanted a job or to advance in your career. Despite their feeling of belonging to the various collectives and doing what was expected of them some children still expressed a sense of insecurity, worrying that adults might in the end not fulfil their role, either because they were unable to or because they for some reason did not want to.

In school, at home and in their religious institution Birabiro children learned to conceptualise knowledge as something immutable, that existed in limited amounts and with which you should try to fill yourself as far as possible. In class children were taught to learn their facts by heart through repetition but very few would assimilate or process what they had learned. Thus they were not taught to use information to revise or question what they already knew or to ask new questions. The thought that there could be information or knowledge not yet discovered but waiting to be developed and understood did not seem to be part of the children's conceptualisation of it.

The ways in which the children learned to communicate and act in their society and the content of what they learned together helped to instantiate already existing modes of thinking in their own minds. According to the discussion by Strauss and Quinn (1997), referred to earlier, we take in new information through learned and innate structures and sort new information according to previous knowledge and categories; information processing thus in itself tends to emphasize what is already established in our minds and is part of our ways of thinking and acting. The knowledge we have and the feelings we tend to connect with various events that triggered it are furthermore strengthened by the fact that much of what is learnt in early childhood is connected with strong emotions, of love, survival, security and their opposites. Much information thus becomes deeply buried in the child and is later taken for granted and considered 'natural'. These factors appear to be some of the reasons why we often do not reflect upon why we think or act in certain ways, but take it for granted while at the same time the lack of reflection, in itself, tends to promote continuity.

The content of what the Birabiro children learned and integrated with their previous experiences thus became part of their identity; positive events provided them with a sense of security while negative incidents could be the cause of anxiety, fear or worry. Children tended to emphasize the flexibility in the hierarchical system probably because it offered them an opportunity to become what they wanted. They also expressed a feeling of security in the collective and seemed to enjoy the thought that one day they would be responsible for others who would look up to them for help. The acceptance of the hierarchy was more pronounced among the boys, however; yet only a few girls questioned it openly. Established ideas and rules of behaviour were difficult to contest, both because questioning in itself could bring about harsh sanctions, as the treatment of Messelesh bore witness to, but also because there was very little alternative information or experience that could make them query that which was already in existence.

Mechanisms and processes promoting schema and organisational continuity

From acts of individual children it is possible to understand how a system of understanding or a cultural schema can develop. Despite the fact that the experiences of each child were personal, and as such affected by her or his gender, class and religious background, acts, negotiations and discussions carried out by individual children could still promote similar cultural schemas. What seems to have facilitated the sharing was that even when reflections, readings, observations of people or of TV programmes were conducted individually, they were later discussed with other children or compared with previous experiences thereby creating more or less shared understandings among the children. As discussed by Strauss and Quinn (1997), individual experiences also tend to cluster together and become themes with similar interpretations. In this way, the processes, according to which cultural schemas were developed, adapted and changed, showed many similarities with organisations.

Like cultural schemas the work of organizations is premised upon specific patterns of behaviour established among their members. According to Clegg, the system of rules guiding behaviour in organizations informs the members of 'who may do what, how, where, when and in which ways to whatever objects or agents' (1989:196). And, even if all the members are not equally well acquainted with the rules and rulings of other departments in an organisation or among people sharing a cultural schema there are always supervisors who act as gate-keepers at different levels and see to it that rules are followed and individual influences or disturbances minimized.

Most organizations, including the state, are based on some kind of employer–employee relationship and, depending on their size, they will have few or many positions in between. They are thus hierarchical with explicit lines of order and decision-making. An example of this hierarchy is the career structure in the police or army, where orders are taken without questioning. In the Birabiro school we could similarly see how teachers learned to be responsible to their superiors, like the school director and team leader, through written documentation the importance of which they also taught the children in class.

Organizations obtain and perpetuate their patterned system of rules, according to Clegg (ibid.) through control, mainly acquired through 'disciplinary power' (Foucault 1977). Disciplinary power is a form of surveillance, which helps perpetuate the subordination in the organization through for example personal supervision, the routinization of work, division of labour, mechanization and legislation. Surveillance can, in other words, be personal, technical, bureaucratic or legal and, Clegg argues, seeks 'to effect increasing control of employees' behaviour, dispositions and embodiment' (ibid.:191). Disciplinary power works in such a way as to make individuals and subgroups internalise dominant rules and principles preferably to such a degree that they even frame their ways of thinking and prevent the emergence of thoughts considered to be outside the scope of the organization. Strauss and Quinn (1997) offer similar arguments for how cultural schemas work.

What further promotes the continuity of an existing system of rules in organizations is repetition. Interactions take place repeatedly both between individuals and collectives. This implies a steady repetition of the relations between various social identities as well as of the rules and rituals, which guide their work, making both the positions people inhabit and the rules guiding their interactions ever more firmly established and taken for granted.

Repetition is also what makes cultural schemas so durable. The children's repeated practice in interactions with others resulted in what Bourdieu calls habitus (1977), flexible dispositions rather than rules, which guided them in new encounters. These dispositions became both mentally and physically embodied in the children since even bodies tend to remember what they have done and what has happened to them. The embodiment was further emphasized when, as discussed by Strauss and Quinn (1997), experiences were associated with strong emotions. In this way it became difficult, as Connerton (1989) reminds us, to separate the past from the present since we tend to recollect and reflect on the past in the light of present factors and to experience the present through our knowledge of the past.

In organizations time further provides, according to Clegg (1989:227–230), for 'institutional isomorphism', referring to how an innovation once made can become widely adopted. The concept and discussion are referenced to DiMaggio and Powell (1983) who identified three different processes, which have a strong bearing on how institutions become more or less similar, all of which were also conspicuous in Ethiopian history. The first has to do with *coercive* pressure like state legislation, routines and similar control mechanisms. These can be applied to dependent agencies, which as a result over time tend to conform. Then there is what is called *mimetic* pressure, which means using a well-known and well functioning example as a model. The innovation will thereby in fact not be abrupt since it at least partly becomes a repetition of something already in existence. This is exemplified by the 'Japanization' of the industrial arena. Finally there is what is called *normative* pressure, meaning the spread of for example minimum or standardized qualifications from their areas of origin, like universities, to spheres where these qualifications were earlier not required.

Mann's theory of 'organizational outflanking' (1986) is, according to Clegg (1989), another reason why radical change is so rare. The theory refers to why the dominated so frequently consent to their subordination.[1] According to Mann

---

1. This subject was also discussed with respect to gender in Chapter 6.

(ibid.), this is because the subordinate lack collective organizations to do otherwise. There may be a number of reasons for this, like ignorance of how organizations function, of strategy, of how to get or change an agenda, of how to handle and change routine procedures and, not least, of how to build alliances or even the possibility and necessity for building them (Clegg ibid.:220).

This absence of action on behalf of themselves, which according to Mann (ibid.), characterizes the dominated and was noted for women and girls in the Birabiro setting, is strongly emphasized by Barnes (1993), who argues that we perpetually validate a knowledge system when we re-enact rather than reject it. To exemplify the stability of an established knowledge system Barnes takes the case of Stalin, whose name can be substituted with that of any other authoritarian leader, saying:

> Stalin's underlings had knowledge of Stalin and of each other. They knew he was everywhere obeyed. Knowing what they did, they obeyed him. By their obedience they confirmed the validity of what they knew, and continued to accept it as valid. Acceptance of the knowledge generated confirming instances of it. Rejection of the knowledge would have led to disconfirming instances. As a system, knowledge of the power structure was self-referring and self-validating; indeed knowledge of the power structure was the power structure. The overall system of domination and obedience had the character of a vast monumental self-fulfilling prophecy.

> If social life is constituted by the actions of responsible knowledgeable agents, then this is how we should understand the basis of such stability and orderliness, as it possesses. Not just crude systems of domination and obedience, but all manner of organisations, institutions and hierarchies are constituted as systems of self-referring knowledge, and persist as self-fulfilling prophecies (Barnes 1993:215).[1]

The factors discussed above as active in promoting continuity of an existing system of rules in organisations, were also functional in the Birabiro school. In school there were both formal and informal gate-keepers that followed up on what teachers were doing. Control within the hierarchy was rigid and well established. It was easy to effectuate control through the use of the written report system backed by disciplinary power that could result in punishments such as dismissal from school or rewards in the form of a higher salary or an advance in the career. Institutional isomorphism was also functional in the Birabiro school and teachers observed and made comments on how they were forced to keep silent and not discuss certain subjects in different kinds of meetings, thereby being subjected to both coercive and normative pressure. The mechanisms involved in organisational outflanking, like the absence of collective organisation to question the existing system of rules, were partly applicable to the Birabiro school situation. Ethiopian teachers used to have their own independent Teachers' Association but their chairperson had been put in prison and their organisation outlawed and replaced by one controlled by the government party. Although some

---

1. See also Vaughan and Tronvoll (2003:29ff) for a further discussion on this subject.

teachers did not want to participate in the new organisation the harsh control made it difficult for them to stay outside. The knowledge system as discussed above by Barnes (1993), was thus reconfirmed through daily practices in the Birabiro school as well as in surrounding schools and in society at large.

The situation was similar in the Ethiopian state where cadres, police and the army acted as gate-keepers at all levels of society. Control through personal, technical, bureaucratic and legal measures has been extremely elaborate. Institutional isomorphism, especially through coercive pressure, has been upheld and organisational outflanking has been the order of the day, as described in, for example, a number of election reports (Pausewang 1994, 2001, Pausewang et al. 2002, Aspen 1995, Donor Election Unit 1995, Tronvoll and Aadland 1995, Poluha 1997). The general sense of insecurity and unpredictability, or lack of social and institutional capital at the national and regional levels, with quick reprisals from the political hierarchy for deeds considered unacceptable, have further acted to reconfirm the existing knowledge system. The present organisation has furthermore been difficult to challenge since the government controls the major media and the few published private newspapers do not reach outside Addis Abeba. New information, whether it would have challenged the government or provided alternative ideas or not, has thus been difficult to come by and the government's need to control the spread of information has worked against a general acquisition of new knowledge. The authoritarian rule of the Ethiopian state has been further promoted by the very limited economic and technological change that has taken place over the past 150 years. The power of continuity in an Ethiopia which discourages individual initiatives and encourages obedience is thus impressive.

PRECONDITIONS FOR CHANGE

Some cases

As everywhere there are signs of change both in individuals, cultural schemas and the state. Change perpetually occurs in individuals who all have their own personalities and do change as a result of their experiences. Sometimes these changes may be of major importance but even when the change is minor it may be significant to the individual. As discussed by de Saussure (1974) it is never possible to freeze the meaning of a relationship between what is called 'the signified and the sign'. There is always ambiguity, where each exchange is exposed to a new interpretation and various forms of resistance. This can be exemplified with the daily interactions of the Birabiro children who changed and became more knowledgeable as a result of their new experiences and practices

More radical transformations than what individual difference may imply can, as argued by Strauss and Quinn (1997), take place as a result of changes in living conditions, which, for example, may occur between generations. Thus, what mothers or fathers did may not be possible or even desirable for their children.

Or the other way around, Birabiro children went to school while most of their parents had not been able to attend classes. In the West, parents used to take care of their children at home until school started. Today this is no longer possible since both the mother and the father need to earn an income to maintain their standard of living or even to survive. Another reason for a change of practices may be due to new living conditions when members of a younger generation no longer find it motivating to do what their parents and they themselves previously did and start doing something else instead. Consequently there may be a number of reasons why people change depending both on the individuals and the circumstances in which they find themselves. The girls and boys who in their essays questioned the gendered division of work and the tasks girls had to perform and those girls who refused to accept the adult distrust of children and what they had learnt in school about AIDS, are examples of such change.

To go a little further in this very preliminary discussion about preconditions for change I shall briefly summarize a few cases from the anthropological literature. All the cases deal with social change, but from somewhat different perspectives. My interest in the cases is related to what they can tell us about the preconditions for change in the contexts where they took place; how these experiences relate to what has been discussed as mechanisms and processes promoting continuity; and what the cases can tell us about preconditions for change in general, including in Ethiopia.

In a discussion about language shift in a Papua New Guinea village Kulick (1992) illustrates the complexity of what we may call unintended large-scale change. In the small village of Gapun, where he did fieldwork, each generation used their vernacular in ever fewer situations thereby gradually losing it. They were aware of what was happening, blamed it on their children and regretted it because they liked their own language. Kulick depicts how over the years the villagers had contact with white Christians, who were conspicuous for having money, machines, factory-made clothes, medicines and such like. The whites always talked about development and slowly the Gapun people began forming and formulating their own ideas of development relating it to what the whites owned and said. The Gapun children furthermore started going to schools where only English was allowed as a means of communication. Tok Pisin, one of the official languages, was frequently but secretly used but never the vernacular. In school the children also learned about people in foreign countries but never about their own headmen, or their own myths or rituals, knowledge which consequently appeared less important. In addition, the vernacular could not help the Gapun develop because to communicate with any person of significance they needed to use Tok Pisin. Their vernacular did not even have words for the Christian religion. Unconsciously the vernacular became associated with the past while the Gapun were looking to the future, they wanted to 'kam-ap'. In everyday practice and through setting their minds to a 'developed' future the Gapun therefore made little use of the vernacular even when they communicated with their own offspring.

The change and loss of the Gapun vernacular thus came about as a result of a number of complex factors, but all revolved around the implications of development by which they were attracted.

In another case Freeman (2002) approaches change from a somewhat different perspective. Comparing the impact of outside influences on two types of decision-making systems in the Gamu Highlands in southern Ethiopia, Freeman argues that the quality of social relations within a decision-making system has a great impact on whether change will take place or not. In the decision-making system people used for initiations social relations were egalitarian and based on network relations. This system was, according to Freeman easy to change and it changed fast because minor changes had repeated effects at several levels of the system. The decision-making system used for sacrificial rituals, on the other hand, had a pyramidal form and did not result in change. The reason, according to Freeman, was that it had many nodes and each level was fairly independent of the others (compare Clegg 1989). Change at one level therefore had few repercussions on the system as a whole and change at the lower levels had very little impact on those above them. This Freeman attributes to the fact that those at higher levels had more contact with those at the lower than the other way round thereby preventing those at the bottom from knowing about how things functioned beyond their own level, and also making it difficult for them to influence their own level and even harder to have an impact on levels higher up. Accordingly, Freeman argues that change in a system with egalitarian decision-making is relatively easy, fast and may involve many people, while in a system where decision-making is hierarchical it is difficult, slow and will only involve a few people.

In his discussion on change Clegg (1989) argues that change will only be successful if important agencies that dispute old discourses are able to have an impact on key arenas in their respective organizations. Clegg depicts the functioning of organizations, like the establishment and implementation of rules, regulations, orders and hierarchies, as taking place within 'circuits of power' where the traffic follows pre-established routes. Along these routes there are what Clegg calls 'nodal points', something like key arenas, positions or places with people who do what is expected of them. As links in a chain they follow and redistribute rules and orders they have received to their respective departments and further in the chain thereby reconfirming and validating the system. It is only when some such agency succeeds in establishing new nodal points or in changing the order or content of those which exist, that the whole organization may change and take on new practices, discourses or routines.

To understand about change we must therefore, if we follow Clegg, study how such 'nodal points' function. We must learn to identify them, together with the practices and knowledge that exist within them, and distinguish what is taken for granted, as well as recognize what may already be contested. Contradictions between different discourses at such 'nodal points' seem, according to Clegg, to be the key to change. Illustrating how such 'nodal points' can be identified and analysed without referring to them in these terms, Wright (1998b:3) argues that:

> A particular way of seeing or of thinking gains authority from being placed in particular sites, like a national museum or gallery or by being spoken from particular places, like national television or parliament, or by being written into legislation. At its most authoritative a particular meaning of a key concept or symbol becomes 'natural' or 'common sense', 'taken for granted' as if it were nothing to do with politics and power. At this stage, the idea can be called hegemonic. However, even the most hegemonic ideas can be contested, unsettled and changed. The dominance of one way of thinking about an idea or symbol is only sustained as long as all alternative ideas are made 'unimaginable' or 'unspeakable'.

Gusterson (1998) provides another example although along similar lines in a discussion about nuclear armaments. In his study Gusterson analyses the case of how one "totalizing discourse' – an account which depicts existing political and ideological systems as true' (ibid.:3) – is contested by an emerging and quickly growing opposite discourse which eventually succeeds in gaining the upper hand. The first discourse described by Gusterson revolves around the axiomatic understanding that to prevent nuclear war you must have nuclear arms as these will act as a deterrent to any war; in other words, you must arm yourself to obtain peace. The emerging discourse, which questioned the hegemony of the first, not only argued that the production of nuclear arms in itself was dangerous but also that it did not have the capacity to prevent war.

Gusterson illustrates how the struggle between defenders and opponents of nuclear arms was carried out in waves with advances and withdrawals on both sides. The number of people engaged on each side was highly disproportionate since more personal engagement and many more people were required to contest the hegemonic discourse than to defend it. It was a political and ideological struggle about public finances and about the state's investment priorities. The nuclear physicists and politicians tried to keep the 'deterrence' argument as an axiom to retain the hegemonic discourse while the opposition provided the public with an alternative discourse, showing how nuclear arms were dangerous, expensive and could not prevent war, arguments which even politicians had to take into consideration when making decisions.

Using Clegg's terminology we can say that the anti nuclear war camp had to establish new circuits and nodal points for their specific discourse to emerge, take form and gain acceptance by a wider public. To keep their own arguments at the top of the agenda the struggle required an enormous amount of energy from a large number of people, much more than was required from those who defended the established knowledge system. The opponents momentarily succeeded in reducing the amount of money that the state invested in nuclear arms. They did not, however, succeed in changing major circuits of power or nodal points or in establishing a new hegemonic discourse or knowledge system, since investments in nuclear arms are again on the government's agenda in the USA.

In a less successful case Susan Wright discusses how an attempt to 'unsettle' the negative associations adhering to a key concept failed. Arguing that change can be seen as a process where contestations 'over the meaning of key terms and concepts' (1998a:9) takes place, Wright distinguishes three stages in this process. The first occurs when some agents attempt to redefine key symbols, which give a particular view of the world. The second stage takes place when such a view becomes institutionalised through for example laws or regulations, and works through non-agentive power, shaping perceptions, values and behaviour. The third stage occurs when a key term, which carries a new way of thinking about one aspect of life, enters other domains and becomes part of a way of thinking. Wright exemplifies the first two stages with the case of a contest over the state's attitude to homosexuality in Britain.[1] To counter the negative attitude to homosexuals prevalent in British schools a group started to campaign for 'positive images'. Their term 'positive' was, however, hijacked by conservative MPs and reinterpreted as 'promoting homosexuality'. Successive parliamentary debates confirmed the interpretation that 'promote' actually meant the seduction of 'normal' children and was an attack on 'the family', equated with 'subversion'. The MPs later managed to introduce a new clause in the legislation barring the use of resources to 'promote' the acceptability of homosexuality as a 'pretended family relationship'. This clause later also resulted in fewer funds for gay people and the further spread of negative stereotyping.

PRELIMINARY CONCLUSIONS

What then, can these examples tell us about preconditions for change? First it seems as if access to new critical and/or attractive information is necessary for an established discourse to be opened up and identified. The new information must either contradict or, at least, pose an alternative to the old knowledge or the already established practices. This is for example what happened in the case of language change in Papua New Guinea, where people learned about and were attracted by all that they associated with 'development'. It was also the case in the anti-nuclear movement, where the discourse stating that 'nuclear arms are necessary to prevent nuclear war' was opened up and questioned. New, critical information made it possible for people to see previously established truths in a new perspective.

New knowledge was also what promoted change according to Freeman's (2002) description of the Gamu Highlands. But knowledge proved, in this case, not to be enough. It was, according to Freeman only in the decision-making system which was egalitarian that change could take place. Although all organizations can be said to have nodal points it appears obvious that the more there are, the more difficult it is to introduce change. Each nodal point and its guardians

---

1. Taken from a study by Reinhold 1993.

will act to prevent the spread of new information and to reduce the number of people who will engage in the activities. In the Gamu Highlands where the decision-making system for initiations had few nodal points and few guardians change was fast and reached many people while in the hierarchical system it did not have the same effect.

In the USA the fight against nuclear arms would not have succeeded had the anti-nuclear camp not been able to use the media. Information was available but the activists also knew that although there were many and various guardians trying to prevent the nuclear research programme from being questioned, they still had the legal right to contest it and do so openly. The rules of the game were known to all and similar, irrespective of person or position. In such a secure political situation the activists were able to criticise and question established views, including those of the government. They could predict the consequences of their chosen actions and interventions, gauge their options and estimate the effects of their acts. For these reasons accessibility to media and an 'open' society were preconditions without which the movement could not have expanded. In spite of these preconditions being in place, to incur change, not only in the discourse but to actually reduce the budget for nuclear research and gain the upper hand over all the gate-keepers, it was necessary for a large number of people to fight not only in different arenas but also for an extended period of time.

In the last case, which constituted an attempt to promote the situation for homosexuals in Britain, the required information was available; the rules of the game were clear, predictable and well known, yet the attempt failed. The reason, I think, has to do with the power of continuity as discussed earlier, the institutional isomorphism, the way the organisation was rule-bounded and, not least, a general awareness of the knowledge system where informed gate-keepers worked actively to prevent change.

To conclude I would like to say that even when there is access to alternative, attractive and manageable information; when there is a system which, even if hierarchical, allows for discussion and spread of information, and there are secure and predictable rules of the game, these circumstances can only be seen as preconditions which make change possible, in Ethiopia and elsewhere. They do not imply that change will follow. Rather it seems as if the mechanisms and processes that promote continuity in cultural schemas and organisations are so powerful that change becomes an exception rather than a rule.

References

Abu Lugod, L., 1991, "Writing Against Culture", in Fox, R. (ed.), *Recapturing Anthropology.* Santa Fe: School of American Research Press.

Alemayyehu Moges, 1973, "Language teaching and curricula in traditional education of the Ethiopian Orthodox Church", *Ethiopian Journal of Education,* Vol. 6, No. 1:87–115.

Alula Abate, 1983, "Peasant Associations and Collective Agriculture in Ethiopia: Promise and Performance", *Journal of African Studies,* 10(3):97–108.

Ambjörnsson, Fanny, 1997, "Med kroppen som fiende: om fem unga kvinnors upplevelse av kropp och identitet", *Antropologiska Studier,* Nr. 58–59, pp. 53–61.

Anderson, Benedict, 1991, *Imagined Communities: Reflections on the Origin and Spread of Nationalism.* London: Verso.

Ardener, Edwin, (1972) 1977 , "Belief and the Problem of Women", in Ardener, Shirley (ed.), *Perceiving Women.* London: J.M. Dent and Sons Ltd.

Ardener, Shirley, 1977, "Introduction", in Ardener, Shirley (ed.), *Perceiving Women.* London: J.M. Dent and Sons Ltd.

—, 1993, "Ground Rules and Social Maps for Women: An Introduction", in Ardener, Shirley (ed.), *Women and Space. Ground Rules and Social Maps.* Oxford: Berg.

Ardener, S. and S. Burman, (eds), 1995, *Money-Go-Rounds. The Importance of Saving and Credit Associations for Women.* Oxford: Berg.

Aspen, H., 1995, *The 1995 National and Regional Elections in Ethiopia: Local Perspectives.* The University of Trondheim, SMU, Working Paper, No. 10.

Bailey, F.G., 1978, "Tertius Gaudens aut Tertium Numen", in Barth, Fredrik (ed.), *Scale and Social Organization.* Oslo: Universitetsforlaget.

Barnes, Barry, 1993, "Power", in Bellamy, R. (ed.), *Theories and Concepts of Politics.* Manchester University Press.

Bartholdsson, Å., 2003, "På jakt efter rätt inställning – att fostra positiva och reflekterande elever i svensk skola", in Persson, A. (ed.), *Skolkulturer – vägar till framgång?* Lund: Studentlitteratur.

Bauman, Gerd, 1996, *Contesting Culture, Discourses of identity in multi-ethnic London.* Cambridge: Cambridge University Press.

Bayart, J.-F., 1993, *The State in Africa: The Politics of the Belly.* London and New York: Longman.

Beckman, B., 1992, "Whose Democracy? Bourgeois versus Popular Democracy", in Rudebeck, L. (ed.), *When Democracy Makes Sense: Studies in the Potential of Third World Popular Movements.* Uppsala: AKUT.

Bengtsson, Bo, 1983, *Rural Development Research and Agricultural Innovations: A comparative study of agricultural changes in a historical perspective, and agricultural research policy for rural development.* Uppsala: Swedish University of Agricultural Sciences.

Béteille, André, 1994, "Inequality and equality", in Ingold, T. (ed.), *Companion Encyclo-pedia of Anthropology, Humanity, Culture and Social Life*. London and New York: Routledge

Blanchet, Thérése, 1996, *Lost Innocence, Stolen Childhoods*. Dhaka: The University Press Limited /Rädda Barnen.

Bourdieu, P., 1977, *Outline of a Theory of Practice*. Cambridge: Cambridge University Press.

—, 1992, *The Logic of Practice*. Cambridge: Polity Press.

Bratton, M., 1989, "Beyond the State: Civil Society and Associational Life in Africa", *World Politics*, 41/3:407–30.

Bridges, D. and B. Ridley, 2000, "Tradition and modernity: educational development and teacher training in Ethiopia", in Bridges, D. and Marew Zewdie (eds), *Secondary Teacher Education in Ethiopia*. The British Council, Addis Ababa in association with Addis Ababa University and University of East Anglia, Norwich.

Broch-Due, V., I. Rudie and T. Bleie, (eds), 1993, *Carved Flesh – Cast Selves, Gendered Symbols and Social Practices*. Oxford: Berg Publishers.

Brock-Utne, Birgit, 2001, "Education for all – in whose language?", *Oxford Review of Education*, Vol. 27, No.1, 2001:115–134.

Butler, J., 1990, *Gender Trouble: Feminism and the subversions of identity*. London: Routledge.

Callon, Michel and Bruno Latour, 1981, "Unscrewing the big Leviathan: How actors macro-structure reality and how sociologists help them to do so", in Knorr-Cetina, K. and A.V. Cicourel (eds), *Advances in social theory and methodology. Toward an integration of micro- and macro-sociologies*. Boston: Routledge and Kegan Paul.

Chazan, N., 1988, "Ghana: The Problems of Governance and the Emergence of Civil Society", in Diamond, L. et al., *Democracy in developing countries. Vol. 2, Africa*. Boulder: Lynne Rienner Publishers.

Cho, Hae-Jong, 1995, "Children in the examination war in South Korea: cultural analysis", in Stephens, Sharon (ed.), *Children and the Politics of Culture*. Princeton: Princeton University Press.

Clapham, Christopher, 1969, *Haile Sellassie's Government*. New York: Frederick A. Praeger.

—, 1990, *Transformation and Continuity in Revolutionary Ethiopia*. Cambridge: Cambridge University Press.

Clegg, Stewart, R., 1989, *Frameworks of Power*. London: Sage Publications.

Cohen, J. and D. Weintraub, 1975, *Land and peasants in imperial Ethiopia: The social background to a revolution*. Assen: Van Gorcum.

Cohen, J. and N.I. Isaksson, 1987, *Villagization in the Arsi Region of Ethiopia*. Uppsala: Swedish University of Agricultural Sciences.

Connell, R.W., 1987, *Gender and Power. Society, the Person and Sexual Politics*. Cambridge: Polity Press.

—, 1996, "New Directions in Gender Theory, Masculinity Research, and Gender Politics", *Ethnos*, 1996:3–4.

Connerton, Paul, 1989, *How Societies Remember.* Cambridge: Cambridge University Press.

Cornwall, Andrea and Nancy Lindisfarne, 1994, "Introduction", in Cornwall, A. and N. Lindisfarne (eds), *Dislocating Masculinity. Comparative Ethnographies.* London and New York: Routledge.

—, 1994, "Dislocating masculinity: Gender, power and anthropology", in Cornwall, A. and N. Lindisfarne (eds), *Dislocating Masculinity. Comparative Ethnographies.* London and New York: Routledge.

Cowen, M. and L. Laakso, 2002, "Election and Election Studies in Africa", in Cowen, M. and L. Laakso (eds), *Multi-party Elections in Africa.* Oxford: James Currey.

Crummey, Donald, 1983, "Family and Property amongst the Amhara Nobility", *Journal of African History,* XXIV, No. 2.

—, 1988, "Theology and Political Conflicts During the Zämänä Mäsafint: the case of Esté in Begemder", in *Proceedings of the Ninth International Conference of Ethiopian Studies,* Moscow.

Dahl, R.A., 1982, *Dilemmas of Pluralist Democracies. Autonomy vs. Control.* New Haven: Yale University Press.

Daniel Haile, 1979, *Law and the status of women in Ethiopia.* Unpublished manuscript prepared for FAO/UNDP Project ETH73/003.

DiMaggio, P. and W. Powell, 1983, "The Iron Cage Revisited: Institutional Isomorphism and Collective Rationality in Organizational Fields", *American Sociological Review,* 48(2):147–60.

Donham, D., 1986, "Old Abyssinia and the new Ethiopian empire: Themes in social history", in Donham, D. and W. James (eds), *The Southern Marches of Imperial Ethiopia. Essays in History and Social Anthropology.* Cambridge: Cambridge University Press.

Donor Election Unit's Report 1995, *The Ethiopian Register,* July: 41–55.

Douglas, Mary, [1966] 1992, *Purity and Danger. An analysis of the concepts of pollution and taboo.* London and New York: Routledge.

Dumont, Louis, 1966, *Homo hierarchicus.* Paris: Gallimard.

—, 1977, *Homo aequalis.* Paris: Gallimard.

Educational Statistics Annual Abstract. 1993 E.C./2000–01/2001. Ministry of Education. Addis Ababa.

Eide, Øyvind, 2000, *Revolution and Religion in Ethiopia: Growth and persecution of the Mekane Yesus Church, 1974–85.* Oxford: James Currey.

Einarsdottir, Jónína, 2000, *"Tired of Weeping" Child Death and Mourning among Papel Mothers in Guinea-Bissau.* Stockholm Studies in Social Anthropology, No. 46.

Encyclopaedia Brittanica 1994. 15th edition.

Eriksen, Thomas Hylland, 1995, *Small Places, Large Issues. An Introduction to Social and Cultural Anthropology.* London: Pluto Press.

Erlich, Haggai, 2003, *Islam and revolution in today's Ethiopia.* Paper presented at the 15th International Conference of Ethiopian Studies, Hamburg.

Eshetu Chole, 1994, "A Preliminary Appraisal of Ethiopia's Economic Reforms 1991–93", in Marcus, H. (ed.), *New Trends in Ethiopian Studies, Papers of the 12th International Conference of Ethiopian Studies*. Vol. II. Lawrenceville: The Red Sea Press.

Ethiopian Economic Association, EEA, 1999/2000, *Annual Report on the Ethiopian Economy*. Editors: Befekadu Degefe and Berhanu Nega. Addis Ababa: United Printers.

—, 2000/2001, *Second Annual Report on the Ethiopian Economy*. Editors: Befekadu Degefe, Berhanu Nega and Getahun Tafesse. Addis Ababa.

Evers Rosander, Eva, 1992, "People's Participation as Rhetoric in Swedish Development Aid", in Dahl. G and A. Rabo (eds), *Kam-Ap or Take-Off, local notions of development*. Stockholm Studies in Social Anthropology, No. 29.

—, 1997, "Introduction", in Evers Rosander, Eva (ed.), *Transforming Female Identities: Women's Organizational Forms in West Africa*. Uppsala: Nordiska Afrikainstitutet. Seminar Proceeding 31.

Fassil Kiros, 1984, "Mobilizing the Peasantry for Rural Development: The Ethiopian Experiment in Progress", in Rubenson, S. (ed.), *Proceedings of the Seventh International Conference of Ethiopian Studies*. Uppsala: Scandinavian Institute of African Studies.

Fatton, R., 1992, *The State and Civil Society in Africa*. Boulder: Lynne Rienner Publishers.

Field, Norma, 1995, "The child as laborer and consumer: The disappearance of childhood in contemporary Japan", in Stephens, Sharon (ed.), *Children and the Politics of Culture*. Princeton: Princeton University Press.

Foucault, Michel, 1977, *Discipline and Punish: The Birth of the Prison*. Harmondsworth: Penguin.

—, 1980, *Power/Knowledge*. New York: Pantheon Books.

Freeman, Deena, 2002, *Initiating Change in Highland Ethiopia, Causes and Consequences of Cultural Transformation*. Cambridge: Cambridge University Press.

Frick, Peter, 1997, "What Is Man?", *Antropologiska Studier*, Nr. 58–59, pp. 63–73.

Frisell Ellburg, Ann, 1997, "Jakten på den perfekta näsan", *Antropologiska Studier*, Nr. 58–59, pp. 39–51.

Fuglesang, Minou, 1994, *Veils and videos, female youth culture on the Kenyan coast*. Stockholm Studies in Social Anthropology, No. 32.

Gaventa, J., 1987, "Makt och deltagande", in Petersson, O. (ed.), *Maktbegreppet*. Stockholm: Carlssons Förlag.

Gennet Zewdie, 1991, "Women in Primary and Secondary Education", in Tsehai Berhane-Sellassie (ed.), *Gender Issues in Ethiopia*. Addis Ababa: Institute of Ethiopian Studies.

Gilligan, Carol, 1993, *In a Different Voice – Psychological Theory and Women's Development*. Cambridge, Massachusetts: Harvard University Press.

Girma Amare, 1967, "Aims and purposes of Church education in Ethiopia", *Ethiopian Journal of Education*, Vol. X, No. X, pp. 1–11.

Goodenough, Ward, 1967, "Componential analysis", *Science*, 156:1203–1209.

Gusterson, H., 1998, *Nuclear Rites. A weapons laboratory at the end of the cold war.* Berkeley and Los Angeles: University of California Press.

Hailu, Fulass, 1974, "Knowledge and its attainment in the Ethiopian context", *Ethiopian Journal of Education,* Vol. VII, No. 1, pp. 19–24.

Halliday, F. and M. Molyneux, 1981, *The Ethiopian Revolution.* London: Verso.

Hannerz, U., 1993, "When Culture is Everywhere. Reflections on a Favourite Concept", *Ethnos,* Vol. 58:1–2, pp. 95–111.

—, 1996, *Transnational Connections: Culture, People, Places.* London: Routledge.

Harris, G., 1989, "Concepts of Individual, Self and Person in Description and Analysis", *American Anthropologist,* Vol. 91, No. 3. Sept. 1989, pp. 599–612.

Hastrup, Kirsten, 1992, "Writing ethnography: State of the art", in Okeley, J. and H. Callaway (eds), *Anthropology and Autobiography.* ASA Monographs 29. London and New York: Routledge.

Haugerud, A., 1995, *The Culture of Politics in Modern Kenya.* Cambridge: Cambridge University Press.

Heath, S.B., 1983, *Ways with Words. Language, Life and Work in Communities and Classrooms.* Cambridge: Cambridge University Press.

von Hirsch, Eva, 1996, *Beliefs and Ideas Concerning Childhood and Child Rearing. A study amongst Arabic speaking Christian and Muslim families at Råby.* Västerås: ProAros.

Hirschmann, D., 1991, "Women and Political Participation in Africa: Broadening the Scope of Research", *World Development,* 19(12):1679–1694.

Hirschon, Renée, 1993, "Open Body/Closed Space: The Transformation of Female Sexuality", in Ardener, Shirley (ed.), *Defining Females. The Nature of Women in Society.* Oxford: Berg.

Holy, Ladislav, 1984, "Theory, methodology and the research process", in Ellen, R.F. (ed.), *Ethnographic Research, A Guide to General Conduct.* London: Academic Press.

Hooks, Bell, 1981, *Aint't I A Woman. Black Women and Feminism.* Boston: South End Press.

Hydén, G., 1992, "Governance and the Study of Politics", in Hydén, G. and M. Bratton (eds), *Governance and Politics in Africa.* Boulder: Lynne Rienner Publishers.

Ingold, T., 1993, "The Art of Translation in a Continuous World", in Pálsson, G. (ed.), *Beyond Boundaries: Understanding, Translation and Anthropological Discourse.* London: Bergh.

James, Allison, 1999, "Learning to be Friends: Participant Observation amongst English School-Children (The Midlands)", in Watson, C.W. (ed.), *Being there. Fieldwork in anthropology.* London, Sterling, Vk: Pluto Press.

James, Wendy, Donald Donham, Eisei Kurimoto and Alessandro Triulzi, (eds), 2002, *Remapping Ethiopia, Socialism and after.* Oxford: James Currey.

Jarvie, I.C., 1967, *The Revolution in Anthropology.* London: Routledge and Kegan Paul.

Kassahun Berhanu, 2000, *Returnees, Resettlement and Power Relations. The Making of a Political Constituency in Humera, Ethiopia.* Amsterdam: VU University Press.

Kondo, D., 1990, *Crafting Selves: Power, Gender and Discourse of Identity in a Japanese Workplace.* Chicago: University of Chicago Press.

Knorr-Cetina, K., 1981, "Introduction: The micro-sociological challenge of macro-sociology: Towards a reconstruction of social theory and methodology", in Knorr-Cetina, K. and A.V. Cicourel (eds), *Advances in social theory and methodology. Toward an integration of micro- and macro-sociologies*. Boston: Routledge and Kegan Paul.

—, 1988, "The micro-social order. Towards a reconception", in Fielding, Niel (ed.), *Actions and Structure. Research Methods and Social Theory*. London: Sage.

Kulick, Don, 1992, "'Coming up' in Gapun. Conceptions of Development and their Effect on Language in a Papua New Guinea Village", in Dahl, G. and A. Rabo (eds), *Kam-Ap or Take-Off. Local Notions of Development*. Stockholm Studies in Social Anthropology, No. 29.

Laketch, Dirasse, 1978, *The Socio-Economic Position of Women in Addis Abeba: The Case of Prostitution*. Boston Graduate School, Ph.D. dissertation in cultural anthropology.

Lefort, R., 1983, *Ethiopia: An Heretical Revolution?* London: Zed Press.

Levine, Donald, (1965) 1972, *Wax and Gold. Tradition and Innovation in Ethiopian Culture*. Chicago: The University of Chicago Press.

Lewis, Herbert, 1989, "Values and Procedures in Conflict Resolution Among Shoan Oromo", in Taddesse Beyene (ed.), *Proceedings of the 8th International Conference of Ethiopian Studies*. Addis Abeba: Institute of Ethiopian Studies.

Lewis, Herbert, [1989] 1994, *After the Eagles Landed, The Yemenites of Israel*. Prospect Heights, Illinois: Waveland Press.

Mann, M., 1986, *The Sources of Social Power*, Vol.1: *A History of Power from the Beginning to A.D. 1760*. Cambridge: Cambridge University Press.

Marcus, Harold, 1995, *The Life and Times of Menelik II. Ethiopia 1844–1913*. Lawrenceville: The Red Sea Press.

Markakis, John, 1975, *Ethiopia, Anatomy of a Traditional Polity*. Addis Abeba: Berhanena Selam Printing Press.

Markakis, John and Nega Ayele, 1978, *Class and Revolution in Ethiopia*. Nottingham: Spokesman.

Mascia-Lees, "Sharpe and John Cohen 1989–90. The postmodernist turn in anthropology: Cautions from a feminist perspective", *Signs*, 15:1–2.

McCann, James, 1987, *From Poverty to Famine in Northeast Ethiopia. A Rural History 1900–1935*. Philadelphia: University of Pennsylvania Press.

Mekonnen Getu, 1987, *Socialism, Participation and Agricultural Development in Post-Revolutionary Ethiopia*. Stockholm University, Stockholm Studies in Economic History, 11.

Mendoza-Denton, Norma, 1996, "'Muy macha': Gender and ideology in gang girls' discourse about make–up", *Ethnos*, 61:47–63.

Mengistu Woube, 1986, *Problems of Land Reform Implementation in Rural Ethiopia: A case study of Dejen and Wolmera districts*. Uppsala: Department of Human Geography.

Messay Kebede, 1999, *Survival and Modernization: Ethiopia's Enigmatic Present: A Philosophical Discourse*. Lawrenceville: The Red Sea Press.

Mikell, G., 1997, "Introduction", in Mikell, G. (ed.), *African Feminism, The Politics of Survival in Sub-Saharan Africa*. Philadelphia: University of Pennsylvania Press.

Ministry of Education, 2000, *Education System: Policies, 5 Years Basic Education (2001–2005)*.

Monga, C., 1996, *The Anthropology of Anger. Civil Society and Democracy in Africa*. Boulder: Lynne Rienner Publishers.

Morton, H., 1996, *Becoming Tongan. An Ethnography of Childhood*. Honolulu: University of Hawai'i Press.

Narrowe, Judith, 1998, *Under One Roof. On Becoming a Turk in Sweden*. Stockholm Studies in Social Anthropology, No. 43.

Negusse Woldemicael, 1984, *A Review of Agrarian Reform and Rural Development in Ethiopia*. Asella: ARDU publication No. 25.

Newbury, C., 1994, "Introduction: Paradoxes of Democratization in Africa", *African Studies Review*, Vol. 37:1–8.

Norman, Karin, 1991, *A Sound Family Makes a Sound State: Ideology and Upbringing in a German Village*. Stockholm Studies in Social Anthropology, No. 24.

—, 1996, *Kulturella Föreställningar om Barn – Ett socialantropologiskt perspektiv*. Köping: Rädda Barnen Förlag.

Ortner, Sherry B., 1984, "Theory in Anthropology since the Sixties", *Comparative Studies in Society and History*, 26(1):126–66.

—, 1996, "Making Gender, Toward a Feminist, Minority, Postcolonial, Subaltern, etc., Theory of Practice", in Ortner, Sherry B., *Making Gender. The Politics and Erotics of Culture*. Boston: Beacon Press.

Ortner, Sherry and Harriet Whitehead, (eds), 1981, *Sexual Meanings: The Cultural Construction of Gender and Sexuality*. Cambridge and New York: Cambridge University Press.

Ottaway, David and Marina Ottaway, 1978, *Ethiopia: Empire in Revolution*. New York: Africana.

Palme, Mikael, 2001, *En man med respekt som undervisar på hieroglyfer. Skolläraren, skolkulturen och det lokala samhället på den mozambikiska landsbygden*. Unpublished ms.

Pankhurst, Helen, 1992, *Gender, Development and Identity, an Ethiopian Study*. London: Zed Press.

Pankhurst, Richard, 1990, *A Social History of Ethiopia*. Addis Abeba University: Institute of Ethiopian Studies.

Pausewang, Siegfried, 1994, *The 1994 Election and Democracy in Ethiopia*. Oslo: Norwegian Institute of Human Rights, Human Rights Report No. 4.

—, 2001, *Ethiopia 2001: In between Elections in Southern Region*. Oslo: University of Oslo/ Norwegian Institute of Human Rights, Working Paper 2002:14.

Pausewang, S., K. Tronvoll and L. Aalen, (eds), 2002, *Ethiopia since the Derg. A Decade of Democratic Pretension and Performance*. London: Zed Books.

Phillips, A., 1992, "Democracy and Feminist Theory", *Political Quarterly*, Vol. 63, No. 1., pp. 79–90.

Poluha, Eva, 1989, *Central Planning and Local Reality. The case of a producers' cooperative in Ethiopia*. Stockholm Studies in Social Anthropology, No. 23.

—, 1990, *Risks, Trees and Security. A baseline study of Beddedo, a peasant association in Wollo, Ethiopia.* Working Paper 111. Rev. ed. Uppsala: Swedish University of Agricultural Sciences, International Rural Development Centre.

—, 1994, "Publicity and the Wielding of Power – A Case from Gojjam, Ethiopia", in Marcus, Harold (ed.), *New Trends in Ethiopian Studies. Papers of the 12th International Conference of Ethiopian Studies.* Lawrenceville:The Red Sea Press.

—, 1997, "Genus, förändring och jämställdhet – ett etiopiskt perspektiv", in Thurén, B.-M. and K. Sundman (eds), *Kvinnor, Män och Andra Sorter. Genusantropologiska frågor.* Stockholm: Carlssons.

—, 1998, "Ethnicity and Democracy – A Viable Alliance?", in Salih, M. and J. Markakis (eds), *Ethnicity and the State in Eastern Africa.* Uppsala: Nordiska Afrikainstitutet.

—, 2002a, "Learning Political Behaviour: Peasant-State Relations in Ethiopia", in Poluha, E. and M. Rosendahl (eds), *Contesting 'Good' Governance. Crosscultural Perspectives on Representation, Accountability and Public Space.* London: Routledge-Curzon.

—, 2002b, "Beyond the Silence of Women in Ethiopian Politics", in Cowen, M. and L. Laakso (eds), *Multi-party Elections in Africa.* Oxford: James Currey Ltd.

Poluha, E. and M. Rosendahl, 2002, "Introduction: People, Power and Public Spaces", in Poluha E. and M. Rosendahl (eds), *Contesting 'Good' Governance. Crosscultural Perspectives on Representation, Accountability and Public Space.* London: Routledge-Curzon.

Popper, E.R., 1963, *The Open Society and Its Enemies.* Vol. II. London: Routledge and Kegan Paul.

Prout, A. and A. James, 1990, "A new paradigm for the sociology of childhood? Provenance, promise and problems", in James, A. and A. Prout (eds), *Constructing and Reconstructing Childhood. Contemporary Issues in the Sociological Study of Childhood.* London: The Falmer Press.

Reinhold, Sue, 1993, *Local conflict and ideological struggle: 'positive images' and Section 28.* Unpublished D.Phil. thesis, University of Sussex.

Richards, Paul, 1996, *Fighting for the Rain Forest. War, Youth and Resources in Sierra Leone.* Oxford and Portsmouth: The International African Institute in association with James Currey and Heineman.

Robinson, P., 1994, "Democratization: Understanding the Relationship between Regime Change and the Culture of Politics", *African Studies Review,* 37/1:39–68.

Rosaldo, Michelle and Louise Lamphere, (eds), 1974, *Woman, Culture and Society.* Stanford: Stanford University Press.

Rosendahl, Mona, 1985, *Conflict and Compliance: Class Consciousness among Swedish Workers.* Stockholm Studies in Social Anthropology, No. 14.

—, 1997, "The Ever-Changing Revolution", in Rosendahl, Mona (ed.), *The Current Situation in Cuba: Challenges and Alternatives.* Stockholm: Institute of Latin American Studies.

—, 2002, "Sounds of Silence: Uncertainty, Language and Politics in the Cuban Economic Crisis", in Poluha E. and M. Rosendahl (eds), *Contesting 'Good' Governance.*

Crosscultural Perspectives on Representation, Accountability and Public Space. London: RoutledgeCurzon.

Rouse, Joseph, 1994, "Power/Knowledge", in Gutting, Gary (ed.), *The Cambridge Companion to Foucault*. Cambridge: The Cambridge University Press.

Rubenson, Sven, (1976) 1991, *The Survival of Ethiopian Independence*. Addis Ababa: Kuraz Publishing Agency.

Rydström, Helle, 1998, *Embodying Morality. Girls' Socialization in a North Vietnamese Commune*. Linköping: Linköping University Press.

Sahlins, M., 1972, *Stone Age Economics*. Chicago: Aldine-Atherton Inc.

de Saussure, F., 1974. *Course in General Linguistics*. London: Fontana.

Scheper-Hughes, Nancy and Carolyn Sargent, (eds), 1998, *Small Wars. The Cultural Politics of Childhood*. Berkeley and Los Angeles: University of California Press.

Schwab, P., 1972, *Decision-Making in Ethiopia: A study of the political process*. London: C. Hurst and Co.

Shiraishi, Saya, 1995, "Children's Stories and the State in New Order Indonesia", in Stephens, S. (ed.), *Children and the Politics of Culture*. Princeton: Princeton University Press

Shire, Chenjerai, 1994, "Men don't go to the moon: Language, space and masculinities in Zimbabwe", in Cornwall, A. and N. Lindisfarne (eds), *Dislocating Masculinity. Comparative Ethnographies*. London and New York: Routledge.

Simons, Anna, 1995, *Networks of Dissolution. Somalia Undone*. Oxford: Westview Press.

Smith, Anthony, 1994, "The Politics of Culture: Ethnicity and Nationalism", in Ingold, T. (ed.), *Companion Encyclopaedia of Anthropology*. London and New York: Routledge.

Stambach, Amy, 2000, *Lessons from Mount Kilimanjaro. Schooling Community and Gender in East Africa*. New York, London: Routledge.

Staudt, K., 1986, "Stratification: Implications for Women's Politics", in Robertson, C. and I. Berger (eds), *Women and Class in Africa*. New York: Africana Publishing Company.

Stephens, Sharon, 1995, "Children and the Politics of Culture in 'Late Capitalism'", in Stephens, S. (ed.), *Children and the Politics of Culture*. Princeton: Princeton University Press.

Strauss, C. and N. Quinn, 1997, *A Cognitive Theory of Cultural Meaning*. Cambridge: Cambridge University Press.

Ståhl, Michael, 1974, *Ethiopia: Political Contradictions in Agricultural Development*. Stockholm: Rabén & Sjögren.

—, 1988, *New Seeds in Old Soil: a study of the land reform process in Western Wollega*. Research Report, No. 40. Uppsala: The Scandinavian Institute of African Studies.

Swedish Save the Children, 1988, *Spare the rod and spoil the child*. Addis Abeba: mimeo.

Tamrat, Taddesse, 1972, *Church and State in Ethiopia 1270–1527*. London: Oxford University Press.

Tekeste Negash, 1990, *The Crisis of Ethiopian Education: Some implications for nation-building*. Uppsala: Uppsala University, Department of Education

—, 1996, *Rethinking Education in Ethiopia*. Uppsala: Nordiska Afrikainstitutet.

Terrel, J., 2000, "Anthropological Knowledge and Scientific Fact", *American Anthropologist*, Vol. 102:4:808–817.

Thorne, B., 1993, *Gender Play. Girls and Boys in School*. New Brunswick, New Jersey: Rutgers University Press.

Thurén, Britt-Marie, 1996, "Om styrka, räckvidd och hierarki, samt andra genusteoretiska begrepp!", *Kvinnovetenskaplig Tidskrift*, 1996, årg17, nr 3–4:69–85.

Toren, C., 1990, *Making Sense of Hierarchy. Cognition as Social Process in Fiji*. London and Atlantic Highlands: The Athlone Press.

—, 1993, "Making History: The significance of childhood cognition for a comparative anthropology of mind", *Man* (N.S.) 28 (3–4):461–477.

Trimingham, J. Spencer, 1965, *Islam in Ethiopia*. London: Frank Cass & Co. Ltd.

Tripp, A., 1994, "Gender, Political Participation and the Transformation of Associational Life in Uganda and Tanzania", *African Studies Review*, 37(1):107–133.

Tronvoll, K. and O. Aadland, 1995, *The Process of Democratisation in Ethiopia – An Expression of Popular Participation or Political Resistance?* Oslo: Norwegian Institute of Human Rights.

Tsegaye Tegenu, 1996, *The Evolution of Ethiopian Absolutism. The Genesis and the Making of the Fiscal Military State, 1696–1913*. Uppsala Universitet, Studia Historica Upsaliensia, No. 180.

Tsehai Berhane-Sellassie, (ed.), 1991, *Gender Issues in Ethiopia*. Addis Ababa: Institute of Ethiopian Studies.

—, 1997, "Ethiopian Rural Women and the State", in Mikell, G. (ed.), *African Feminism. The Politics of Survival in Sub-Saharan Africa*, Philadelphia: University of Pennsylvania Press.

Vaughan, S. and K. Tronvoll, 2003, *The Culture of Power in Contemporary Ethiopian Political Life*. Stockholm: Sida Studies, No.10.

de Vylder, Stefan, 2002, *Utvecklingens drivkrafter. Om fattigdom, rikedom och rättvisa i världen*. (The propelling forces of development. On poverty, wealth and justice in the world.) Stockholm: Forum Syd.

Wallman, Sandra, 1984, *Eight London Households*. London: Tavistock Publications.

Wikan, U., 1992, "Beyond the Words: The Power of Resonance", *American Ethnologist*, 19:460–482.

Wright, S., 1998a, "The Politicization of Culture", *Anthropology Today*, Vol. 14. No. 1:7–15

—, 1998b, "Cultural diversity and citizenship: Report of the seminar and agenda for future research", in *Cultural Diversity and Citizenship*. Report of a joint UNESCO/ University of Birmingham Seminar. The University of Birmingham.

Yanagisako, Sylvia and Jane Collier, 1987, "Toward a Unified Analysis of Gender and Kinship", in Collier, J. and S. Yanagisako (eds), *Gender and Kinship Essays toward a Unified Analysis*. Stanford: Stanford University Press.

Yeraswork Admassie, 1995, *Twenty Years to Nowhere. Property Rights, Land Management and Conservation in Ethiopia*. Uppsala: Department of Sociology, Uppsala University.

Index

through written word, 104–6
Cornwall, A., 148–9
counter-discourse, 91–102, 148
Crummey, D., 176
cultural schemas, 17–21, 37, 191
   continuity, 192–7
culture, concept of, 17

Derg regime, 163, 165, 178–83
development, participation, 113–14
diaries, children's, 39
discourse analysis, 18–19
division of labour, gendered, 46–50,
   141–2, 148–9
Donham, D., 175–6
Dumont, L., 94, 97

Easter, 161
edel (luck), 98, 166, 192
education
   Derg policies, 181–2
   EPRDF policies, 32, 187
   Imperial era, 176
   quality of, 31–2, 190
   religious, 99–102
   see also teaching
EFFORT (Endowment Fund for the
   Rehabilitation of Tigray), 186
Eide, Ø., 163
e'kuja (peer group), 153, 154, 159
Elfenesh, 26
embodied behaviour, 119–20
equality
   friendships, 155–6
   and hierarchy, 94
Eritrea, war with, 186–7
Eritrean People's Liberation Front
   (EPLF), 183
Ermias, 51, 54, 69, 89, 90, 118, 128–9,
   137
Etalam, 119
ethical values, children, 37, 54–65
Ethiopian Democratic Union (EDU),
   179
Ethiopian Economic Association (EEA),
   185–6
Ethiopian Orthodox Church (EOC),
   99–101, 121, 160–5, 166

Ethiopian People's Revolutionary
   Democratic Front (EPRDF), 183–8
Ethiopian People's Revolutionary Party
   (EPRP), 179
ethnicity, 165–70, 171, 183–4
Evers Rosander, E., 114
evil eye *see Buda*

Fatima, 49–50, 62, 63, 76, 83, 148,
   167–8
female circumcision, 137
fieldwork, 32–6
Freeman, D., 199
friends
   characteristics, 159
   choice of, 152–6, 170–1
   disputes, 156–8
   mediation, 158–9

gate-keeping, gender system, 144–7
Gebrehiwot Baykedagn, 177
Ge'ez language, 99, 100
gender divisions
   classroom, 117–18
   diary entries, 43
   division of labour, 46–50, 141–2,
   148–9
   embodied behaviour, 119–20, 143
   friendships, 153–5
   hierarchy, 15–16, 122–3
   perpetuation of, 144–8
   self-awareness, 142–4
   space, 138–9
   stereotypes, 124–37
   time, 139–40
Gilligan, C., 57, 59
Girma, 46, 79
Girma (teacher), 70, 77, 87–8, 88–9,
   104, 112, 114–15
Gojjam, 64, 141–2, 148, 164, 169
Goodenough, W., 33
Gusterson, H., 200

Habiba, 26
habitus, 20, 37, 195
Haile Sellassie, 162, 175–8
Hailu Fulass, 99